The A–Z of
Victorian
Crime

The A–Z of Victorian Crime

Neil R. A. Bell, Trevor N. Bond,
Kate Clarke and M. W. Oldridge

AMBERLEY

ACKNOWLEDGEMENTS

We are lucky to be able to express our gratitude to the following people for their support and assistance in the creation of this book: Robert Anderson, Debra Arif, John Bennett, Nick Connell, Chris Jones, Nick McBride, Katja Nieder, Mark Stevens, Neil Storey, Linda Stratmann, Jo Vigor and Adam Wood. Any errors which remain are ours, rather than theirs.

M. W. Oldridge, on behalf of Neil R. A. Bell, Trevor N. Bond and Kate Clarke, March 2016

First Published 2016

Amberley Publishing
The Hill, Stroud
Gloucestershire, GL5 4EP

www.amberley-books.com

Copyright © Neil R. A. Bell, Trevor N. Bond, Kate Clarke and M. W. Oldridge, 2016

The right of Neil R. A. Bell, Trevor N. Bond, Kate Clarke and M. W. Oldridge to be identified as the Authors of this work has been asserted in accordance with the Copyrights, Designs and Patents Act 1988.

ISBN 978 1 4456 4786 9 (paperback)
ISBN 978 1 4456 4787 6 (ebook)

British Library Cataloguing in Publication Data. A catalogue record for this book is available from the British Library.

Typesetting and Origination by Amberley Publishing
Printed in the UK.

CONTENTS

Contents

INTRODUCTION

Little is more evocative of the Victorian period than its criminal subculture. Several of the great criminal personalities of the era are still vivid in the communal memory, although the pre-eminence among them of Jack the Ripper – judged at least by the number of words devoted to him in the dozens of Ripper books which appear every year – cannot be overlooked. Perhaps it is something less than an irony, and something more than a coincidence, that, in the case of Jack the Ripper, the 'personality' behind the crimes is still up for grabs; perhaps he belongs to us now because we can still 'create' him to suit our own changing image of him; perhaps our options are more limited in other cases. Still, I know people who will open this book and turn directly to the entries on Florence Maybrick or Charles Peace, and we hope that *your* favourite criminal of the period – for lack of a better expression – will be lurking here somewhere, too.

This is not to say that this is, or ever could be, an all-encompassing record of Victorian crime. In the style of the very best self-denying Victorians, we have had to impose certain limitations on ourselves, settling, for example, on a very literal demarcation of the Victorian period, which, for our purposes, ran from 20 June 1837 to 22 January 1901 – the respective dates of Queen Victoria's accession to the throne and her death. The cases which appear in this book occurred between those two dates. Even so, we recognised that social and cultural continuities typically transcended these rather arbitrary parameters, and this required us to make certain additional decisions in borderline cases. Thomas Wainewright misses out at the beginning of the period because his crimes occurred before Victoria's accession, although his trial occurred during the early days of her reign; James Greenacre and Sarah Gale – perhaps *the* criminal luminaries of early 1837 – were, likewise, narrowly cut at the leading edge; at the other end, both George Chapman and Samuel Herbert Dougal killed during the Victorian era, but they were convicted and executed under Edward VII. We recognise the artificiality of these restrictions but it would have been impossible to proceed without them. On a personal note, I was disappointed to omit the Chilwell Ghost, whose manifestation – a Victorian phenomenon – had the effect of drawing very belated attention to a crime which had been committed during the reign of George IV.

Elsewhere, other sacrifices had to be made. We have perforce stayed almost entirely out of the civil courts, although it is hard to write about the Tichborne Claimant without setting foot there very briefly; the result of this decision was the loss, on the one hand, of the Royal Baccarat Scandal, and, on the other, of poor Emily Lavinia Wilkinson, whose plaintive tale deserves to be told somewhere. We have also confined our attention to – broadly speaking – British cases, although Frederick Bailey Deeming, Edith Carew and a few others take us overseas in the course of their stories. Regrettably, Lizzie Borden, Ned Kelly and a menacing array of Mexican serial killers all had to be dropped in accordance with this rule.

Occasionally, happenstance softened the edges of our intentions. Kate set out to write about Mary Ann Ansell; she ended up writing about Bertha Peterson, whose case occurred at much the same time. Ms Peterson emerged into view from a thicket of newspaper reports which commented on the two cases, and Kate, quite properly, liked her better, so in she went. Charles Dobell and William Gower similarly came to Trevor from the ether. For all the rules we had established, we wanted to remain open to discovery and to curiosity. In the same spirit, we hope that you will find something new in the pages that follow: something which is unfamiliar to you, or interesting beyond the few words which we are able to devote to it. Our suggestions for 'Further Reading', which occur at the end of most entries, are not meant to be utterly comprehensive, but they are starting points – ones we can vouch for, or which are somehow dear to us – for anyone wishing to learn more.

A

Abberline, Frederick George (1843–1929)

Every so often a real-life detective becomes so well known that their surname alone conjures up images of the period within which they worked. The name of Leonard 'Nipper' Read (the Krays' nemesis) evokes heavies in sharp-tailored suits amidst the faux-Mafioso gangland warfare of London in the 1960s, whilst Chief Inspector Walter Dew epitomised the dapper Edwardian-era detective, tapping the potential of modern technology as he captured his man, Dr Crippen. And if one non-fictional 'tec' is synonymous with the gas-lit streets of the Victorian period, then that detective is undoubtedly the former apprentice clockmaker from Blandford in Dorset, the pursuer of Jack the Ripper, Chief Inspector Frederick George Abberline.

Abberline, born on 8 January 1843, was the youngest of four surviving children. His father, Edward, a humble saddler, rose to undertake a variety of responsible roles within the community, from sheriff's officer to clerk of the market, along with numerous minor local governmental positions. His influence on his youngest son was to be brief, however – six years to be precise – as Edward sadly passed away in 1849, leaving his wife Hannah, a shopkeeper, to raise their children alone.

Nothing is known of Abberline's education but it seems to have been sufficient to prepare him for his manufacturing apprenticeship (itself interrupted by a thirty-five-day spell in the Dorset Militia). However, it was his next career move that really defined him, as, in late 1862, Frederick decided to travel to London to join the Metropolitan Police as a constable. After 'passing out' with the warrant number 43519 just a day prior to his twentieth birthday, his first posting as constable was in Islington's N Division. Two years of impeccable service made him eligible for the sergeant's examination, which he duly passed; this brought about a transfer to another division, and in August 1865 Abberline became the newest sergeant in Highgate's Y Division. There then followed eight years of hard work in uniform branch, with a secondment in 1867 which Abberline spent in plain clothes, assisting with investigations into Fenian activities (see Terrorism). 1867 also saw Abberline marry Martha Mackness, a union which was sadly cut short the following year by Martha's death from consumption.

The stint in plain clothes gave Abberline a taste for detective work, and upon his promotion to Inspector in 1873 he was immediately transferred into the most notorious division in the Metropolitan area: H Division, Whitechapel. So began a fourteen-year association with London's East End, the echoes of which endure to this day. More stellar work saw Frederick rise to the rank of H Division's Local Inspector of CID in 1879. Here, Abberline ran the rule over the criminals of Whitechapel; however, it was his experience with the Fenians that undoubtedly aided him in his investigation of two notorious Fenian activists, James Cunningham and Harry Burton, who had succeeded in blowing up part of the Tower of London, which stood within H Division's jurisdiction. Abberline's appearance at the Old Bailey in 1885, in what was to be known as the 'Trial of the Dynamitards', singled him out as the subject of death threats, but it seems that the senior men at Scotland Yard were also beginning to take notice of this portly, soft-spoken native of Dorset, who reminded one of his young H Division detectives, the aforementioned Dew, of 'a bank manager or solicitor' rather than the scourge of the hardest of East End criminals.

Abberline was instructed to appear at King Street Police Station, Whitehall, on 26 July 1887, to be transferred to the prestigious A Division, but within months he had moved yet again, this time to Scotland Yard itself as a First Class Inspector. The year was 1888 – a year during which a series of murders, occurring in Whitechapel, wrote themselves indelibly into the dark psyche of a nation and its people.

The murders of Jack the Ripper caused widespread panic throughout the East End and made a world sensation like no other crimes before them. Scotland Yard's response was to return Abberline to his old stamping ground, as it was felt that local knowledge would be an essential component of the investigation. Alas, Abberline was unable to track down the elusive murderer.

However, his involvement at the head of ground operations ensured that his name would be forever associated with this case.

With the exception of the Ripper case, the 1889 Cleveland Street Scandal was probably Abberline's best known inquiry. He led the investigation into the secrets of a homosexual brothel, many of whose clientele were derived from the higher echelons of society: during this period, of course, homosexuality was a crime.

Abberline retired from the Metropolitan Police in 1892 and became a private enquiry agent until 1898, when he moved on to Pinkerton's European Agency. In 1901, he and his second wife, Emma, retreated to full retirement in Bournemouth, where, on 10 December 1929, one of the most famous and feared detectives of his time passed away.

NRAB

Adams, Fanny (1859–1867)

Contemporary accounts of the murder of Fanny Adams are harrowing and impossible to forget. It is difficult to comprehend an act of such senseless barbarity.

Eight-year-old Fanny met her death on a summer afternoon in 1867, in fields not far from her home in the Hampshire town of Alton. She had been playing with her seven-year-old sister, Lizzie, and their friend, Minnie Warner. At about half past one, they were approached by Frederick Baker, a twenty-nine-year-old solicitor's clerk; tall and clean-shaven, he was wearing a black hat and frock coat over light-coloured trousers. He appeared to have been drinking. Engaging the girls in conversation, he offered Minnie and Lizzie a halfpenny each to buy sweets, but only on the condition that they would go away, leaving him alone with Fanny. The two little girls took the money and ran off; Fanny also accepted a halfpenny, but – even when she was promised a further inducement (perhaps twopence) – she refused to go with Baker along a lane known as The Hollows. Frustrated, he grabbed her and carried her off to a nearby hop field.

Lizzie and Minnie stayed out playing until five o'clock that afternoon, returning home without Fanny. They told Fanny's mother, Harriet, what had happened, and she and a neighbour went in search of the child. At the edge of a nearby meadow they encountered Frederick Baker, who was coming from the direction of The Hollows. Interrogated by the two women, Baker calmly admitted that he had given the girls some money to buy sweets – he often did it, he said, with children he met.

At about seven o'clock that evening, while it was still light, a search party was formed; before long, it met with a scene of carnage in the hop field. Fanny's killer had butchered her, severing her head and scattering other parts of her body over a wide area. Her abdominal cavity had been plundered and the viscera discarded. Her eyes had been gouged out and thrown into a nearby stream. A bloodied stone, found later, was thought to have been used to stun the child.

Superintendent William Cheyney arrested Frederick Baker at the offices of a local solicitor, William Clements. Baker was found to be in possession of two small penknives, and his clothes bore traces of blood. He was charged with the killing of Fanny Adams and taken to Winchester Gaol. A later search of his desk revealed a diary in which the entry for Saturday 24 August read, 'Killed a young girl. It was fine and hot.'

Such was the animosity aimed at Baker that, during the subsequent inquest at the Duke's Head and the magistrates' hearing at the town hall, the police had to restrain the crowds gathered outside; a lynching was threatened. Mr Justice Mellor presided over the murder trial, which was opened on 5 December at the Hampshire Assizes in Winchester. Baker was easily identified in court, and compelling evidence was given by Harriet Adams and several others who had seen him in the relevant area that Saturday afternoon. One young lad had actually seen Baker washing blood from his hands in a spring close to the scene of the murder. Baker's work colleague, Maurice Biddle, was able to confirm that Baker had left the office soon after midday on the day of the murder and had returned at about half past three. But then he went out again at about five o'clock, apparently to distribute Fanny's body parts around the fields in an attempt to impede the identification of the victim. After completing this task to his satisfaction, he set off back towards the office. It was at this point that he was confronted by Fanny's distraught mother and her neighbour.

A plea of inherited insanity was raised in Baker's defence, founded on the premise that no sane person could have slaughtered an innocent child in such a brutal fashion. Attention was drawn to the fact that several members of Baker's family were mentally unstable, and he himself had once threatened to commit suicide. So damning was the evidence against him, however, that the jury returned a verdict of guilty within fifteen minutes. Sentenced to death, he walked from the dock without displaying any emotion.

Whilst awaiting execution, Baker made a nauseatingly detailed confession. He also wrote to Fanny's father, seeking forgiveness – the murder, he said, was unplanned – he had been 'enraged at her crying, but it was done without pain or struggle'. He also emphasised that he had not sexually violated the child and had not attempted to do so.

On Christmas Eve that year, Frederick Baker was hanged outside Winchester Gaol by William Calcraft; a crowd of more than 5,000 spectators watched it happen. It was reported that Baker had slept well on the night before his execution and ate a hearty breakfast the following morning. He showed no fear until he was pinioned, hooded and positioned on the scaffold with the noose around his neck. When he heard the chaplain intoning the last prayer – only then did his knees begin to tremble violently.

Fanny's remains were buried in Alton's cemetery, marked in 1874 by an elaborate headstone funded by public donations. But perhaps the saddest epitaph to the memory of Fanny Adams is that 'Sweet Fanny Adams', a term first used by the Navy in 1869 to express their disgust at the unappetising lumps of mutton they were given to eat, has since passed into popular usage as a derisory expletive, denoting nothing of value, nothing at all.

KC, MWO

Adkins, Eliza (dates unknown)

The tragic case of Eliza Adkins provides a poignant example of not only the devastating effect of poverty, but the gulf between the rich and poor in the Victorian era. On the morning of Saturday, 30 July 1865, the body of a small boy was found at the bottom of a communal well at Pegg's Green, near Ashby-de-la-Zouch, in Leicestershire. A post-mortem revealed that the four-year-old child, Zadock Adkins, had been alive before being pushed down the well; his death had been caused by drowning. His feet were badly blistered and his stomach contained nothing but a few wild gooseberries.

The boy's mother, Eliza, was arrested and charged with his murder. Her subsequent confession was disturbing: she explained that she had become destitute after her husband died and, with a child in tow, she was unable to secure work as a live-in maid. Therefore, in order to qualify for parish relief, she and her son were obliged to enter the Loughborough Union Workhouse. She stayed but a few days, for the treatment she received was harsh and, according to workhouse rules, she was separated from her son by an iron grid. Unable to bear to hear him constantly crying for her, she managed to grab him and together they escaped from the workhouse, aimlessly trudging the lanes. As she said in her statement, 'I did not know what to do with the child. I had no home, nothing to eat, and no friend to go to. I could get a situation for myself, but not if I had the child. So I did not know what to do with it.' She had drowned her son, she explained, out of desperation and to save him from further suffering; she was also convinced that he was 'now in Heaven'. It is distressing to consider that Eliza's helplessness was not secondary to either youth or inexperience; she was reported by the newspapers to be forty-two years of age, and may even have been older.

Eliza Adkins was tried for the murder of her son (see Infanticide) at the Leicester Assizes on Saturday, 16 December 1865, before Mr Justice Mellor. Between her arrest and the trial the press published numerous letters and articles commenting on Eliza's tragic situation, and there was much sympathy expressed for her plight. Her defence counsel proposed that the stress of her dire circumstances had triggered a temporary state of insanity that had led to the murder. Rejecting this plea, the jury returned a guilty verdict, and Eliza was sentenced to death. Under pressure from public opinion, however, the Home Secretary, Sir George Grey, issued a reprieve, and the death sentence on Eliza was commuted to penal servitude for life. Had she been convicted a few years earlier, she would probably have been transported to the penal colonies in Australia, where life would have been unbearably harsh for a woman as frail and worn down by hardship as Eliza.

The Poor Law Board instigated an inquiry into her allegations of cruelty in the Loughborough Union but, perhaps predictably, the workhouse staff made self-serving statements, which were published in the *Pall Mall Gazette*. They indignantly refuted the accusations made against them, denied any culpability in the tragedy and insisted that whilst in the workhouse Eliza and her son had been treated humanely.

One can only speculate on the last moments of Zadock's life. Did Eliza, mentally and physically exhausted, struggle to the well at the top of the hill at Pegg's Green that night, carrying the sleeping child in her arms, and did he have a few wild gooseberries – the only food he'd eaten all day – clutched in his hand? And did they fall as he crashed down into the murky depths of the well? Or did Eliza hoist him up to peer over the rim of the shaft and drop the few berries they had left into the water to hear them splash – a tragically macabre final game to amuse the little boy who was about to die?

KC

FURTHER READING

Clarke, K., *Deadly Dilemmas* (London: Mango Books, forthcoming)

Anderson, Sir Robert (1841–1918)

When the stolid English go in for a scare they take leave of all moderation and common sense. If nonsense were solid, the nonsense that was talked and written about those murders would sink a Dreadnought. The subject is an unsavoury one, and I must write about it with reserve ... I spent the day of my return to town, and half the following night, in reinvestigating the whole case, and next day I had a long conference on the subject with the Secretary of State and the Chief Commissioner of Police. 'We hold you responsible to find the murderer,' was Mr Matthews' greeting to me. My answer was to decline the responsibility. 'I hold myself responsible,' I said, 'to take all legitimate means to find him.'

So wrote Sir Robert Anderson about the nemesis of his particular policing era: the murderer known as Jack the Ripper.

Anderson was born in Dublin on 29 May 1841, into an Ulster Scots family whose head, Matthew, was a solicitor and a distinguished elder in the Presbyterian Irish Church. Despite the strongly religious tone of the Anderson household, young Robert struggled with his own faith until his late teens, when he converted to evangelical Christianity and thereafter devoted the remainder of his spiritual life to his religion, authoring a number of books upon the subject.

A private education took Anderson as far as Boulogne-sur-Mer and Paris, and his path may have led him in quite a different direction had he stuck with a business apprenticeship at a large brewery in Dublin, where the role of cashier filled him with a sense of pride which, alas, could not outweigh his deficiencies in bookkeeping. Realising that he was somewhat lacking, Anderson returned to education at Trinity College after eighteen months of floundering at the brewery and began reading law. Here, he excelled: he was called to the bar in 1863, received his Bachelor of Law degree in 1875, and in between times became an expert in Fenian terrorist activity. In 1868, he was made a Home Office Advisor on that subject.

Throughout the 1870s, Anderson combined his legal and governmental duties, liaising between the newly formed Irish Bureau and Scotland Yard from 1883. Political manoeuvrings saw Anderson's career stutter somewhat in the mid-1880s, but, on 31 August 1888, Queen Victoria appointed him to be 'during our pleasure, one of the Assistant Commissioners of Police of the Metropolis' with responsibility for the Criminal Investigation Department. On the very same day, a murder occurred in London's Whitechapel area – the third to take place there within a matter of weeks. Anderson, acting upon his doctor's advice, promptly took overseas sick leave, and found himself trying to remotely manage the investigation into the murders of Jack the Ripper – perhaps the most notorious crimes the country had ever seen.

When he did return, Anderson discovered that, despite the best efforts of his men, the investigation had not reached a satisfactory conclusion: the perpetrator had not been captured. This was to remain the official line for some years after the murders had ceased – and forever more, or so it seemed. However, in his 1910 book, *The Lighter Side of my Official Life*, Anderson tantalisingly reported that he was

> almost tempted to disclose the identity of the murderer and of the pressman who wrote the letter above referred to [a reference to the infamous Dear Boss letter, supposedly written by Jack the Ripper]. But no public benefit would result from such a course, and the traditions of my old department would suffer. I will merely add that the only person who had ever had a good view of the murderer unhesitatingly identified the suspect the instant he was confronted with him; but he refused to give evidence against him.

The degree to which these enigmatic assertions can be substantiated remains a topic of fascination for Ripperologists. Is Anderson a reliable source, or is he puffing himself up? In his favour are the privileges of his role as chief of CID, which conferred the authority to see all the information gathered on the case. Perhaps the situation was not one which yielded to the lawful obligations of the police: one of Anderson's predecessors, Sir Howard Vincent, summed up the frustrations of detective work when he stated that it 'is often easy to find out the author of an offence, but it is quite another matter to be able to prove the legal guilt of the delinquent by legal means'. Perhaps healthily, however, consensus on this matter remains a very distant prospect.

After his retirement in 1901, Anderson remained in the public eye. In 1903, he provided an article for *T. P.'s Weekly*, entitled 'Sherlock Holmes, Detective, as seen by Scotland Yard', in which he compared the great fictional detective with his real-life counterparts. Anderson concluded, in relation to Holmes and Moriarty's epic cat-and-mouse tale, 'The Final Problem', that 'the reader's last impressions are in line with Dr. Watson's first impressions, that Sherlock Holmes is insufferable, egotistical and tiresome' – the irony of these words may not have been lost on some of Anderson's enemies.

Sir Robert Anderson died in Switzerland on 15 November 1918, a victim of the Spanish influenza pandemic. He was a man who divided, and still divides, opinion. To take just one of these – one which exemplifies the importance of knowing one's source – the journalist and film actor Raymond Blathwayt, in the evangelical penny weekly *Great Thoughts*, observed that 'Sir Robert Anderson is one of the men to whom the country, without knowing it, owes a great debt'.

NRAB

FURTHER READING

Anderson, Sir R., *The Lighter Side of my Official Life* (London: Hodder & Stoughton, 1910)
Moore-Anderson, A. P., *Sir Robert Anderson and Lady Agnes Anderson* (London: Marshall, Morgan & Scott, 1919 and 1947)

Arran Murder, The (1889)

Few Victorian murder victims can have been as complacently cheerful and gregarious as Edwin Rose. A resident of Tooting and by profession the clerk to a Brixton builder, thirty-two-year-old Rose set off on his summer holidays in July 1889, aiming for the hydrotherapy centres of Scotland. On a ferry to the Isle of Arran, on the twelfth of the month, he formed an instantaneous friendship with a young man named Annandale. They decided to spend some time together on the island, beginning the next day, when a lowly lean-to adjoining Mrs Walker's guesthouse would be made available to them.

The thing to do on Arran was to climb the island's dominating peak, Goatfell; since it was the height of the tourist season, plenty of folk were up and down the mountain all day. On Monday, 15 July, Rose and Annandale set out to do exactly this. They were in contrasting humours: Rose his usual self, chatting to anybody he encountered as if he had known them all his life; Annandale silent, morose, and stalking the slopes ahead of his companion.

Then the men became separated; then Annandale left Arran without paying Mrs Walker for his ramshackle accommodation. When Rose did not reappear in London on his return train, the alarm was raised and search parties were sent up Goatfell to try to establish what had become of the vanished holidaymaker. Inclement weather prevented the discovery of Rose's body until Sunday, 4 August; it was in a badly degraded condition, although – with the exception of the head, which had been thoroughly smashed in – it was generally uninjured. Oddly, it had been concealed in a cavity beneath one of the mountain's innumerable boulders, and a screen of rocks and vegetation had been erected to obscure it from the view of passers-by. The volunteer who discovered it had been drawn to the rotting body's location by its putrid stench.

Curiosity now turned to the whereabouts of the elusive Annandale. As it turned out, the ostentatious appearance of one John Watson Laurie, who was swanning around Glasgow dressed in Rose's missing yachting cap and distinctive tennis jacket, left little doubt as to who had been using the name 'Annandale' as an alias. One of Laurie's associates, a man named Aitken, had begun to put two and two together. 'Surely,' Laurie said to Aitken, 'you don't think me a ...' There the sentence trailed off. Aitken thought that Laurie would have gone on to say 'thief', because the dubious ownership of the yachting cap was a particular point of suspicion; but surely 'liar' and 'murderer' were also available – and not unfitting – options.

John Watson Laurie (see **The Arran Murder**). (Authors' collection)

Realising that Glasgow was getting too hot for him, Laurie fled, first to Liverpool, and then, perhaps, to Aberdeen. He was eventually arrested in a wood near Hamilton, having made an ineffectual attempt to commit suicide, saying, enigmatically, 'I robbed the man, but I did not murder him.' At his trial, which began in Edinburgh on Friday, 8 November, his defence, partly out of necessity, ran the same line, parsing Laurie's remark in a way that could not be considered entirely natural. In this reading, Laurie had left Rose (alive and well) at the summit of Goatfell, and had then stolen the possessions that Rose had left in the lean-to when he became (rather presciently) convinced that his temporary room-mate was not coming back. Since the corpse had been divested of its valuables before it was concealed underneath the boulder, it was difficult to avoid the conclusion that Laurie's comment had not been meant to carry quite so specific a meaning.

The verdict of the court depended partly on whether one thought that Rose's head injuries were inflicted in an attack or whether they were the result of an accidental fall. Medical opinions were divided, and the jury's decision closely mirrored this uncertainty, since Laurie was convicted only by eight votes to seven. He was sentenced to death, but reprieved after a popular outcry predicated partly on the merciful precedent of the other key criminal figure of the moment, Florence Maybrick. He was never released and spent the last twenty years of his life in a facility for the criminally insane.

Laurie never admitted his guilt, but did change his story after the trial, saying that Rose had, in fact, died from a fall, and that he, Laurie, had been struck by the instant realisation that the whole thing looked very strangely like murder; he therefore decided, hastily, to hide Rose's body and to hope for the best. It is difficult to believe a word that issued from Laurie's mouth – he *was* a liar, if nothing else – but we ought to note William Roughead's observation that, 'in the skilled hands of the Dean of Faculty [Laurie's advocate],' this argument probably 'would, if adopted, have resulted in an acquittal'.

MWO

FURTHER READING

Roughead, W., 'The Arran Murder' in *Classic Crimes* (New York: New York Review Books, 2000)

Arsenic

In its natural form arsenic is relatively harmless, and indeed exists in the body in trace amounts. Combine two atoms of arsenic with three of oxygen, however, and you have created arsenic trioxide, otherwise known as white arsenic. What you choose to do with it then is up to your own conscience. Whilst medically-trained poisoners such as Thomas Neill Cream and William Palmer often favoured strychnine, arsenic became the method of first recourse for many Victorian domestic murderers due both to the ease with which it could be obtained and its potentially devastating effects.

In fact, while arsenic was often prescribed as a component of medicines for a wide range of conditions (or as an aid to virility), it was also a common ingredient in all sorts of domestic products, comestibles and synthetic preparations. Arsenic could also be found papering the walls – Scheele's Green was a particularly dangerous colour, as it transpired – hanging from the ceiling to catch flies, preserving clothes, aiding the complexion, and even as an additive in sweets.

Once a lethal quantity of arsenic has been absorbed into the bloodstream, it will begin to attack every organ except for the brain, which will be affected indirectly. It will collect in particularly high levels in the liver, kidneys, spleen, and heart – but, in truth, no part of the body is safe, as the poison begins to inhibit cellular processes which contribute to keeping tissues alive.

This will have a particularly powerful, and rapid, effect on the stomach and bowels – perhaps within half an hour, the victim will experience profound sickness and abdominal pain; vomiting is to be expected, as is diarrhoea. This will be pale and watery at first, but may soon contain large quantities of fresh blood due to haemorrhaging within the colon. For this reason, cholera and infective colitis are often initial misdiagnoses in many cases of murder by arsenic.

Within four hours, further effects will start to be felt. A loss of sensation in the hands and feet may develop due to nerve damage; conversely, painful involuntary twitching and cramp may also occur, due not only to neural compromise but also to the disruption of the natural blood chemistry – the victim's blood is now quite literally becoming acidic. They will start to breathe in a rapid and unsustainable manner in an attempt to correct this by disposing of excess carbon dioxide; this will be unsuccessful, but will rapidly lead to exhaustion. If the other effects of the poison do not get there first, this excessive effort will eventually lead to acute respiratory failure and a cessation of any meaningful breathing.

In the meantime, bladder control may be lost and the urine becomes blood-stained. The liver and kidneys will also shortly start to deteriorate, but for now the victim has more pressing concerns. A painful headache sets in, and the swelling of the brain may cause visual disturbances and dizziness (perhaps accompanied by the onset of uncontrollable seizures, or even lapses into unconsciousness). All of this exacerbates the nausea and vomiting to which the victim is already subject.

Disturbance of the careful balance of calcium and potassium in the blood is now beginning to affect the function of the heart. The good news, if there is any, is that, typically, the victim is comatose before the heart attack arrives.

Representative Victorian cases are legion: see, for example, Florence Maybrick, Edith Carew, and Christiana Edmunds; there are plenty more. A less iconic case – but one which raises interesting questions – occurred in June 1855, when a woman from Darlington named Jane Wooler died after a lingering illness. Suspicion fell on her husband, Mr Joseph Wooler, who, it was revealed, had been responsible for enemas which Jane had been receiving throughout her decline. When the presence of arsenic was confirmed in his late wife's urine, stomach, and beyond, Mr Wooler was brought to trial. However, character evidence convinced the jury that he had no reason to wish to murder his beloved, and thus he was acquitted. The origin of the arsenic in Mrs Wooler's body remains an enigma.

By the close of the nineteenth century, the dangers of arsenic were much better understood. It was more likely to be detected by improved forensic techniques, and its appeal as a poison was accordingly diminished. Still, there was time for one more interesting case, which occurred late in Queen Victoria's reign. In 1900, doctors at Manchester Royal Infirmary became curious about an increase in the number of Lancashire beer drinkers presenting with partial paralysis due to nerve damage. It turned out that production errors at a sugar refinery had seen several local breweries supplied with ingredients containing arsenic. A number of brewers were prosecuted, as was a Nantwich publican who continued selling contaminated beer to his customers even after he had been informed of the issue. He was fined £2. The sugar refinery was liquidated.

TNB

FURTHER READING

Whorton J. C., *The Arsenic Century* (Oxford: Oxford University Press, 2010)

Assassination

The nineteenth century may have begun with the assassination of British Prime Minister Spencer Perceval in the House of Commons (in 1812), but the subsequent reign of Queen Victoria was relatively free of high-profile assassination attempts; except, that is, for those targeted at the monarch herself. After taking the throne in 1837, Victoria was the subject of no fewer than seven attempts on her life during her sixty-four-year reign.

The first came just three years into her reign, and has become the most well known due to a highly fictionalised portrayal in the 2009 film *Young Victoria*. As Victoria, twenty-one years old and pregnant, passed through Green Park accompanied by her husband, Prince Albert, an eighteen-year old unemployed potman named Edward Oxford fired two pistols in the direction of their carriage, before being overpowered by members of the watching public.

In a bizarre trial, more attention was paid to the previous behaviour of Oxford's father and grandfather, both alcoholics, than to his own actions, while the prosecution were unable to prove that his pistols had even been loaded. Eventually, he was acquitted due to insanity and ordered to be detained at Her Majesty's pleasure.

For her part, Queen Victoria does not appear to have taken much pleasure in the decision. She would later state her conviction that, had Oxford been hanged, his fate would have served as a deterrent to future aspiring assassins, be they of sane mind or those whose 'diseased brain[s]' had led them to commit 'supposedly involuntary acts'. Her cynicism about the verdict, which she demanded to be removed as an option for the judiciary in later years, is clear, and her opinion on the matter, taken from a letter to Prime Minister William Gladstone some forty-two years later, could be seen as indicative of her attitude to peacekeeping in general. 'Certainty that [such men] will not escape punishment,' she wrote, 'will terrify them into a peaceful attitude towards others.'

Oxford was sent to the Royal Bethlehem Hospital, where he remained for twenty-four years before being transferred to the criminal lunatic asylum at Broadmoor in 1864, becoming one of that institution's first male patients (at both institutions, he would have been a contemporary of patricide Richard Dadd). His case notes reveal a studious and well-behaved man, who on arrival at Broadmoor was noted to be 'apparently sane'.

Finally, aged forty-five, Oxford was released from Broadmoor and allowed to travel to Australia to begin a new life, on the condition that he would be immediately arrested if he attempted to re-enter Britain. He died in 1900, aged seventy-eight, eight months before Queen Victoria herself.

It was not only the plots involving actual violence with which those charged with protecting the monarch had to contend. During this same period, a constable was dispatched to Margate to observe a man who had written menacingly to the palace (as well as to the Duke of Wellington, and to the Home Secretary).

Later, a former lieutenant named Frederick Mundell monopolised a significant amount of police attention, with a number of officers detailed to follow him, intermittently, over a seven-year period. At one point, in 1849, two constables assigned to observe him kept it up, without undertaking any other duties, for an unbroken period of 229 days between them. Hampered by recent legislation which meant they could no longer arrest suspected 'lunatics' without evidence of a planned crime, the police were forced to conduct daily searches of Mundell's homes and to continually question his friends and acquaintances. Having tracked him countrywide, the police finally left him in peace in 1853.

In the event, the Queen was next fired on in 1842, on two separate occasions – in May, again in Green Park, by John Francis (who had also pointed a pistol at her the previous day, accounting for the sometimes-quoted number of eight attempts on her life), and also in July by John William Bean, this time in St James's Park, perhaps provoked or inspired by the commutation of Francis's initial life sentence to one of transportation the day before. Bean's pistol, however, contained only gunpowder and tobacco. Bean was sentenced to eighteen months' imprisonment after the intervention of Prince Albert, who argued that he should not be tried for treason – still punishable by death – but simply with having endeavoured to 'alarm' his intended victim.

Despite the consort's mercy, Bean's subsequent life does not seem to have been a happy one. On 19 July 1882, he was discovered in his bed at his home in Camberwell, having committed suicide by drinking a large quantity of opium. Reporting on his death, *Lloyd's Weekly Newspaper* stated that he had been living in an asylum five years previously, and that a note was found near his body in which he declared himself an 'incumbrance' to his wife and was therefore 'only too glad' to die.

In 1849, once again in Green Park, Victoria was fired on by an Irishman named William Hamilton. As with Bean, however, Hamilton's weapon was not fully loaded, and he was sentenced to transportation for a period of seven years. Like Oxford and Francis, he seems to have taken full advantage of the opportunity to build himself a new life in Australia.

The same sentence was handed down to retired Army officer Robert Pate, who in 1850 ambushed the Queen's carriage in Piccadilly and, clutching a brass-tipped cane, beat her around the head hard enough to leave a mark on her forehead which reportedly remained for a decade. Pate returned to England in 1865, and died thirty years later.

Victoria would have only two more assassination attempts to endure. In 1872 a young Irishman named Arthur O'Connor pointed a pistol at the Queen as she exited her carriage outside Buckingham Palace; he had hoped to force her to sign a document agreeing to free numerous Irish prisoners, but he was swiftly overpowered by the Queen's attendant, John Brown. Again, O'Connor's pistol was found to be without bullets, and he was also sent to Australia. Incredibly, the following year, he wrote a letter to his intended victim from his new home. In it, O'Connor explained that (in addition to his political aims) he had hoped that, upon meeting him, Victoria would appoint him to replace Alfred Lord Tennyson as Poet Laureate. The letter never reached its intended recipient.

Another frustrated poet, Roderick Maclean, was responsible for the final act of attempted regicide, when he shot into the royal carriage as it left the platform at Windsor station in 1882. Like Oxford a generation before him, Maclean was declared not guilty by reason of insanity and sent to Broadmoor, where he died thirty-nine years later. It was this final perceived insult that led the Queen to write to the Prime Minister demanding a change in the law; although, never one to underestimate her own importance, she also famously declared that 'it was worth being shot at – to see how much one is loved'.

The only other notable assassination attempt in mainland Britain during the Victorian age was Daniel M'Naghten's shooting of civil servant Edward Drummond, secretary to then Prime Minister Sir Robert Peel, in 1843. Overseas, Italian Felice Orsini's attempt to assassinate the French Emperor Napoleon III in Paris, in 1858, using a bomb made in England and assisted by English accomplices, is perhaps notable for the serious repercussions felt, after the event, by the British government.

TNB

FURTHER READING

St Aubyn, G., *Queen Victoria: A Portrait* (London: Sinclair-Stevenson, 1991)
Hibbert, C., *Queen Victoria: A Personal History* (London: HarperCollins, 2000)
Murphy, P. T., *Shooting Victoria* (London: Head of Zeus, 2012)

B

Balham Mystery, The (1876)

It is little wonder that the mystery surrounding the death of Charles Bravo in 1876 has become one of the most intriguing cases of the Victorian period. It has all the hallmarks of crime fiction: here, the handsome, thirty-year-old barrister, Charles; there, his wealthy and beautiful wife, Florence – who, before their marriage, had engaged in a scandalous affair with sixty-two-year-old Dr James Gully, the celebrated hydropath, at his fashionable clinic in Malvern. After meeting Bravo on Brighton promenade, Florence soon ditched Gully and set up home with Charles – by now her husband – in the Priory, a quaint, pseudo-Gothic villa in rural Balham, which came complete with stables and extensive grounds. They employed a butler, a cook, a maid, and a groom for the carriage horses; also in residence was a widowed former governess, Mrs Jane Cox, who had befriended Florence during her affair with Gully. She enjoyed an annual salary of £80 and received preferential treatment far beyond that of any of the other servants in the household. With financial help from Charles's stepfather, Joseph Bravo, she even invested in property, and enrolled her three boys in a private school.

On 17 April, whilst Charles was out riding on Tooting Common, his horse, Cremorne, bolted; Charles returned to the Priory in a foul mood. Mrs Cox joined her employers for dinner, having spent the day on the south coast looking for a villa in which Florence could convalesce after suffering a recent miscarriage. Charles said very little during the meal and, as soon as it was over, he retired for the night, taking the spare bedroom as Florence, who was feeling unwell, had decided to share her bed with Mrs Cox. Having consumed a quantity of wine over dinner, Florence was soon fast asleep, with Mrs Cox sitting devotedly by her bedside. Suddenly Charles flung open the door to his room and cried, 'Florence! Florence! Hot water! Hot water!' Staggering back into the room, he vomited out of the window before collapsing on the floor.

Mrs Cox took control in a manner so laboured and deliberate that it left her open to suspicion, as if she had intended the irritant which Charles had ingested to remain in his system long enough to kill him. When Florence eventually roused herself and saw her husband's condition, she became hysterical and screamed for Rowe, the butler, to fetch a local doctor; Mrs Cox, by contrast, had suggested one who lived some distance away.

Charles Bravo went on to suffer the most appalling agony as the poison took hold, but he repeatedly denied that he had tried to commit suicide. Mrs Cox (again out of tune with the Bravos) insinuated that Charles had been unable to get over his jealousy of Florence's pre-marital affair with Dr Gully. In desperation, Florence sent for the celebrated physician, Dr William Gull, who confirmed that Charles had been poisoned and would soon die. It was only then that Mrs Cox mentioned the vomit on the roof tiles. Had this information been available earlier, an analysis might have been made, and an antidote found. But Gull's prognosis proved correct, and Charles died in the early morning of 21 April 1876.

Several of Charles's friends were convinced that he would never have committed suicide, and they voiced their disquiet after this unlikely conclusion was reached by the discreet inquest held at the Priory on Friday 28 April. Their concern was echoed by Joseph Bravo, especially after an analysis of the vomit on the roof tiles had identified the poison as antimony. The most likely vehicle seemed to be the carafe of water from which Charles invariably drank before sleeping. Both Florence and Mrs Cox fell under increasing suspicion. They were soon advised to make voluntary statements to the Treasury, but whatever was said during this meeting caused a catastrophic rift between them. The household dissolved and they went their separate ways, Mrs Cox to Birmingham and Florence (by way of Brighton) to the countryside seat of her family.

A second inquest was ordered. Joseph Bravo secured the services of George Lewis, a fearless legal interrogator, and Florence's father, Robert Campbell, hired Sir Henry James QC, a former Attorney General, to represent Florence. The proceedings were held in the upstairs billiards hall at the Bedford Hotel, in Balham, and lasted for twenty-three days. Press coverage was extensive, with newspapers publishing daily reports of the hearing; crowds surged to gain entrance, and the room was so crowded that a surveyor had to be brought in to check that the floors could withstand the load. Members of both the Bravo and Campbell families were interrogated; so, too, were the Priory's servants, including the former groom, George Griffiths, who admitted that he had used antimony on Florence's horses to maintain their healthy coats, and had done the same when he had worked for Dr Gully in Malvern. Both Florence Bravo and Mrs Cox were questioned at length – the nerveless companion effectively stonewalled the questions put to her, but Florence suffered the humiliation of having her affair with Dr Gully made public, and she wept bitterly throughout. Despite it all, the jury decided that, although Charles had died by poisoning (rather than by his own hand or by misadventure), they were nevertheless unable to 'fix the guilt on any person or persons'. Mrs Cox retreated to Birmingham. Florence, calling herself Mrs Turner, went to live in Southsea where, eighteen months later, on 17 September 1878, she died, having literally drunk herself to death at the age of thirty-three.

Shortly before Charles Bravo's death, Mrs Cox, upon learning that she had been left some properties in Jamaica, had asked Joseph Bravo whether she should travel to the Caribbean to consolidate her affairs. Knowing that his son was considering getting rid of her to save money, he had urged her to go, but she had eventually decided against it. The timing was all wrong. She was not ready to give up her life of luxury as Florence's confidante, and she was determined that her sons should complete their elite English education. She knew that if she had made that visit Charles would never have taken her back. However, within months of Charles's death and the abrupt cessation of friendly relations with Florence, Mrs Cox travelled to the West Indies to take charge of her inheritance. She and her sons settled for many years in Jamaica, but she eventually returned to England, dying in 1917, her ninetieth year, in Lewisham.

We may never know who poured the lethal dose of antimony into Charles Bravo's water jug that night. Did Florence suspect that Mrs Cox had poisoned Charles – or were they both involved? The question remains formally unsolved. But if there had been a conspiracy, surely Florence would have retained Mrs Cox, her close friend and confidante of privileged status, joined to her by their complicity in the crime? That Florence chose to sever all links with her erstwhile companion would seem to hint towards Florence's innocence and Mrs Cox's guilt. But the mystery remains, and some writers on the case have yet to be convinced.

KC

FURTHER READING

Clarke, K. and Taylor, B., *Murder at the Priory: The Mysterious Poisoning of Charles Bravo* (London: Grafton, 1988)
Ruddick, J., *Death at the Priory* (London: Atlantic Books, 2001)

Ball, Mary (1818–1849)

It is doubtful that thirty-one-year-old Mary Ball was the only woman who tricked her errant husband into inadvertently killing himself with a pinch of arsenic, at a time when it was easily obtained for killing all manner of pests and its presence in the home was commonplace. Thomas Ball married Mary in 1838, and within twelve years they had produced six children – only one daughter, Mary Ann, survived. The family was living in Nuneaton, in a tight-knit community of ribbon weavers that included several other family members; Mary's father ran a beer-house known as the White Hart and Thomas worked as a labourer, so they were by no means destitute. Mary made it known that her husband was a bully, a drunkard and a philanderer, and she often threatened to kill him. His dalliances with other women seemed the likely cause of her anger, although it was rumoured that she was having an affair herself with a relative, the nineteen-year-old Will Bacon. Whether or not she seriously intended to get rid of Thomas, the perfect opportunity arose on Friday 18 May when he returned after a fishing trip with friends. He had been drinking heavily at the White Hart, and by the time he staggered home his 'inside was very queer'. Clearly, the usual remedy for such attacks was a dose of 'salts' kept, it seems, behind a teapot on the mantel above the fireplace.

Two weeks before, on 4 May, Mary had purchased a pennyworth of arsenic 'to kill bugs' in the house, leaving the package on the mantel. Now, she gave the nauseated Thomas some bread and gruel, and left the house. Upon her return, she found that his condition had worsened; he was vomiting violently. A doctor made two calls, and, after Thomas Ball died on Sunday 20 May, issued a certificate giving the cause of death as inflammation of the stomach. Local gossip, however, fuelled the need for a post-mortem; this revealed that Thomas's body contained between three and four grains of arsenic. Mary was arrested on suspicion of poisoning her husband. Bizarrely, she made three conflicting statements. In the first, she said that she had mixed the poison in a cup (as an insecticide), thrown the cup away and burned the paper wrapping. When no cup was found, she changed her story, saying that she had become confused, and may have inadvertently mixed some of the arsenic powder into Thomas's gruel. In her third statement, she admitted that she *had* added some of the arsenic to his gruel – but only as a purging agent.

On 22 May she was charged with the murder of her husband. The case came before Mr Justice Coleridge at the Warwickshire Assizes, held in the County Hall, Coventry, on 28 July 1849. Although she pleaded not guilty and was ably defended by Mr Miller (who suggested that Mary's 'forgetfulness', not malevolence, was to blame), she was sentenced to death. Petitions were sent to the Home Secretary, Sir George Grey, begging the Queen to sanction a reprieve, but none was given. Whilst in the condemned cell, Mary was subjected to the fervent (some might say overzealous) ministrations of the prison chaplain who, on 4 August, in an attempt to extract a confession, held her hand over a lighted candle so that she might fully comprehend the fires of eternal damnation; this act of religious enthusiasm lost him his job. Mary did, however, make a final statement in which she admitted that she had put the arsenic on the shelf knowing that Thomas would mistake it for the 'salts' to ease his stomach pains. Had she said, when she was first arrested, that he took it by mistake while she was, conveniently, out of the house – and therefore absolved of blame – she might have been released without charge or, at worst, found guilty of manslaughter, not murder.

Mary Ball was executed on Thursday, 9 August by William Calcraft on a scaffold in front of the county hall, in Cuckoo Lane. Thousands were said to have gathered to watch her die; many would have bought a copy of a broadside entitled, *Life, Trial and Awful Execution of Mary Ball*. A death mask of Mary's face was made, which remains on display at the West Midlands Police Museum in Coventry. Her public execution was the last to be carried out in the town, and a plaque to that effect is situated on the wall of the County Hall.

The murder of Thomas Ball was not one of the more sensational cases of Victoria's reign, but it serves to illustrate the plight of thousands of women shackled to unsatisfactory partners at a time when divorce was not an option; without the support of a male wage-earner, the workhouse beckoned. The majority of women chose to tolerate their situation and, despite the mid-century paranoia over the rise in the number of women accused of poisoning their husbands (which culminated in the Arsenic Act of 1851 – see Sarah Chesham), comparatively few resorted to murder. On the other hand, men wishing to rid themselves of their wives had no need to resort to murder by stealth; they could, and did, use brute force to kill or subjugate the women who were classed as mere chattels.

KC

FURTHER READING

Muscutt, R., *The Life, Trial and Hanging of Mary Ball* (Dereham: Broadlands Books, 2011)

Bambrick, Valentine (1837–1864)

In 1858, at the age of twenty-one, Private Valentine Bambrick of the 1st Battalion of the 60th Regiment of the King's Royal Rifle Corps was awarded the Victoria Cross for 'conspicuous bravery' during the so-called Indian Mutiny. Just five years later, the medal – the highest possible military honour that any British soldier could attain – was rescinded. Bambrick was by then a convicted criminal. Another year later he would be dead, by his own hand, in Pentonville Prison.

A rifleman, and seemingly a talented shot, Bambrick had been born on 13 April 1837 in Cawnpore (now Kanpur), in northern India. He was the son of Major John Bambrick, and the nephew and brother of military men. Coincidentally, in June 1857, Cawnpore would itself be the scene of one of the most controversial battles of the Mutiny.

Eleven months on, in Bareilly, around 160 miles to the south, Bambrick and his comrades were attacked. The details are vague, but it would appear likely that his assailants were local fighters who objected to the colonial rule of the East India Company, which had once been a private company (or a 'delinquent behemoth', in John Pemble's words), and was now 'a non-trading Indian civil service under parliamentary control'. Bambrick fought back, reportedly repelling three men and killing one despite being wounded himself.

Bambrick remained a soldier until 1863, even transferring regiments to remain in India once his battalion was stood down. The final months of his military service were spent in Ireland, before events took a turn for the worse.

On 16 November 1863, Valentine Bambrick landed at Hampshire, his army service finally at an end. Soon after, he got into a fight with a soldier named Henry Russell in a nearby public house. By his own account, Bambrick had attempted to intervene when he witnessed Russell arguing violently with a woman.

Both Bambrick and the woman were arrested, accused not only of assault but of the theft of Lance Corporal Russell's medals, which had gone missing during the altercation. Bambrick's life outside the army, at least as a free man, had lasted less than twenty-four hours.

A few weeks later, on 3 December 1863, a brief trial ended with the former hero convicted and disgraced. Bambrick – who reportedly made aggressive outbursts towards both Russell and the court – was ordered to surrender his medals as well as his claim to an army pension, and was taken away to begin three years of imprisonment. The woman, Charlotte Johnson, was sentenced to twelve months' imprisonment.

In the event, Bambrick could only bear the first four months of his sentence. On 1 April 1864, he left a note in his Pentonville cell and then hanged himself, just days short of his twenty-seventh birthday.

Bambrick remains one of only eight men to suffer the indignity of having the Victoria Cross removed; although, interestingly, two more of that number were also granted their medals during the battles of the Mutiny in 1858 (James McGuire and Michael Murphy). One other, Frederick Corbett, was also granted his for service with the King's Royal Rifle Corps. In fact, the period accounts for a disproportionately large number of Victoria Cross awards, with a record-breaking twenty-four being distributed for acts on a single day during the campaign's most controversial incident, the siege at Lucknow.

In 2002, a plaque commemorating Bambrick's valour was placed in the chapel of St Pancras Cemetery. No reference was made to his forfeiture of the Victoria Cross. The exact location of his grave remains unknown.

TNB

Bartlett, Adelaide (1855–?)

What could be more intriguing than an unsolved crime involving an alluring young woman suspected of murdering her husband – and, for good measure, the added frisson of an extra-marital affair? The Victorian era saw two such mysteries: the poisoning of Charles Bravo in 1876, whose wife, Florence, was suspected of, but not charged with, his murder (see The Balham Mystery); and, ten years later, that of Adelaide Bartlett, who was tried for killing her husband with liquid chloroform, a death more usually associated with suicide.

Adelaide Blanche de la Tremoille was born in Orléans in September 1855; her father's name was given as Adolphe Collet de la Tremoille, Comte de Thouars d'Escury, a thirty-five-year-old widower; her mother was Clara Chamberlain, the nineteen-year-old daughter of a clerk in London's Stock Exchange. However, according to Edward Clarke's memoir, published in 1918, Adelaide was the 'unacknowledged daughter of an Englishman of good social position' who funded her defence when, some thirty years later, she was charged with murder. This shadowy father-figure had also arranged Adelaide's marriage to Edwin Bartlett, a south London grocer, in 1875. After spending two years at a school in Stoke Newington, Adelaide started married life with Edwin in a flat above the shop in Herne Hill. They were an ill-matched couple and, after moving to rural Merton, Adelaide embarked on an affair with a young Wesleyan preacher, the Reverend George Dyson. Edwin had hired him to tutor his young wife and, it seemed, harboured no resentment when their friendship became intimate.

By 1885, Edwin and Adelaide had moved to Claverton Street, Pimlico, where Adelaide's lessons with Dyson continued. When Edwin became weary and depressed and a blue line started to appear along his gums, Adelaide called in a gullible young physician, Dr Alfred Leach (he died in 1896 whilst recklessly experimenting with sewer gas). In thrall to the pretty young Frenchwoman, he failed to recognise the symptoms of slow lead poisoning and prescribed, instead, mercury for syphilis. As Adelaide's affair with Dyson accelerated, so Edwin's health declined. Having convinced the young preacher that she needed some chloroform to sprinkle on a handkerchief and wave under Edwin's nose to deflect his amorous advances, Dyson gallantly obliged by buying a quantity of the drug from two chemists' shops in Putney, ostensibly for 'cleaning purposes'.

On the afternoon of 31 December, Edwin underwent some gruelling tooth extractions, but nonetheless was able to enjoy a cosy supper with Adelaide, who had ordered some of his favourite treats – nuts, fruitcake and brandy. The air was filled with the shrill laughter of folk celebrating the New Year. During the night, in a more private scene, Edwin was restless, and Adelaide spent several hours by his bedside, holding his toe to calm him. When she woke the next morning, Edwin was dead, and there was a strong smell of chloroform and a hint of brandy on his pillow and nightshirt. The bottle of chloroform was in its usual place on the mantelpiece, although Adelaide said later that, after Edwin's death, she had emptied the contents and tossed the empty bottle from a train window into the waters of Peckham Rye pond. This was, in fact, a lie, as the pond was frozen over that day: the bottle was never found.

Both Adelaide and Dyson were arrested and stood trial at the Old Bailey for the murder of Edwin Bartlett on Monday 12 April 1886. The presiding judge was Mr Justice Wills; the Attorney General, Sir Charles Russell, appeared for the prosecution and Edward Clarke for the defence. The newspapers ensured their readers were amply supplied with detailed accounts of the drama, complete with drawings of the main players. There was a scramble for seats in the public gallery and many were turned away; those fortunate enough to gain access to the courtroom waited in anticipation for the proceedings to begin. Adelaide, already considered scandalous by the public, compounded her notoriety by appearing in the dock not only hatless but with her hair cropped; both these displays of independent spirit were considered shocking, but even the severity of the cut could not disguise her feminine charms. Dyson, although he had procured the chloroform that had caused Edwin Bartlett's death (and possibly disposed of the empty bottle), was soon released, guilty only of gullibility and foolishly misplaced trust.

Adelaide therefore faced the charge alone. Her mysterious father's engagement of Edward Clarke had, however, been fortuitous, for he defended her with passionate commitment. His rhetoric was mesmerising, and his closing speech monumental. The crux of the case for the prosecution was that, although the post-mortem findings had revealed that Edwin's stomach was full of liquid chloroform, there were no blisters on his mouth or gullet. It was suggested, therefore, that the chloroform reached his stomach by way of a tube. Adopting the stance of a great actor on the stage, Clarke addressed the jury, sure of the rapt attention of every person in the court. How, he argued, could Adelaide have administered the poison? How, without any medical knowledge, could she have inserted a tube through her husband's mouth and into his stomach? Even professionals would attempt such a tricky and potentially dangerous procedure with trepidation. How, then, could the young woman in the dock have achieved such a technically difficult task?

Clarke steered the jury towards the suggestion that suicide was a more plausible explanation. The bottle of chloroform was left within easy reach of the patient – in all probability, distressed by his chronic ill-health, riddled with anxieties about having worms crawling inside him and, furthermore, excluded from his wife's affections, he was unable to sleep. In desperation, he had swallowed the fatal dose.

Such was the case for the defence; yet some might suggest a more sinister scenario. Could it be that Adelaide had begun to find the prospect of a lifetime married to Edwin, with his peculiar notions and rotten teeth, too repugnant to contemplate? She knew that his state of mind was extremely fragile, and he was already susceptible to the idea of being mesmerised: so did she suggest that he should end his suffering by swallowing the lethal dose of chloroform – perhaps with a little brandy to help mask the sickly taste and excruciating pain on impact?

There was great rejoicing when the jury delivered its verdict of not guilty. Thousands of cheering spectators lined the roads outside the Old Bailey and a triumphant Edward Clarke, whilst on a visit to the theatre that evening, was greeted with tumultuous applause – indeed, his lucrative career as a defence lawyer flourished on the back of his success in securing Adelaide's acquittal. Elsewhere, curiosity about what had actually happened remained unsatisfied. Lord Coleridge, who unsuccessfully defended Louise Masset in 1899, recorded the much-quoted remark made by Sir James Paget, Serjeant-Surgeon to Queen Victoria, on leaving the Old Bailey that day: 'Mrs Bartlett was no doubt quite properly acquitted, but now it is hoped in the interests of science she will tell us how she did it!'

Adelaide's family connections must have been instrumental in ensuring that her movements from that day remained uncharted. She may have returned to France, where she had spent her early childhood, or she may have travelled to America – but, to date, no proof of her whereabouts has been found. As for George Dyson, recent research has suggested that he went to America, changed his name to John Bernard Walker, became editor of *Scientific American*, married a socialite, and died in 1928.

KC

FURTHER READING

Clarke, K., *In the Interests of Science* (London: Mango Books, 2015)

Hall, Sir J., *Trial of Adelaide Bartlett* (Edinburgh: William Hodge and Company, 1927)

Clarke, Sir E., *The Story of My Life* (London: John Murray, 1918)

Bennett, Herbert John (1879–1901)

Herbert John Bennett was a restless soul whom modern theorists are often inclined to exonerate, in spite of the absence of any contemporary doubt about his culpability.

Bennett's early history was unimpressive. He seemed to be very conscious of this, affecting an aura of intellectuality and sophistication to which his unspectacular education and background did not entitle him. This false persona was only likely to be persuasive to someone with a rather naïve outlook on things, and, in 1897, Bennett married a woman – only slightly older than himself – who met this condition admirably. This was Mary Anne Clark, a music teacher with a great deal of interest in her new husband's grand visions of the future. The reality was a gloomier one, in which Bennett moved through lowly occupations as a newsagent's assistant, then a grocer's assistant, and then a salesman of sewing machines, apparently losing his grip on these positions whenever he was required to exhibit trustworthiness with money.

By 1900, the couple were living separately. Bennett had married in haste and was now, by custom, obliged to repent at leisure; Mary Anne was in rooms at Bexley Heath, Kent. He sent her a little money every so often, earned either through his new, legitimate work at the arsenal at Woolwich or, as Edgar Wallace speculated, because he was running 'one of his get-rich-quick schemes as a side-line'. He had also become acquainted with a young lady named Alice Meadows; feigning respectability, he met her family, and took her briefly to the seaside, at Yarmouth, where the demure pair occupied separate rooms.

Clearly, the time had come to erase Mary Anne from this overpopulated picture. On 23 September 1900, it transpired that a woman's body had been discovered, asphyxiated, on Yarmouth beach. The immediate difficulty facing the local police was in establishing her identity. She had been staying in a guest house in Yarmouth since 15 September under the name of 'Mrs Hood', but it was soon realised that this was an alias. Scrabbling around for details, the police ascertained that the victim's silver chain and antique watch – family heirlooms – were missing when the body was discovered, and that she had, earlier that week, received a letter with a Woolwich postmark.

There was also the small matter of the laundry mark on the victim's clothing. These were commonly added to garments that were sent to wash houses for cleaning, and the victim's number, distinguishing her clothing from everybody else's, was 599. A tireless survey of the Woolwich wash houses, however, produced no result. Eventually, a laundry manageress in Bexley Heath saw a photograph of the laundry mark in a newspaper, recognised its origin, and, scanning through her records, found that it belonged to a Mrs Bennett.

Back in London, Herbert Bennett evinced 'a mild interest' in the case, discussing it with Alice Meadows and her sister and wondering aloud about the police's failure to catch the murderer. Little did he realise that the laundry manageress's evidence had turned the tide. When he was arrested, he exclaimed, 'Yarmouth? Why, I have never been to Yarmouth in my life!' But this was only the first of a string of unsupportable statements to which he stuck for the duration, irrespective of the facts ranged against him. Even the noted barrister Edward Marshall Hall could not bring about his acquittal, and Bennett was eventually executed at Norwich Gaol on 21 March 1901. His body twitched on the end of the rope for two minutes and then was still.

The case was notable for several reasons. The evidence of the laundry mark exemplified the new value of the media: once, the police could hardly have hoped for assistance of this sort, but an increasingly literate public and advances in printing technology enabled clues such as these to be presented to the masses (see Forensics). Without the somewhat fortuitous intervention of the laundry manageress, the true identity of 'Mrs Hood' may never have been revealed. The absence of the watch and chain also intrigues: it has to be supposed that Bennett stole them, but whether for their monetary value or because they were distinctive is not known. In an ideal world, perhaps Bennett hoped to argue that the Yarmouth victim could not have been Mary Anne, who was never without her precious artefacts; but her seaside landlady had noticed them and, besides, they had been snapped in situ around their owner's neck by a beach photographer earlier that week.

Bennett's apologists sometimes insist that a later murder at Yarmouth beach – committed in 1912 – bore similarities to the death of Mary Anne, enough to justify reasonable doubt. It would seem to be the case that both murders were committed with bootlaces; but – taking into consideration the inexplicable twelve-year gap – one wonders whether this fact is sufficient to outweigh the strong circumstantial evidence against Bennett. On the other hand, Paul Capon, in his sweetly titled 1965 book, *The Great Yarmouth Mystery*, also felt that Bennett was innocent, and his scenario did not rely on the allusive properties of the second bootlace murder. A new monograph is required, exploring this intricate case more fully than is possible here.

MWO

FURTHER READING

Wallace, E., *The Murder on Yarmouth Sands* (London: George Newnes, n.d.)

Capon, P., *The Great Yarmouth Mystery* (London: George G. Harrap, 1965)

Eddleston, J. J., *Blind Justice* (Oxford: ABC-CLIO, 2000)

Berry, James (1852–1913)

It might be supposed that any man who offers his services as a state executioner must have in his nature a brutish streak, and harbour a sadistic desire to punish his fellow men and women in a manner both terrifying and ignominious. This assumption might be endorsed by the image we have of James Berry, employed as an executioner between 1884 and 1892, during which time he executed 125 men and five women, for which he was paid £10 a time plus expenses. Yet behind the physical image lay a man not without feelings of compassion or sensitivity, seemingly at odds with the career he had chosen. He was fond of presenting those he was about to hang with sentimental religious tracts urging repentance in the face of imminent death. He was also a family man and particularly fond of pigeons and rabbits.

James Berry was born in Heckmondwike, Yorkshire, in 1852, one of eighteen children born to Daniel Berry, a wool-stapler, and Mary Ann Kelly. A little over five feet and eight inches tall, he was of stocky build with a florid complexion. His bewhiskered face was scored with two scars, one caused in childhood by a kicking horse, and the other inflicted in later life whilst arresting a thug in Bradford. After serving in the police force for eight years, he was working as a poorly paid shoe salesman when, in 1884, he applied and was accepted for the post of executioner. He was proud of his office and as an ex-policeman saw his role as a link in a 'chain of legal retribution', providing an essential service in upholding law and order. Having learned aspects of the procedure from his forerunner, William Marwood, he sought to ensure that death was as near-instantaneous as possible. He perfected a *Table of Drops*, correlating the weight of the convict against the pendant

James Berry. (Authors' collection)

length of the rope, a calculation that would ensure that enough force was produced as the body fell to break the neck and avoid strangulation. Berry took pride in his work and ensured that the apparatus was rigorously tested using dummy weights prior to the execution. He has been quoted as saying that 'Calcraft hanged them; I executed them'. Most of the executions he performed were without incident, but his abortive attempt to hang John 'Babbacombe' Lee, in 1885, descended into a fiasco distressing for both Berry and Lee (although a subsequent inquiry blamed the faulty mechanism operating the trap doors rather than any error on the part of Berry). That same year, Robert Goodale was decapitated during his execution by Berry at Norwich Castle.

James Berry resigned from his post in 1892 after a disagreement with Dr James Barr, medical officer of Kirkdale Gaol, over the length of the drop in the execution of John Conway, in 1891. Conway was nearly decapitated, and the incident sparked renewed public clamour for the abolition of capital punishment. Berry remained a troubled man, wrestling with his conscience having, he said, hanged some who he felt had been wrongly convicted. He nevertheless travelled the country giving talks about his work; in time, however, he became increasingly religious, professing to question not only the morality of hanging but also its effectiveness as a deterrent. After suffering a breakdown in 1894, he became an evangelist, regularly preaching at a mission hall in Bradford whilst working as a salesman and part-time barman.

In his memoir, *My Experiences as an Executioner*, published in 1892, he advocated the introduction of a court of appeal for criminal cases, preferring the idea to the emotive reprieve appeals which then had to be presented to the Home Secretary. In his opinion, appointing three judges to reassess a case seemed a much fairer system, as those who signed petitions were often lacking a full grasp of the law or were incapable of understanding the factors informing a guilty verdict. He also considered that the three-week period between conviction and execution – to allow time for either a confession or a reprieve – was far too long and extremely harrowing for both the condemned and the prison staff assigned to attend them. Though not (at least at that time) against capital punishment per se, he advocated that consideration should be given to various degrees of murder and a sentence of death reserved for the most heinous.

James Berry died in 1913 at the age of sixty-one.

KC

FURTHER READING

Berry, J., *My Experiences as an Executioner*, edited and with an introduction by Jonathan Goodman (London: David & Charles, 1972)

Bond, Thomas (1841–1901)

Somewhere in the background of several cases cited in this book appears the character of Dr Thomas Bond, who was, among other professional appointments, police surgeon to A Division (Westminster) of the Metropolitan Police from 1867 until his death, by suicide, in 1901. He examined the disarranged body of Harriet Lane, the victim of Henry Wainwright; he gave evidence at the Old Bailey regarding the death of Harriet Staunton, and at Maidstone regarding the death of Frederick Isaac Gold (see Percy Lefroy Mapleton); he studied the remains of Julia Thomas, and then found her killer, Kate Webster, who was reluctant to be executed without a struggle, to be fabricating her claims of pregnancy. His examination of the anatomy of Percy John (see George Henry Lamson) failed to reveal the cause of death, although a chemical analysis later uncovered the poisonous secret in John's organs; he meticulously scoured the body of Phoebe Hogg, the adult victim of Mary Pearcey, and checked Pearcey's hands (and, indeed, her kitchen) for evidence to substantiate his observations. He gave testimony at the trial of Louise Masset, mentioning that he had afforded 'special attention' to the means by which medical men could determine the time of death of the bodies which crime or happenstance brought before them. This was, he said, not 'part of the practice of an ordinary practitioner'; his opportunities had been different, outside the norm, and he had seen 'so many hundreds of dead bodies' along the way. Eighteen months later, after jumping from a third-floor window, Bond joined the dark parade, to the dismay of his friend and coroner, John Troutbeck, who described him as 'one of the best known men in Westminster, noted for his courage and determination'.

It was not until the late 1980s, however, that Bond was raptured into the constellations, and even then he figured primarily (almost exclusively, in fact) on the quirky celestial maps of Ripperologists. In October 1888, he had been commissioned to review the post-mortem paperwork of the first four victims of Jack the Ripper, and it so happened that the murder of Mary Jane Kelly, in November, provided Bond with a chance to see the remains of a Ripper victim for himself. His report, filed on the day following Kelly's murder, survived in (at least) two pieces: one section, previously unknown to historians, was sent anonymously to Scotland Yard in 1987 (it had, no doubt, been snaffled decades before), and this seems to have reignited interest in the only *other* known section, which had never left the police files, and which had been publicly available in transcript since the 1970s. The late 1980s, of course, were the halcyon years of the criminal profiler, and famous (and frequently infallible) iterations of this already cultish figure had begun to appear in the popular media. Elsewhere in society, programmatic and deterministic interpretations of human behaviour had begun to falter, but serial killers, some of whom were as conscious of their media image as their pursuers, felt like fair game. The work of the FBI at Quantico had begun to impose a form of scientific logic on the apparently schizoid nature of serial homicide, and, in this atmosphere, Thomas Bond emerged as an unlikely forefather of the profiling discipline.

We ought to be cautious about this attribution, however. While it was true to say that Bond's report escaped the usual confines of medico-legal discretion (positing, for example, that the Ripper was 'a man of physical strength and of great coolness and daring', 'quiet', inoffensive' and 'respectably dressed'), many of his deductions were couched in very cautious language, well below evidential thresholds, and of limited practical utility to the police of the day, whose enquiries are not known to have been steered in any particular direction by his observations. There was a qualitative distinction to be made between Bond's insights and those of the FBI, and, ironically, this consisted in the *quantitative* methods of the latter. The FBI's VICAP database emerged from statistical sampling, and its growing dataset was expected to lead to an increasingly detailed picture of serial offending behaviours, their formative indicators, and their expression in real-time by modern America's most disturbed individuals. To abstract the quantitative basis of this activity is to change its character entirely; it follows that, whatever it was that Thomas Bond was doing, it was not criminal profiling.

MWO

Boucher, Eliza (1825–1878)

In 1854, Eliza Boucher, a maidservant in her late twenties, was working for John Barnard and his wife, Susan, at Myrtle Cottage, near Barnstaple, Devon. Early in the morning of 18 October, Eliza gave birth to premature twins; the male child died shortly after delivery, but the female, though weak and underweight, lived for a few hours. When bathed in hot water, she opened her eyes and whimpered, but she died soon afterwards. An inquest was held and it was reported that 'the two little corpses were pitiful to behold'. Charles Morgan, a local surgeon, confirmed that there were marks of bruising on either side of their windpipes as though their throats had been squeezed between finger and thumb.

In March 1855, Eliza Boucher was sent for trial, charged with infanticide. A plea in her defence suggested that the injuries to the babies' necks were caused during their delivery and 'were not the consequence of the deliberate murderous act of the prisoner'. Having heard the judge's summing up, the jurors delivered a verdict of not guilty without even leaving the courtroom.

After Eliza's perfunctory acquittal, it was rumoured that John Barnard may have fathered the doomed infants; the source of the gossip was supposed to be the surgeon, Morgan, repeating some derogatory remarks which Eliza had made. In this rendition,

Barnard had made 'disgraceful overtures' towards Eliza soon after she had joined the household, and there had been a 'disgusting occurrence' – perhaps a coerced abortion attempt – at Myrtle Cottage three weeks before the fateful birth. Barnard took great umbrage at these insinuations and subjected Morgan to a ferocious attack with a horsewhip. He was subsequently charged with assault and fined £25. As a man of property, he was able to pay the fine immediately and thereby avoided imprisonment; a man of lesser means would, of course, have gone to prison.

Eliza's backstory intrigues. In 1853, two short years before her murder trial, she had served a six-month sentence for 'concealing the birth' of a new-born, whose body she admitted she had burned in a wash-house furnace. It is not known whether she went on to have more children, but, bearing in mind the absence of efficient birth control at the time, it seems likely that she did. She died in 1878, in her mid-fifties, full of secrets.

KC

Further Reading

Clarke, K., *Deadly Dilemmas* (London: Mango Books, forthcoming)

Bousfield, William (*c.* 1825–1856)

A man of thespian inclinations, William Bousfield eventually made it to the public stage – but only in the most unfortunate way. He is remembered now for the utter horror of his execution.

William Bousfield was an inattentive husband, prone to bouts of worklessness and happy to leave to his wife, Sarah, the task of running their shop on Portland Street, in Soho, London. As it turned out, Sarah took to the role quite naturally, and did a good job, but still William's apathy may have rankled with her. There were times, it was said, when Sarah was 'heard designating him a worthless idle fellow' – and one suspects that fruitier language is concealed in the decorous retelling. On William's side, it was thought that he may have become jealous of his wife, 'accusing her of being too familiar with the customers'. Seven years (and three children) into the marriage, itches were being felt.

William's aimlessness, though unshakeable during daylight hours, gave way to sudden activity after sundown, and, according to those who knew him, he would head for the theatres of London's West End. Perhaps no more than occasionally, he made a pittance 'at the Princess's Theatre [on Oxford Street], as a supernumerary' – put more simply, he was an extra, rarely (if ever) picked out by the limelight, and all for a shilling a night, or a shilling and sixpence if he was lucky.

On the morning of Sunday, 3 February 1856, William appeared in a corridor at Bow Street Police Station. PC Alfred Fudge, coming the other way, asked him where he was going. 'In here,' said William, 'to give myself up. I have murdered my wife.' He was taken to see Inspector Dodd, who noticed that William had made an attempt to cut his own throat, had a deep cut on his hand, and was missing one of the sleeves of his bloodied shirt.

Hurrying to the shop in Portland Street, the police found that the door to the back parlour, in which the family normally slept, was locked. They forced it open. The interior disclosed that William's confession to murder had been incomplete: he had mentioned Sarah, but omitted the children. A doctor who was brought to the scene from his home in nearby Berwick Street found no life in any of them. The missing shirtsleeve was also discovered, saturated with blood; it was compared with the shirt which William had been wearing when he handed himself in, and it fitted perfectly.

The hanging was set for Monday, 31 March 1856, to be conducted – per the custom of the time – in public, outside Newgate Prison; William Calcraft was engaged to pull the lever. Bousfield had not stood up to the strain of events: some said that he had thrown himself into the fire in his cell on the evening before he was due to be executed; some said that when the gathered officials arrived to accompany him to the scaffold, he fainted, recovered, vomited, and then fainted all over again. He was carried halfway to the rope by two turnkeys, and then placed on a chair, and seated insensible on the drop, with the rope around his neck.

Back went the lever, down went the chair; Bousfield was suspended for a second or two. And then there was a shout from the crowd – 'He is up again!' – and Bousfield, regaining consciousness, was seen to have managed, somehow, to get his feet back onto the edge of the trap; he was trying to raise his hands to the rope. One of the officials dislodged Bousfield's feet, and he dropped again – but again he rose, restoring his feet to their previous position. Calcraft, who had made a hasty exit thinking that his job was done, now returned to the scene, and pushed Bousfield's feet back into the nothingness; Bousfield dropped again, suspended by the rope. And then for a third time the feet wriggled back up, and again Bousfield's hands lifted, trying to clutch at the rope. And now Calcraft grabbed one leg, with difficulty gained control over the other, and held on, keeping Bousfield over the drop, hanging by his neck, until he stopped struggling for life. Four minutes the whole thing took – *at least* four minutes – and *The Times* reported the next day that Bousfield had been 'tortured to death'.

All the while, the bells in the nearby churches had been pealing joyously: peace with Russia had come.

MWO

Britland, Mary Ann (*c.* 1847–1886)

In 1886, thirty-nine-year-old factory worker Mary Ann Britland, her husband, Thomas, and their two teenage daughters were living in the Lancashire town of Ashton-under-Lyne. Mary Ann was described as 'a neat, industrious woman who always discharged her duties to her family in a thoroughly creditable manner'. As the house they rented in Turner Lane was supposedly overrun with vermin, Mary Ann purchased some 'mouse powders', sold as Harrison's Vermin Killer, at 3*d* a packet; these contained 14 grains of strychnia and 10.5 grains of arsenic (as little as half a grain of strychnia or less than four grains of arsenic could prove fatal to humans). When handing over the powders the chemist had made a macabre joke of unintended perspicacity, advising Mary Ann that, to avoid detection and claim the burial 'club' money, she should only give her intended victim a series of small doses.

On 9 March, the eldest daughter, nineteen-year-old Elizabeth, died suddenly – ostensibly from natural causes – and her parents claimed £10 from her life insurance. Mary Ann had recently gone in person to the insurance broker and paid 1s 8d in advance for insurance on both her husband and daughter, instead of waiting for the agent's usual home visit to collect payment of a few pence each week. Thomas Britland spent some of the money buying a new hat to wear to his daughter's funeral, little knowing that he would be the next victim. On 3 May, he died, having suffered a series of catastrophic epileptic seizures. The following day, Mary Ann, in the company of a neighbour, twenty-five-year-old Thomas Dixon, went to claim £11 17s on her husband's life insurance. The pair proceeded to exchange the deceased's hat with one that fitted Thomas Dixon and was of 'better quality', the transaction being completed by Mary Ann on payment of an extra 5s.

It was already rumoured that Mary Ann and Thomas Dixon had an illicit 'connection', and it was noted that Dixon spent a great deal of time at the home of Mary Ann whenever her husband was working. He had even said that he wished he had married someone like Mary Ann, and made derogatory remarks about Mary, his wife of six years and the mother of his two children; she, however, was either unaware or unfazed by the gossip for, taking pity on the newly bereaved Mary Ann, she invited her and her daughter, Susannah, to sleep at the Dixon home. Predictably, when Mary Dixon died on 14 May, and Thomas Dixon promptly collected £19 17s 6d from the Union Friendly Society, foul play was suspected in all three deaths. The police questioned Mary Ann, and a subsequent post-mortem on Mary Dixon's body confirmed the presence of strychnine and arsenic. The bodies of Thomas and Elizabeth Britland were exhumed and found to contain evidence of both poisons.

Mary Ann Britland was arrested, brought before the magistrates, and charged with three counts of murder. Initially, Thomas Dixon was also charged with complicity in the murder of his wife, but he was released after convincing the authorities of his innocence. The murder trial was opened on Thursday, 22 July 1886 before Mr Justice Cave at Manchester Assizes and, although Mary Ann denied the charges, she was found guilty and sentenced to death. Her piercing screams echoed around the courtroom and, once confined to the condemned cell, she was distraught and barely able to eat or sleep. There was no hope of a reprieve, and Mary Ann spent her last night on earth singing hymns. When urged to confess to all three murders, Mary Ann denied killing Mary Dixon but hung her head at the mention of her husband and daughter. She was hanged on 9 August by James Berry, becoming the first woman to be executed at Strangeways Prison. She had to be dragged, crying piteously, to the scaffold but, once secured, she died instantaneously.

The motive for these murders remains a mystery, but it was rumoured that Elizabeth was killed because she threatened to expose her mother's adulterous liaison with Thomas Dixon. It seems inexplicable that Mary Ann, who, it seems, had led a normal life without exhibiting any bizarre or criminal behaviour, should suddenly inflict an agonising death on three people. Some contemporary reports suggested that Mary Ann and Thomas Dixon, despite the difference in their ages, intended to marry once they were free of their respective spouses.

KC

FURTHER READING

Berry, J., *My Experiences as an Executioner*, edited and with an introduction by Jonathan Goodman (London: David & Charles, 1972)

Broadmoor

Located in the Berkshire village of Crowthorne, Broadmoor Criminal Lunatic Asylum (now Broadmoor Hospital) was opened on 27 May 1863. Today it is one of a trio of British psychiatric hospitals offering the highest level of security. Both of the others – Rampton Hospital, near Lincoln, and Ashworth Hospital, approximately ten miles outside of Liverpool – were opened in the twentieth century to deal with an increase in patient numbers at Broadmoor. Superseding the ancient charitable institution of the Royal Bethlehem Hospital, Broadmoor was the premier destination for 'criminal lunatics' during the last four decades of the Victorian era: in a neat example of historical symmetry, it was, in its turn, the growing pressure on places in 'Bedlam' – to give the popular corruption – which had led to the creation of Broadmoor in the first place.

Notable Victorian residents of Broadmoor included not only artist-turned-patricide Richard Dadd, doctor-turned-murderer-turned-lexicographer William Chester Minor, and James Kelly (first admitted in 1883, he famously absconded in 1888 and was readmitted at his own request in 1927), but also Daniel M'Naghten, who murdered Edward Drummond in 1843, as well as the architects of two assassination attempts against Queen Victoria – Edward Oxford, the first to commit such an outrage in 1840, and his comrade-in-treason Roderick McLean, who did so in 1882. In fact, it was McLean's trial, in 1883, which led to the invention of the legal tautology by which certain people could be considered 'guilty but insane'. Last (in this list), but by no means least, was Christiana Edmunds, who in 1872 was found to have poisoned an assortment of her fellow residents of Brighton with arsenic and strychnine inserted into chocolates.

On the outside, the idea that confinement in Broadmoor was preferable to incarceration in a conventional prison was not unpopular; although all Broadmoor's inmates were held indefinitely, they had to be released when they regained their sanity. To some folk – those with criminal ambitions and a degree of confidence in their ability to act – this seemed like an interesting gambit to entertain, but it was easy to underestimate the difficulties of proving one's sanity in an asylum (a truism of which David Rosenhan's 1973 experiment demonstrated the durability). In practice many patients were never liberated since it was difficult to foresee the consequences of reuniting them with their peers in society: how was it possible to tell whether any characteristics of sanity which they had begun to exhibit within Broadmoor's controlled environment would be sustained in the dynamism of the world beyond its walls? In 1897, a Kent man named Rollo Richards stood trial at the Old Bailey for causing an explosion at a post office in Lewisham. Rollo's arresting officer testified that the prisoner had told him, 'I would sooner do five years at Broadmoor than at Portland,' an apparent reference to Portland Prison in Dorset. Rollo's wish went unfulfilled – he was sentenced to seven years, to be spent in a mainstream prison, but one sees the equation underpinning his thinking. Perhaps, all things considered, he got the better end of the deal.

Then there was the question of diagnosis and treatment planning. The Victorians found themselves caught between post-Enlightenment philosophical advancements – in which insanity was humanely reclassified as a disease, rather than a moral failure – and an antiquated pharmaceutical and therapeutic milieu which could do almost nothing to manage patients' symptoms. In 1884, a twenty-five-year-old woman from Notting Hill named Annie Player was committed indefinitely after throwing her seven-month-old son from a window; the testimony of Broadmoor's superintendent, Dr William Orange, who stated that he had 'formed a clear opinion that she was of unsound mind', was influential in deterring the imposition of a prison sentence or worse. Nonetheless, Annie was certainly still in Broadmoor in 1911, and probably died there in 1929. Nowadays, she would be diagnosed with a post-partum condition, monitored closely by midwives, health visitors and social workers, and treated by doctors and psychologists, almost certainly in the community (presuming, at least, that these prophylactic interventions were sufficient to avert tragedy). In the 1880s, however, nearly seventy-nine per cent of the women who had been found insane by a court and admitted to Broadmoor arrived in the wake of a child-murder – this amounted to seventy-four cases altogether (see also Infanticide). Similarly alarming ratios were recorded right up until the 1950s, but by the 1980s the ratio had dropped below four per cent, representing three cases.

TNB

FURTHER READING

Gordon, H., *Broadmoor* (London: Psychology News Press, 2012)
Stevens, M., *Broadmoor Revealed* (Barnsley: Pen and Sword, 2013)

Brown, Elizabeth Martha (1811/12–1856)

When forty-one-year-old Martha Bearnes married twenty-one-year-old John Brown at Wareham, Dorset, in January 1852, it was a second marriage for both. She was later described as 'a rather mild-looking woman with short black curls [and] a quiet appearance', and John was portrayed as 'a fine, good-looking young fellow, standing near six feet high' with 'very long, thick hair'. The pair had met whilst working at Blackmanston Farm, on the Isle of Purbeck. Once married they moved to Birdsmoorgate, some seven miles from Beaminster, and with the £50 Martha had inherited from her former husband, John equipped himself with a horse and wagon and, while he worked as a tranter (that is, a carrier of goods), Martha set up a small grocery shop. John travelled far afield in his work and it was common knowledge that he usually stopped for a drink or two at various pubs before making his way home. On the evening of 5 July 1856, John parted company with another carrier, George Fooks, after completing a delivery of poles to Beaminster, and went home.

Early next morning, a relative who lived close by was awoken by Martha, who was banging on his bedroom window and pleading with him to come to the house; John's horse, she said, had kicked him in the head. He found John dead, lying on the floor with a catastrophic wound to the back of his head. After an inquest, held the next day at the Rose and Crown inn, Martha Brown – now known as Elizabeth – was arrested, charged with the murder of John Brown and taken to Dorchester Gaol. Her subsequent murder trial was held at Dorchester Crown Court on 21 July 1856, before the judge, Serjeant William Fry Channell, and a jury representing a cross-section of local artisans – a tailor, a printer, a farmer and a shoemaker among them. Witness statements demonstrated that, during the journey to Beaminster that day, John and George Fooks had encountered Mary Davis, a rival for John's affections. It was not clear, however, whether Mary had left them on the road or whether she had joined them in the pub later, drinking and playing skittles until midnight. Although Elizabeth still denied murdering her husband, the medical evidence contradicted her claim that he had been killed by his horse, and she was found guilty of murder and sentenced to death.

On 7 August, whilst awaiting execution in Dorchester Gaol, Elizabeth made a full confession. She described her husband coming home drunk at two o'clock in the morning. When she accused him of consorting with Mary Davis, he reacted violently, and the quarrel escalated: he stunned her with a blow to her head before lashing out with a horsewhip, finally delivering a vicious kick to her side and threatening to knock out her brains. When he bent down to unbuckle his boots, she, in an 'ungovernable passion at being so abused and struck', seized a hatchet and struck him several violent blows to the head. At the first blow he fell unconscious to the floor. 'As soon as I had done it,' she confessed, 'I would have given the world not to have done it. I had never struck him before after all his ill treatment; but when he hit me so hard at this time I was almost out of my senses and hardly knew what I was doing.'

There were concerted efforts to secure a reprieve from the Home Secretary, Sir George Grey, but these were rejected. Elizabeth was executed over the gateway of Dorchester Gaol on Saturday 9 August before a large crowd that, despite the rain, had gathered to watch the grisly spectacle. As they left the condemned cell, the two female warders who accompanied her were clearly upset; but Elizabeth, perfectly composed, paused to shake hands with the prison officials. She climbed the steps to the gallows to meet her executioner, William Calcraft, who, having placed the noose around her neck and covered her face with a white cap, descended from the scaffold. He had forgotten, however, to pinion her legs, and had to return to her to do so – by which time the rain had so dampened the fabric of the hood that it clung to her face, resembling a ghostly mask. Retreating once more, Calcraft withdrew the bolt; Elizabeth's body plummeted and, after struggling for a few moments, became still.

There is no doubt that in today's courts Elizabeth would be treated leniently, for she was clearly a victim of her husband's cruel mistreatment and had acted in self-defence against his drink-fuelled assault. Thomas Hardy, as a lad of sixteen, had witnessed the hanging, and had been so affected that, in later life, he could still recall the scene: 'I remember what a fine figure she showed against the sky as she hung in the misty rain, and how the tight black silk gown set off her shape as she wheeled half round and back.'

KC

FURTHER READING

Thorne, N., *In Search of Martha Brown* (Plymouth: The Dashwood Press, 2000 and 2014)

Buranelli, Luigi (1823–1855)

Today, in Langham Street (formerly Foley Place), close to Regent Street in London, the discerning buyer can purchase a two-bedroom apartment for a price starting at just over £3,000,000. In 1855, however, ownership of property in this area was a more achievable ambition. Men like Joseph Latham could buy houses and in turn rent out space within them to men like Luigi Buranelli, a thirty-two-year-old immigrant from Ancona, Italy. Such stories, however, do not always end well.

Buranelli had arrived in London in either 1849 or 1850, intent upon pursuing a convoluted legal matter involving his late employer. After living for some time in a hotel, Luigi took up lodgings in Soho. Amongst his fellow lodgers were Joseph Latham and a lady named Mrs Jeans; Latham and Jeans claimed, falsely, to be man and wife, going under the names of Mr and Mrs Lambert. Shortly afterwards, Buranelli's own wife Rosa joined him in England. However, early in 1851, Rosa died and Luigi's life, and his sanity, began to unravel. Enigmatically, he was heard to complain on more than one occasion that 'all my troubles happen on a Friday'.

Nevertheless, by the time of the 1851 census, widower Buranelli was to be found in the service of a Charles Joyce, in Paddington, listed alongside another servant, twenty-three-year-old Martha Ingram, who would soon become the second Mrs Buranelli.

A daughter, named Rosa, was born the following year, by which time the couple were in service in Kent. Tragically, however, Luigi was soon to lose his second wife: in 1854, supposedly during childbirth, Martha died. This time, there was no escape from Buranelli's grief.

His physical health also began to deteriorate and he required lengthy treatment for an anal fistula, the symptoms and management of which only added to his mental torment. In August, he finally agreed to have the fistula operated on and was admitted to the Middlesex Hospital. By this time, he was said to be often violent, with an ungovernable temper.

On 2 September 1854, Luigi was discharged from hospital and began renting a room from his former acquaintances 'Mr and Mrs Lambert', first in Newman Street and subsequently in Foley Place. There he met a fellow lodger, Mrs Williamson, and an affair soon began. On 28 December, however, Williamson complained to her landlord that Buranelli had made her pregnant, and, fearing a scandal, Latham asked him to leave. It is unclear whether Williamson was indeed pregnant, although she was said to have been confined to bed for some days afterwards.

Luigi Buranelli. (Authors' collection)

For a time, Buranelli seemed to bear no ill will. He visited the house once more and spoke to Joseph Latham and, briefly, in private, to Mrs Williamson. He also wrote letters to her and enquired about her health from his former neighbours. Nevertheless, on 14 January 1855, Luigi returned to Foley Street with a pistol he had recently bought from Oxford Street, and shot Joseph Latham dead while he lay in bed with Mrs Jeans. Buranelli attempted to commit suicide following the murder, but succeeded only in firing a bullet through his face and into the space behind his nose, where it lodged.

Following his arrest and trial, the objections of celebrated 'alienist' Forbes Benignus Winslow to Buranelli's execution were of no use; nor was the campaigning of the Society Against Capital Punishment, which also believed him to be insane and therefore not responsible for his actions.

On 29 April 1855, Buranelli wrote a letter from the condemned cell in Newgate Prison thanking the woman who had been caring for his daughter; at five o'clock the following morning, he woke and spent two hours speaking to a Catholic priest. At seven, he was led to the gallows, where he was pinioned by executioner William Calcraft in front of a large crowd. His final request was that a letter be forwarded to his mother, and an image of himself and a ring sent to his daughter. The bullet from his attempted suicide would remain with him to the end, as attempts to remove it while he was imprisoned had proved too painful.

Buranelli's death was not a good one. 'He appeared to struggle convulsively for two to three minutes', according to one report, with other accounts claiming that Calcraft resorted to hanging onto the prisoner's legs to hasten death. Other sources claim that this was not uncommon for Calcraft, and even suggest that he may have done so partly for the amusement of those watching. On this occasion, at least, such theatrics did not go down well with the assembled crowd. When Calcraft returned to the scaffold to cut the body down, he was jeered, at which point the executioner reportedly gave a sarcastic bow to the crowd, which can hardly have helped to defuse the situation.

Buranelli's 'death mask' today sits within the collection of Scotland Yard's Crime Museum.

TNB

FURTHER READING

Winslow, F. B., *The Case of Luigi Buranelli, Medico-legally Considered* (London: John Churchill, 1855)

Buswell, Harriet (1845–1872)

At ten o'clock on Christmas Eve 1872, a twenty-seven-year-old woman, Harriet Buswell, also known as Clara Burton, borrowed a shilling from a friend and left her lodgings in Great Coram Street, Russell Square. Wearing a black silk dress, a velvet jacket and a jaunty green hat with a red feather, she walked to the Alhambra Theatre in London's Leicester Square. Although she professed to being a dancer on the stage, she was working (or at least moonlighting) as a prostitute at the time, touting for business on the streets in the West End (see Prostitution). She was deeply in debt and, in addition, needed to pay for the care of her eight-year-old daughter. She returned to her lodgings in the early hours of the following morning, accompanied by a man. She was carrying a bag of nuts and fruit, and stopped to pay her week's rent to the landlady with a half sovereign (ten shillings), receiving change of one shilling before joining the man upstairs.

When Harriet had not made an appearance by the afternoon of Christmas Day – although a maid had seen her client leave the house at about seven o'clock that morning – they broke open the door: it had been locked from the outside, and the key was missing. They found Harriet lying on the bed with her throat cut. A pair of borrowed earrings and a purse containing the shilling change were missing. On the bedside table was an apple with a bite taken out of it. Subsequent tests showed that Harriet's stomach did not contain any apple, so it must have been consumed by her murderer. Police enquiries located two men, a greengrocer named Fleck and a waiter named Stalker, who had seen Harriet in male company on the last evening of her life. The police offered a reward of £200 for information and issued the following description of the man they sought to question:

> Age 25, Height 5 feet 9 inches, Complexion swarthy, red spots on face, Black Hair, no Whiskers or Moustache, but not shaved for two or three days, Stout Build; Dress, dark tight-fitting Coat, dark Billycock Hat, a Foreigner (supposed German).

Down at Ramsgate, the *Wangerland*, a German brig, was docked and undergoing repairs after becoming stranded on the Goodwin Sands. One Karl Wohlebbe, an apothecary who had sailed to England on the stricken ship, had somehow come to the attention of the police, who now suspected him of being Harriet's killer. An identification parade was arranged, taking place in the town hall, and, among other passengers, a Dr Gottfried Hessel volunteered to make up the numbers. He was a Lutheran minister on his way to Brazil to fulfil a ten-year missionary assignment; his offer of help at the parade was merely a courtesy, extended voluntarily; but, to his astonishment, he was unhesitatingly picked out of the line-up by both Fleck and Stalker. Although Hessel, his wife and Wohlebbe had all stayed at Knoll's Hotel in London over the Christmas period, he vehemently denied any involvement in the killing. On Tuesday, 21 January, sucked into a nightmare, he appeared before magistrates at Bow Street Police Court charged with the murder of Harriet Buswell. However, while the prosecution witnesses gave vague and conflicting evidence, staff at Knoll's Hotel confirmed that Dr Hessel and his wife had remained in the hotel on the night of Harriet's

Harriet Buswell. (Authors' collection)

death. After drinking camomile tea, Hessel had gone to bed, suffering from a chest infection, leaving his boots outside the door. On Thursday, 30 January, the charge against him was dropped.

The newspapers were generally outraged by Dr Hessel's wrongful arrest and published his graphic account of the time he had spent in police custody. He and his wife sailed for Brazil, carrying with them £1,200 raised by *The Daily Telegraph* and the commiserations of William Gladstone, no less.

The identity of the murderer of Harriet Buswell remains a mystery. Recently, it has been suggested (without real foundation) that her death was the first atrocity committed by Jack the Ripper. H. L. Adam, writing about the case in the 1930s, thought otherwise, and announced that Hessel 'was, in fact, the murderer and that his alibi was a fake'. Supposedly, Adam founded his view on 'facts subsequently revealed', and he is known to have been friendly with several senior police officers who could, in theory, have given him the inside line, but his conclusion remains difficult to assess.

KC

Further Reading

Adam, H. L., *Murder by Persons Unknown* (London: W. Collins Sons & Co., 1931)

C

Calcraft, William (1800–1879)

For a remarkable forty-five years, William Calcraft undertook executions in all corners of the country. Even when this career came to an end in 1874 upon his decommissioning, he wanted to continue.

Calcraft's name is associated with those of many individuals discussed elsewhere in this book. He was, for example, Thackeray's 'tall, grave man in black' at the hanging of François Courvoisier, and he saw off the likes of James Blomfield Rush and Franz Müller. But, like all executioners, he is remembered for his mistakes. In Calcraft's case, the fact that he spent nearly half a century in the role meant that he was able to accrue these in several different areas of his practice.

Sometimes there was clumsiness, or raw bad luck. Edward Pritchard went to his death in 1865 before a huge Glaswegian crowd, and many would have remained to watch the body, which had gradually stilled on the end of the rope, being taken down and returned to the prison for burial. Calcraft, retrieving Pritchard from the level of the platform, allowed the rope to slip through his hands, and Pritchard's corpse crashed into the pit below.

Scenes like this were unfortunate and undesirable, but they might have happened to anybody. On the other hand, some of Calcraft's apparent errors tested the professional expectations of his position. Every executioner was required to recognise and behave in accordance with the peculiar moral and ethical challenges he faced: on this measure, Calcraft's appearance in the crowd outside the Old Bailey at the conclusion of the trial of William Palmer seemed like bad, and possibly bloodthirsty, judgement. Sometimes – as, for example, at the execution of the tragic Sarah Harriet Thomas – he admitted to feeling 'compunction', and he described this particular victim as 'one of the prettiest and most intellectual girls I have met with in any society'. Since, throughout their brief acquaintance, Sarah was in hysterics (a condition hardly conducive to showing off one's intellectuality), this opinion would seem to mask a good deal of suppressed guilt.

Execution. (Authors' collection)

And then there were William Bousfield and John Wiggins, both of whom struggled vainly to keep a grip on life; and then there was Philip Larkin, a Fenian terrorist who hung inertly at the end of the rope, undying, until Calcraft descended into the pit and, reportedly, climbed onto his victim's back to tauten the rope around his neck. Incidents like these were not simply unlucky, and as time crept on they appeared more and more likely to occur. Calcraft's method – the so-called 'short drop' – typically left the prisoner to asphyxiate, and public sentiments about execution were changing. One of Calcraft's last assistants, William Marwood, planned to take the practice to new levels of scientific sophistication, and greater attention was being given to the question of whether the condemned individual suffered before death intervened. The 'long drop', designed to compromise the spinal column and leading, in ideal circumstances, to instant insensibility, was not far away. When hangings moved indoors in 1868, away from the passions of the public, this can have done Calcraft little harm, since his performances were probably better not exposed to mass inspection; but still his victims endured the wretched minutes of trembling on the end of the noose. Marwood promised new horizons. Calcraft's last appointment, on a sunny May morning in 1874, was for the hanging of James Godwin: the prisoner went out of this life, and marked the end of his era, in paroxysms of convulsive breathing, with his hands raised helplessly to his throat.

MWO

FURTHER READING

Abbott, G., *William Calcraft: Executioner Extra-ordinaire!* (Kent: Eric Dobby Publishing, 2004)

Caminada, Jerome (1844–1914)

On 15 March 1844, a child of Italian-Irish stock was born in the poor working-class area of Deansgate, Manchester, an area the child himself was later to describe as 'a very hotbed of social iniquity and vice'. As a policeman in adulthood, he would patrol the very same mean streets in which he grew up. For constables whose strength of character was flawed, these sorts of split loyalties sometimes caused complications; but Jerome Caminada's spirit was strong.

Caminada's childhood home was situated opposite the site of St Peter's Field where, in 1819, reformists demonstrating against the political situation of the time were hacked down by sabre-bearing cavalrymen – an incident to become known as the Peterloo Massacre. At the time of Jerome's birth, local memories were still raw, and distrust of the establishment was still widespread.

In February 1868, after a brief flirtation with engineering, Caminada, finding himself undeterred by the prevailing popular sentiment, became a constable in the Manchester City Police. Within four years, his attributes as an innovative (if slightly unconventional) policeman had seen him move into the Detective Department: here, his reputation was cemented. 'The rookeries of the city held no terrors for him,' reported the *Manchester Courier*, and by 1888 his record showed that he had notched up the imprisonment of 1,255 criminals, along with the closure of around 400 public houses. His run-ins with flamboyantly named shady characters such as 'Jimmy Good-Lodgings', 'Shiny-Trousers Jack', 'Oldham Johnny' and 'Fat Martha' were the stuff of legend, and seem to belong in the pages of a Charles Dickens novel rather than the notebook of a Manchester policeman.

Caminada worked at horse-racing meetings, where he would disguise himself in an attempt to throw off those criminals who had become aware of the notorious 'Detective Jerome'. On one occasion, at the Grand National, whilst patrolling the main grandstand in disguise as a labourer, he and his colleagues saw a gang of pickpockets 'relieve' a gentleman of his pocket watch. Caminada and his men moved in, arrested the gang and frogmarched them to the nearby police station. Here Caminada waited for the victim to arrive, for he was known to the detective; and, lo and behold, minutes later, in walked the man whose watch had been stolen, complaining loudly that he had been robbed. The gentleman really should have been more cautious, for he was none other than the Chief Constable of the Manchester

City Police. A smiling Caminada jumped up, produced the stolen watch from his own pocket, and returned it to a very perplexed Chief Constable. The reason for the Chief's confusion was that Caminada was still heavily disguised and therefore unrecognisable to his superior, who promptly interrogated him as to how he, Caminada, had obtained his watch. The confusion dissipated as soon as the detective explained all, leaving a relieved, if embarrassed, Chief Constable thanking the detective and his team for their good work.

On another occasion, whilst investigating the theft of music sheets from the Free Trade Hall during the concert season there, Caminada secreted himself inside a piano box after making observation holes in it. There he waited until the musicians arrived; then they left for the stage, leaving the conductor and a librarian behind. Soon the conductor left, leaving the librarian and, unknown to him, a concealed Caminada. The detective then watched the librarian leaf through some music sheets, before sliding a few of them into his inside pocket. No sooner had Caminada observed this than the musicians returned, propping their instruments against the very piano box he was hiding in; then they departed for the night, leaving one of Manchester's finest detectives trapped inside, where he remained until the gasman arrived to turn out the lights. 'Shift these fiddles!' boomed Caminada from inside the box. The gasman, believing that he was being spoken to from the other side, stared at the haunted instruments. 'Shift these fiddles from the piano case, man, and let me out!' yelled the detective. 'I'm no ghost, but flesh and blood like yourself!' The gasman tentatively approached and did as he was instructed, trembling as a figure emerged from the piano box. Caminada was unable to explain the situation to the poor fellow, who declined to verbally engage with a ghost and apparently never spoke of the incident again.

It must be noted that Caminada was no mere career copper, and that he mixed his bread-and-butter cases with his work on larger, more complex crimes. His exposure of quack doctors such as Charles Davies Henry, Arthur Chadwick and the former mayor of Nottingham, the Reverend Edward J. Silverton, who profiteered in poor and unhealthy communities, highlighted Detective Jerome's strong sense of right and wrong, and proved that he never lost touch with his roots. Some of his most famous episodes, such as the case of the Birmingham Forger and the Manchester Cab Mystery, would not seem out of place in the world of Sherlock Holmes.

Upon his retirement in 1899, Caminada became a private detective, estate agent and later a city councillor. He died in 1914 at his Manchester home, a result of diabetes, influenza and heart disease. His eulogy, read by Judge Edward Abbot Parry, described Caminada as a 'great character ... a man of resource, energy and initiative ... the Garibaldi of detectives'.

NRAB

FURTHER READING

Buckley, A., *The Real Sherlock Holmes: The Hidden Story of Jerome Caminada* (Barnsley: Pen and Sword, 2014)
Brody, D. and Sawkill, C., *The Police! 150 Years of Policing in the Manchester Area* (Runcorn: Archive Publications, 1989)

Camp, Elizabeth (1863–1897)

'We do not enjoy murders, or, as a rule, like to see the public enjoy them,' wrote *The Spectator* on 20 February 1897 – a sensible position, most would surely agree. 'But the interest in the murder of Elizabeth Camp is in the highest degree natural.'

The facts of this intriguing case were these. On Thursday, 11 February 1897, thirty-three-year-old Elizabeth Camp boarded the 7.42 p.m. train from Hounslow to Waterloo, having spent a half-holiday visiting her two married sisters. Waiting for her in south London was her fiancé, Edward Berry – but when the train arrived, at around 8.25, she did not descend onto the platform.

Variously described as the manageress, housekeeper, or waitress at the Good Intent public house in Walworth (which still survives, on East Street), and as 'intelligent', 'attractive', 'well built', and 'strapping', *The Spectator*'s correspondent suggested that Camp was certainly capable of defending herself in an altercation, 'as well able to take care of herself as any person in London, male or female'. Nevertheless, back at Waterloo her body poked out from underneath the seating in a second-class carriage. Her skull was broken, and the scene would have been as bloody as it was surprising to the cleaner who happened upon it. There was no doubting that she was dead, although this was only confirmed once she had been conveyed to nearby St Thomas' Hospital. Supposedly, Berry had planned to visit a music hall with his fiancée that evening; now, he followed her body to St Thomas' in order to provide a formal identification.

Initial leads were hard to come by – an examination of the carriage in which the body was found discovered nothing more than an umbrella (which was Elizabeth's) and a pair of cufflinks, whose owner could not be identified. A sexual motive was discounted after the body was examined, despite some salacious press accounts to the contrary. One clue, suggesting a motive of robbery, was that Camp's pockets and purse appeared to have been emptied. The closest thing the inquiry would have to a breakthrough, however, came during a search along the railway line. On the embankment between Putney and Wandsworth, a pestle was discovered, akin to those used by chemists during the preparation of drugs. Even without the forensic benefits of DNA analysis or fingerprinting, the investigators were confident that the blood and hair found on the item had belonged to Elizabeth Camp.

The police had a weapon, but there was still no culprit. Rumours of a man with blood-stained hands who was seen running from Vauxhall station came to nothing, and the claims of a man who confessed to the crime during the investigation proved groundless. For a time, attention focused on a man called Brown, a previous romantic interest of Camp's, but this too proved to be a dead end. It is unclear whether Brown matched the only physical description which the police had to work with, that of a man of medium height, aged about thirty, with a dark moustache, wearing a top hat and a frock coat. This depiction had been provided by a pastry cook who had briefly travelled in the same coach as Camp, and who stated that he had seen a man boarding the train at Chiswick before alighting hastily at Wandsworth.

In a way, however, looking into Brown did serve to advance the enquiry, as it was discovered that he had supposedly owed Camp money. In fact, it transpired, Camp had been in the habit of lending money to family and associates on a regular basis. Could this have been a case not of robbery, but of a debtor taking desperate measures to avoid repayment, or avenging themselves on a harsh creditor?

When a man called Thomas Stone was identified, this interpretation seemed increasingly plausible. Stone, it was suggested, had been in the company of Camp and her sister in Hounslow shortly before the former left for the railway station. Described as a 'family friend', Stone too was said to be in debt to Camp. Fighting back against the local rumour mill, he claimed to have left Hounslow immediately after parting with Camp, and, despite apparently questioning him for some time, the police were never able to find enough evidence to file charges. Accordingly, he was released.

And there, effectively, ended the story of the murder of Elizabeth Camp. Except, that is, that the media can never quite let a good story die. Just ten months after Camp's murder, an interesting addition to the tale was published in the American *Butte Weekly Miner*. Written pseudonymously by British journalist Frederick Cunliffe-Owen, the piece is worth quoting at length:

> It may be mentioned that it was at Broadmoor that the blue-blooded perpetrator of the [Jack the Ripper] murders is now admitted by the authorities to have breathed his last, and it is likewise to Broadmoor that will be consigned without trial the well-born hitherto successful member of the Bar whose homicidal mania ... led him to perpetrate the mysterious murder of Miss Camp ... and likewise to put to death in an equally unaccountable fashion a young woman whose body was found some six weeks ago, at Windsor. It is probable that his true name will be kept from the public precisely in the same way as that of the author of the [Jack the Ripper] series of murders.

The 'young woman ... at Windsor' would seem to have been Emma Matilda Johnson, who was presumed murdered along a 'lonely road' between Oxford and Maidenhead on 15 September 1897. Johnson's mutilated body was discovered in the River

Thames, but, despite the arrest of a man (apparently going by the ominous nickname of 'Madman') who owned land near the spot where some of her clothing had been discovered, her killer also evaded arraignment and conviction.

Perhaps the suggestion that the true culprit was known to the authorities is to be taken with a pinch of salt. On the other hand, this was not the only near-contemporary hint of something hidden. Sir Robert Anderson believed that the case would have been officially solved were it not for the inflexibility of the laws of evidence; and the early-Edwardian periodical *Famous Crimes*, while reflecting on the 1884 murder of John Broome Tower in Stoke Newington, said, apropos of apparently rather little, 'We could a tale unfold etc., etc., if we were not bound by the police to secrecy, but the truth about this case, like that of Miss Camp, may yet be revealed.' With such inviting whispers disappearing swiftly into the silence of the past, however, one cannot help but feel that the chances of a definitive revelation are now, unfortunately, rather diminished.

TNB

FURTHER READING

Pearce, C. E., *Unsolved Murder Mysteries* (London: Stanley Paul, 1924)

Carew, Edith May Hallowell (1868–1958)

In 1897, Mrs Edith Carew was sentenced to death for the poisoning of her husband, Walter, in what would come to be known as the 'Japanese Maybrick Case'.

After marrying in Somerset in 1889, Walter and Edith Carew set off for the Far East. Walter aspired to make the best of what little business acumen he possessed, propping himself up with a genuinely gregarious sensibility; Edith was similarly disposed, able to attract men and enjoying their attention. Each partner seemed prepared to overlook the other's flirtations, and Edith, at least, continued to write notes to her husband in the fondest terms.

C

The Carews were the life and soul of the party in the expatriate quarter in Yokohama, Japan, a cosmopolitan city in which British interests were overseen by a consulate.

Behind the scenes, however, the social whirl had begun to spin out of control. Henry Dickinson, ostensibly Edith's bank clerk, had developed a powerful attachment to her, which he poured out in loving letters, many of which she foolishly retained. She had given him the impression that Walter acted violently towards her, and Dickinson urged her to seek a divorce. Others, too, had begun to take sides: Mary Jacob, the governess looking after the Carews' two children, seemed to have become suspicious of her mistress and, through the adroit agency of one of her friends, had come by one of Dickinson's letters, retrieved from the wastepaper basket and pieced together from the shreds into which Edith had torn it.

The pressure began to tell in autumn 1896. Edith reported the presence of a 'woman in black' who had ghosted onto the Carews' property hoping for an audience with Walter; from near-anonymous notes, this seemed to be Annie Luke, with whom Walter, as a single man, had once had a fling. Walter endeavoured to find Annie, although she gave no written indication of her whereabouts and – curiously, in a small Anglophone community – had failed to come to anybody else's notice. While Walter poked at this mystery, which refused to unravel, he became ill, exhibiting painful gastric symptoms. On 22 October, after enjoying a brief respite from his symptoms, he relapsed and died.

It rapidly became apparent that Edith had obtained a large quantity of arsenic from a local pharmacist. She argued that Walter had been in the habit of self-medicating for a liver complaint, and – fleetingly – an inconclusive inquest made it seem likely that she would escape Florence Maybrick's fate. However, a criminal enquiry led to a trial, held, British-style, before a British consular judge. Here, the Dickinson letters were read in open court, and local fascination was mirrored by intense interest around the world. Annie Luke – who had, supposedly, continued to write to all and sundry, even after Walter's death – could not be found or made to attend; nothing was more likely than that she had never been in Japan, and that the rumour of her being there, and all the letters associated with her, had been misleadingly concocted by the defendant. Edith was the worst representative of her unlikely case, and, during the pre-trial hearing, one of her lawyers returned his brief when she tried to conceal one of Dickinson's letters, entered in evidence, within the downturned cuff of her coat.

Edith was found guilty of murder and sentenced to death, but the verdict split opinion, and memories of the Maybrick scandal were quickly recalled. Like Walter Carew, James Maybrick had had extra-marital (or pre-marital) relationships; Maybrick had been violent, and Carew was *supposed* to have been violent, although the evidence for this was far from unambiguous; perhaps Edith, like Florence, was a mistreated wife pushed beyond the limits of her endurance. She was lucky to receive a commutation, issued by the British minister and plenipotentiary to Japan, Sir Ernest Satow. The practice of the Home Office, who took responsibility for homeland cases, was never to grant commutations to sane poisoners – Florence's commutation had been a clumsy compromise for which no legal precedent was available. As it happened, Edith was repatriated to Britain and imprisoned at Aylesbury, alongside Florence.

In 1910, Edith was released. She spent much of the following half-century in retreat from the gossip that still attached to her. One cannot help feeling that she was really fortunate; the circumstances which made the Maybrick affair into a matter of public outrage were only present in miniature in Edith Carew's case, if at all, and the idea that she *might* have been treated poorly by her husband was given too much oxygen. Molly Whittington-Egan, inspecting Edith's diaries long after the event, found that they gave no reason to doubt the justice of the court's verdict.

MWO

FURTHER READING

Whittington-Egan, M., *Murder on the Bluff* (Glasgow: Neil Wilson Publishing, 1996)

Wyndham, H., 'The Carew Case' in Goodman, J. (ed.), *The Lady Killers* (London: Sphere Books, 1991)

C

Cass, Elizabeth (1863–1956)

On 28 June 1887 Elizabeth Cass, a twenty-three–year-old Lincolnshire dressmaker who had moved to London just three weeks earlier, had been working as a forewoman for her employer Madame Bowman at her address in Southampton Row. As was now usual for Miss Cass, she finished her day's work at eight o'clock in the evening. As her workplace also doubled as her residence, and as she was on her own, Cass stuck with the tradition of the age and dutifully asked Madame Bowman if she could leave the premises unaccompanied. Bowman, adopting an almost parental role which was not untypical in its day, gave her permission, and Cass left at around 8.45 p.m. for what was one of the most common of Victorian pastimes, the evening constitutional walk.

Cass commenced her stroll, passing through Bloomsbury Square and by the British Museum, turning into Tottenham Court Road, and on to the shop-lined thoroughfare of Oxford Street. Queen Victoria's Golden Jubilee celebrations had been going on throughout that week: the street was lined with bunting, and good-natured crowds were taking advantage of the fair summer's evening. At the junction with Regent Street the crowd became particularly thick, and as Cass struggled through the throng, she felt a hand on her arm. Snapping her head around, Cass saw that the hand belonged to a Metropolitan Police constable, who immediately spoke to her.

'I want you,' he said.

'What for?' Cass replied.

'I have been watching you for some time,' the constable responded.

The confused Miss Cass retorted, 'You have made a mistake,' but the constable was adamant that he had not, and warned her against telling lies.

The constable was a reserve from Marylebone's D Division, PC 42D(R) Bowen Endacott, an experienced policeman of twelve years' service. Grasping Cass firmly by the arm, Constable Endacott marched her to Tottenham Court Road Police Station, ignoring her pleas to detour via Madame Bowman's so that she could vouch for her young employee. Instead, Constable Endacott asked Cass if

Madame Bowman would bail her out. Cass repeated the question quizzically, as she still did not understand why she had been arrested.

Upon arriving at the station, and whilst waiting for the desk sergeant to arrive so that the act of charging Cass could commence, Endacott – so said Cass, later on – issued her with a thinly veiled threat, advising her that he knew her, and had done for six weeks. Cass was, by this stage, confused and panicking. How could this policeman have known her for six weeks? She had only been in London for three. It was at this point that the situation became too much for Cass and she fainted. Police Sergeant Ben Morgan was already at the station, immersed in reading, when he heard a commotion behind him. Turning around, he saw Constable Endacott standing over a woman lying prone on the floor. He watched Endacott and another constable help Cass into a chair, ordering some water for the young woman as he did so.

Before long, Cass had regained her senses enough for them to proceed, and Constable Endacott explained to the desk sergeant that Cass was a known disorderly prostitute whom he had seen annoying men in Regent Street. Accordingly, she was taken to the cells, where she was held until her hearing at Marlborough Street Police Court the following day. The result of that hearing was mixed. The respectable Madame Bowman appeared in Cass's defence, stating that her young charge had only recently become an inhabitant of London, and that her character was impeccable. The magistrate, Robert Milnes Newton, had little choice but to find Cass not guilty, but nonetheless he poured doubt on her innocence, warning her to take his advice: 'If you are a respectable girl, as you say you are, don't walk in Regent Street at night, for if you do you will either be fined or sent to prison after the caution I have given you.'

Though Cass was now free, Madame Bowman was incensed by the treatment she had received. She put in a formal complaint against the police, which drew attention from Parliament; Home Secretary Henry Matthews ordered an enquiry, the results of which were a six-week suspension for Endacott and a formal reprimand for Newton. With the support of Bowman, Cass took the matter further, pursuing a private prosecution for perjury against the constable who had arrested her. This case was heard at the Old Bailey in October 1887, with Cass, now married and appearing under the name of Langley, taking centre stage in the witness box; months after Cass's ordeal in the dock, it was now Endacott's turn to sweat. His defenders again cast aspersions on Cass's character, but it was want of evidence which made the not guilty verdict – the second such verdict in the case, one for each side – inevitable.

Newton's warning not to walk in Regent Street at night for fear of being mistaken for a prostitute highlighted how young and independent women were perceived during this period; it was this perception, rather than any apparent wrongdoing, which resulted in a unwarranted stay in a police cell for Elizabeth Cass, who merely went out for a walk on a fine summer's evening.

NRAB

Chantrelle, Eugène Marie (1834–1878)

A lapsed medical student and a veteran of the 1851 Paris Commune, Eugène Marie Chantrelle emerged in respectable Edinburgh society in 1866, coordinating neatly with the aspirations of his host community by providing highly rated language tuition to débutantes. The adjectives that became attached to him, even in retrospect, scarcely covered his myriad characteristics: although he was known to be 'good looking', 'cultured', 'polished' and 'debonair', his behaviour actually left much to be desired. On his own devices, he was also 'priapic', 'alcoholic', 'abusive' and 'immoral'. In early 1868 he contrived to impregnate one of his students, sixteen-year-old Elizabeth Cullen Dyer; she was as moved by her teacher's dashing image as he was sickened by the prospect of being forced to endure an unwanted marriage; but married they were, in August 1868. The union, which produced four children, was a calamity from its beginning and, as one commentator put it, 'a more melancholy story of married life has seldom been told'.

Among other forms of mistreatment, Chantrelle frequently told Elizabeth that, given an excuse to do so, he would be able to poison her in some manner undetectable to scientists. Elizabeth intermittently sought protection from the police; once she made hesitant enquiries about the possibility of divorce. More often, she merely voiced her concerns to her mother, who tried to be reassuring, even when Elizabeth saw the end approaching. In October 1877, Chantrelle, having run up enormous debts in pursuit of alcoholic and sexual oblivion, insured against Elizabeth's accidental death; any misfortune that occurred subsequently stood to net him £1,000. On 27 December, Elizabeth, at a low ebb, told her mother, 'My life will soon go after this insurance.' Indeed, she had less than a week to live.

Elizabeth spent the first day of 1878 in discomfort, suffering from vomiting, and retired early to the bedroom which she no longer shared with her *mari*. The next morning, the Chantrelles' servant, Mary Byrne, heard her mistress's moans filling the house. Elizabeth was draped over the edge of her bed, and vomit clung to her hair, her nightdress, and her bedsheets. Mary fetched Chantrelle, who sent her to check the children, saying that he had heard the baby crying. When she returned, she noticed him stepping away from the gas pipe near Elizabeth's window, and when she began to smell gas, she turned off the supply at the source. In an unhurried manner, Chantrelle arranged for a doctor to attend, but Elizabeth died on the afternoon of 2 January 1878.

Chantrelle seemed eager to attribute Elizabeth's death to a chance gas leak, but narcotic poisoning was rapidly suspected. There had been no gas in the room when Mary Byrne first went in, and the gas pipe leaked only after Chantrelle had been left alone with it. Engineers discovered that the rupture to the pipe was not due either to an accident or to general wear and tear. Moreover, although Elizabeth's intestines refused to disclose poison when they were subjected to chemical analysis, the stains on her linen did: by something that could not be called coincidence, they teemed with traces of opium, and Chantrelle had bought a preparation of opium from a local chemist on 25 November 1877. Searching the house, the police found a medicine cabinet containing an assortment of toxic substances, but the opium that Chantrelle had acquired a matter of weeks earlier could not be accounted for.

Inevitably, given the evidence against him, Chantrelle was convicted of Elizabeth's murder. He declined to admit responsibility, selfishly persisting with exculpatory stories which failed to conform to the facts. A public testimonial – animated more by feelings of revulsion about the cultural institution of capital punishment than by sentiments favourable to the prisoner himself – did not stir the Home Secretary, and Chantrelle was hanged by William Marwood on 31 May 1878.

In 1908, an unnamed 'police spy', whose recollections were published in rather literary form in the *Aberdeen People's Journal*, claimed to have met Chantrelle in November 1876. Supposedly, Chantrelle, realising that the 'spy' needed assistance to obtain the estate of an elderly uncle who refused to die, laid out a murder plan involving the use of opium and coal gas; for his efforts, he proposed to take a share of the inheritance. The 'spy' turned down the offer, and, attending Chantrelle's much-publicised trial in May 1878, realised with a mixture of horror and satisfaction that he had been inducted into the homicidal method so many months before. The episode is a pleasing addition to Chantrelle's story, but we need not suppose that it is true.

MWO

FURTHER READING

Smith, A. D. (ed.), *Trial of Eugène Marie Chantrelle* (Edinburgh: William Hodge and Company, 1928)

Whittington-Egan, M., *Scottish Murder Stories* (Glasgow: Neil Wilson Publishing, 1999)

Chesham, Sarah (1809–1851)

Nineteen-year-old Sarah Parker, from Clavering, Essex, married Richard Chesham, a farm labourer, in 1828, and within a decade they had produced six children. In 1845, two of the children, Joseph and James, died after suffering from severe vomiting and stomach pain. The cause of death was given as English cholera – a disease rampant at the time – and they were buried in Clavering churchyard. Suspicion was aroused only when, the following year, a third child died. His name was Solomon, the illegitimate son of Lydia Taylor, who lived in a nearby village.

Lydia Taylor was questioned by magistrates about conversations she had had with Sarah Chesham – conversations about the uses of poison – and this led to the bodies of Joseph and James being exhumed. When the contents of their stomachs were analysed at Guy's Hospital, in London, and arsenic was found, Sarah was charged with murder. In March 1847, at the Essex Lent Assizes, she stood trial at three separate hearings – for the deaths of Joseph, James, and then Solomon Taylor. However, as there was no proof that she had administered poison to any of the children, she was acquitted.

On 24 May 1850, after a long illness, Sarah's husband died. She was soon arrested. She had told neighbours that, on at least one occasion, she had sent him a poisoned mince pie when he was working in the fields, after which he was violently sick. The contents of Richard's stomach were sent to Guy's Hospital for analysis, as was some rice discovered during a subsequent search of Sarah's home. Both samples contained traces of arsenic. Before her first murder trial, *The Times* had criticised the apathetic locals who 'had seen her children buried without remark or outcry, though they were clearly convinced that there had been foul play'; now, the ire of the press was directed at Sarah. She was described as a known poisoner of 'odious fame', branded a 'fiend', given the nickname 'Sally Arsenic', and further demonised by being described as a 'masculine-looking woman'.

Sarah was tried at the Essex Assizes of March 1851. Evidence was given that she allowed no one else to tend to her husband during his final illness, and fed him milk thickened with rice. The jurors were also told that Sarah had advised a local woman, Hannah Philips, on the use of arsenic to end an unhappy marriage. Although Richard Chesham had been suffering from consumption, the post-mortem findings suggested that Sarah had been giving him small doses of arsenic over a period of time, compounding the inflammation of his lungs and hastening his death. Sarah was found guilty of administering poison with intent to kill, and, since this was then a capital offence, she was taken to the county gaol at Chelmsford to await execution. On 25 March 1851, William Calcraft hanged both Sarah Chesham and Thomas Drory (convicted of murdering his girlfriend) from the gallows erected above the gatehouse.

The hideous spectacle was watched by a mainly female crowd of thousands, with pickpockets enjoying a bonanza. Sarah was the last woman to be hanged in public at Chelmsford.

Fully fledged murderers had to be buried inside the prison grounds, but as Sarah's conviction was (rather narrowly) for a lesser crime, family members were permitted to claim the body and to arranlesge for its interment elsewhere. It took two days to get Sarah back to Clavering – overnight, the coffin stopped at the Lion Inn at Dunmow, 'where it attracted a considerable degree of public attention, and many offers were made to obtain a sight of the corpse'. The family, keen to make what profits they could from their situation, were not unmoved by these grisly approaches, even going so far as to sell off 'portions of the hair and clothing, which were eagerly bought as relics by the morbidly curious'. The next day, in Clavering itself, it was discovered that the local clergyman was not inclined to permit the body to rest in the churchyard and had written to the diocese expressing his disquiet. While the dispute was ongoing, a shallow, temporary grave was dug, and the coffin placed into it and covered by boards. After dark, Sarah's body was stolen, apparently by resurrectionists, and was not seen again.

Sarah was known in her neighbourhood as someone with poisonous advice to dispense, whether one was overburdened by multiple births, or troubled by tiresome or over-amorous husbands. If the damning soubriquet was justified, did Lydia Taylor follow her advice in getting rid of little Solomon, only to turn against her former friend when she stood trial for murder?

Perhaps Sarah's sinister public influence spread even further. In 1848, a year after Sarah had been acquitted of poisoning the three boys, a woman called Mary May was executed at Chelmsford for killing her half-brother with arsenic – her motive, to claim his burial fund. At the time, child mortality was high, but it was said that, of the sixteen children born to her, only one survived. Reports like these often exaggerated the numbers involved, but public feeling was clearly running hot. May was also rumoured to be a disciple of the exploits of Sarah Chesham; and Hannah Southgate, supposedly a close friend of Mary May's, was arguably fortunate to be acquitted at Chelmsford of the poisoning of her husband in 1849. The tales of this putative network of poisoners (who were either linked by acquaintance, or merely inspired by press reports or local gossip, and encouraged either by their own successes or by those of their predecessors; or, in another reading, none of the above – the whole thing has something of *The Crucible* about it) provoked considerable moral anxiety, and, on the day before Sarah's execution, the House of Lords ratified the Arsenic Act (1851). This legislation introduced a number of measures designed to regulate the retail of arsenic; a clause forbidding its sale to women – capable of interpretation only in the context of the scandalised atmosphere which had developed in the wake of the Essex poisonings – was prudently removed shortly before the bill passed into law.

KC, MWO

FURTHER READING

Ainsley, J. L., *The Ordeal of Sarah Chesham* (University of Victoria, Canada: MA thesis, unpublished)

Child Abuse

As early as 1827, it was possible to put the words 'child' and 'abuse' together to evoke an appreciable concept. On 19 December that year, as the country prepared for Christmas, a meeting in the town hall at Portsmouth considered the benefits of discontinuing the use of 'Climbing Boys' – who swept chimneys from the inside – and adopting an automated alternative referred to (slightly ominously) as 'the Machine'. The *Hampshire Telegraph* hymned the consensus: 'It requires now only a decided resolution on the part of the public to insist on having the Machine used, instead of the Child, to effect a gradual abandonment of a system of child abuse, which is a reproach to a civilised and Christian community.'

Of course, allusions to Christmas, Portsmouth and child abuse all direct the thoughts of the student of Victorian culture towards the period's greatest novelist, Charles Dickens. In the early 1840s, Dickens was much moved by the cruelty detailed in two governmental reports into children's working conditions. The individual stories were indeed shocking, and a few examples, selected more or less at random, suffice: at Patrick M'Laughlin's tobacco manufactory in Belfast, children as young as eight worked for nearly fifty-four hours a week in the winter, and a little longer in the summer when the skies were lighter; all smoked or chewed tobacco, 'from curiosity'. In Upper Sedgley, in the West Midlands, twelve-year-old factory hand William Hartil was not only illiterate but 'stupefied with work' and 'apparently deaf from the constant hammering'; Thomas Rishter, who was also twelve years old, was working for twelve hours a day in a nail forge – pay: two shillings a week – and was 'very little indeed for his age', 'weak and unhealthy in appearance' and 'poorly clothed'. Children like these were personified in the figures of Ignorance and Want, who emerge from below the folds of the Ghost of Christmas Present's robe in *A Christmas Carol*. Dickens, of course, had survived his own traumatic childhood, including dismal industrial work; his own painful memories found supernatural echoes in his grim reading of the depressing reports.

Economic child exploitation of this sort was primed to stimulate the popular conscience. It was highly visible, and almost every adult lived or worked with children whose education, health or wellbeing had been affected by labour. Behind closed doors, however, things were different. Then, as now, every Englishman's home was his castle, and most parents – even those who bitterly decried the mistreatment of children by others – reserved the right to treat their own children exactly as they pleased. The murder of Fanny Adams, for example, provoked general shock and outrage, and quite rightly so; but its characteristics were, in truth, highly unusual. Very few children would be killed by random predators, so there was, statistically, little to fear in this respect; by contrast, vast numbers would be killed by their parents, who were often the damaged vehicles of their own early traumas (see Infanticide). In October 1843, Edward Dwyer was drinking in a now-vanished pub near Tooley Street in Southwark when his wife and mother-in-law came in to call him various names and to treat him rather roughly; they then left him in charge of his three-month-old son, James. Edward had been upset by the unpleasant behaviour of his wife and her mother, and began muttering darkly about the child, saying, as George Stead – another of the pub's customers – recalled, that 'he would be the death of it before the morning'. Stead tapped Edward on the shoulder and 'told him to take a fool's advice, and not revenge himself on a poor innocent baby'. But the despondent Edward unheedingly swept James up by the legs, and cracked his head on the bar-rail.

The prevalent use of corporal punishment as a means of enforcing domestic discipline also increased children's chances of dying at the hands of their parents. Countless beatings, no doubt, ceased before they had fatal consequences, but some (again, then as now) had the most serious results. Mary Ann Seago was convicted of manslaughter at the Central Criminal Court in July 1854, following the death of her son Billy at their house on York Street (now Myrdle Street, in Whitechapel). She set out to teach him not to fight with his brother Tommy, but Billy – a little short of his sixth birthday – may have been dead even before his punishment (during which he was comprehensively thrashed, struck, humiliated, kicked and thrown about the room) had concluded. The principal witness for the prosecution was Tommy's half-sister (and Mary Ann's stepdaughter) Annie, who described herself in court as 'nine years old last month'. The cross-examination itself seemed bound to re-abuse her. 'I have sometimes been a naughty little girl, and told stories,' she confessed, innocently, to her mother's barrister. But she was not telling stories now, and she had taken her oath seriously. 'I have been taught to say my prayers,' she said. 'They have taught me at the workhouse.' Mary Ann Seago was sentenced to transportation for life, but actually served only a short prison sentence (first in Millbank, and then in Brixton) before she was released on medical grounds on 13 June 1859.

Other forms of abuse were similarly enabled by a social value system in which children's rights were secondary considerations. Sexual exploitation, for example, was simultaneously exposed by the Maiden Tribute affair and energised by a culture in which adult prostitutes were known to be an infection risk. Syphilis, in particular, was endemic in Victorian Britain, and this placed, as Michael Pearson puts it, 'an enormous market premium' on young girls whose virginity promised a disease-free sexual experience – but only for the male participant. Consent was not introduced into the transaction, even if the victim was, in the eyes of the law, old enough to provide it (that is, thirteen before 1885, and twelve before 1875), and 'very young girls were sometimes chloroformed' to ensure their compliance. Beyond personal health considerations, Victorian abusers also exhibited an abstract passion for 'getting there first': much Victorian pornography thrills to the theory and practice of defloration, as if this were the parochial equivalent of the contemporary exploration of sub-Saharan Africa, or of the Polar Regions. In perhaps the most notable pornographic book published during the period in question – *My Secret Life*, by the pseudonymous Walter – the narrator and protagonist's *terra incognita*, which he meticulously documents, would be more conventionally described as the women and children of the backstreets of the West End and the basements of the East End.

Every so often children would abuse other children, but this phenomenon was poorly understood. In the notable case of fifteen-year-old nursery maid Emily Newber, who poisoned ten-month-old Ray Maude Myers with acetic acid in 1893, the motive behind the abuse remained obscure. Emily's age – in an era of later menarche – made it possible to speculate about hysteria, but she had a history of losing nursery positions due to the cruelty with which she treated the children in her care. Today her behaviour would be considered in the context of her own childhood, and treatment, as opposed to punishment, would be the result.

MWO

FURTHER READING

Pearson, M., *The Age of Consent* (Newton Abbot: David & Charles, 1972)

Clerkenwell Explosion, The (1867)

Difficult to believe though it now seems, Victorian Britain was governed by a narrow political class whose overseas misadventures frequently had the effect of provoking the animosity of marginalised partisans. Nowhere was this more true than in Ireland, where, intolerably, it was still popularly held that the representative of God on Earth resided in Rome rather than in Buckingham Palace.

In late 1867, a large and nebulous group of Fenian terrorists – that is, according to Patrick Mullany, a terrorist who spoke up, those who wished 'to establish a republic in Ireland, and to overthrow English rule there' – set about liberating their confrère, Rickard Burke, from the Clerkenwell House of Detention. Burke had originally been arrested for his part in a daring prison-van rescue in Manchester and, on 12 December, while the prisoners were parading silently in the prison yard, he attracted the notice of one of the guards when he broke ranks to adjust his footwear, gazing meaningfully over the wall towards the houses in adjoining Corporation Lane as he did so.

On the outside, however, things were not going according to plan. The gang had acquired a huge weight of gunpowder, packed it into an old petroleum barrel and positioned it against the wall of the prison, but Captain James Murphy, the man nominated to detonate the bomb, struggled in vain to light the fuse. There was to be no explosion that day, and the disappointed terrorists took their weapon away with them.

The next day arrived with renewed promise. Michael Barrett, an intelligent, articulate member of the Fenian Brotherhood, had decided to take over ignition duties, and so all returned to Corporation Lane for another go. This time, the fuse fizzed into life; the terrorists scattered (Barrett went almost directly to shave off his distinctive whiskers); and a huge explosion tore a hole in the prison wall, and ripped Corporation Lane to pieces. At number 3a, the roof was partly blown off; number 2 was 'very badly shattered – so much so as to be unsafe'; the doors and windows of numbers 4, 5, 6 and 7 were blown in, 'and the houses were rendered otherwise dangerous'; numbers 1, 1a, 2a and 3 lost their windows and were 'very seriously damaged'; others did not escape the effects of the blast. Since it occurred in the mid-afternoon in an area of predominantly domestic properties, the explosion disproportionately affected women and children and, as well as the twelve deaths, there were also said to be unhappy long-term effects upon those who had been caught up in the incident:

> One young woman is in a mad house; forty mothers were prematurely confined and twenty of their babies died from the effects of the explosion on their mothers; others of the children are dwarfed and unhealthy, and one mother is now a raving lunatic. One hundred and twenty persons were wounded, fifty going into St Bartholomew's, Gray's Inn Lane and King's College Hospitals; fifteen are permanently injured, with loss of eyes, legs, arms, *etc.*

An assortment of suspects were identified but, after a trial lasting six days, only Barrett was found guilty (the charge – murder – related to the death by haemorrhage and suffocation of poor Ann Hodgkinson at number 3a, who had been horribly injured by flying glass; she had in part choked on a blood clot which had formed in her throat). Montagu Williams, a lawyer representing two of Barrett's co-defendants, commented that he could not recall seeing 'a less murderous countenance than Barrett's'; and Williams was far from the only person to feel some sympathy for the condemned man, although popular feeling was generally divided. There was even a suggestion that he had been in Glasgow at the time of the explosion and that the Clerkenwell witnesses had misidentified him, but his conviction stood and, on 27 May 1868, he became the last man to be executed publicly on the British mainland, by the hangman William Calcraft.

Predictably, an outrage on the Clerkenwell scale had the effect of alienating the masses, who now turned firmly against both the Republicans' cause and their methodology. In fact, the bombing had not even achieved its primary objective: Burke had been taken out to exercise on the *morning* of 13 December, perhaps – it is not quite clear – because the prison authorities realised that something was up, and decided that a change to Burke's itinerary was desirable. He was safely back inside the building long before the explosion took place and could not have escaped through the sixty-foot hole in the prison wall even if he had wanted to. He was subsequently sentenced to fifteen years' imprisonment for 'feloniously compassing to deprive the Queen of the Imperial Crown of Great Britain and Ireland'.

MWO

Further Reading

Williams, M., *Leaves of a Life* (London: Macmillan, 1896)

Cleveland Street Scandal, The (1889)

Charles Hammond was what the criminally minded Victorian would call a bully-boss, the violent landlord of a male brothel. His was located at 19 Cleveland Street, not far from Regent's Park, and it was this location in London's fashionable Fitzrovia which attracted Hammond's rich, and sometimes famous, clientele. However, it was Hammond's fierce reputation as a blackmailer which really paid well for him, as he preyed on his customers' vulnerability – homosexuality was not only illegal, but it also carried a social stigma so great that any hint of scandal would destroy a man's reputation in an instant.

And so the catch-22 continued. Wealthy customers paid their money knowing full well that Hammond could not only provide them with what they desired but could also extract more from them if he wished, with them having little choice but to comply. Hammond knew that these affluent and well-known men could hardly go to the police and admit the misdemeanour of sodomy; the fear really lay in the subsequent court appearance, which would undoubtedly damage their reputation. The matter was also compounded by the fact that some of Hammond's customers had a preference for young men in their mid-teens. Hammond himself could rest assured, knowing that those he was blackmailing would keep quiet; however, it was not the clientele who instigated Hammond's demise, igniting a scandal which would rock the foundations of the Establishment, but rather a fifteen-year-old telegraph boy named Charles Swinscow.

Constable Luke Hanks was assigned to London's Central Post Office, and therefore investigated all crimes connected to that organisation. In early July 1889, he had been looking into a case of theft committed upon post office premises when he received notification that one of the telegraph boys, Swinscow, who was not in a position to handle money, had been found with fourteen shillings upon his person. This was more than a few weeks' wages for such an employee, and so Constable Hanks questioned Swinscow. It was during this exchange that the young lad admitted he had been working as a male prostitute for Charles Hammond, and the money was his takings. The use of telegraph boys as male prostitutes was not uncommon, due to their availability and the quasi-validity of their travelling to deliver telegrams across the metropolis. Constable Hanks's enquiries revealed that Swinscow had been approached by eighteen-year-old post office clerk Henry Newlove, and that the pair had entered into a sexual relationship. Newlove then introduced Swinscow to Hammond. Two other telegraph boys, George Wright and Charles Thickbroom, were also revealed to be working for Hammond at Cleveland Street. Realising that another offence had now come to light, Constable Hanks handed over this specific case to Scotland Yard, who appointed Inspector Frederick Abberline, one of their most accomplished detectives, to the case.

On 6 July, armed with a warrant for the arrest of Newlove and Hammond, Abberline made his way over to 19 Cleveland Street, only to find the place locked up. He was too late; Newlove had already warned his paymaster that the jig was up. Abberline then proceeded to the home of Newlove's mother in Camden Town, where he found and arrested the young post office clerk. Upon his removal to the police station, Newlove admitted to having tipped-off Hammond, and stated that the bully-boss had gone to his brother's home in Gravesend and from there to France. Then came a shocking admission as Newlove, undoubtedly upset at Hammond for leaving him to face the music alone, began listing name after famous name – the dramatis personae of the days and nights at the Cleveland Street brothel – including Lord Arthur Somerset, a close friend of the Prince of Wales, and the Earl of Euston, Henry FitzRoy.

Abberline placed the premises in Cleveland Street under observation, just in case Hammond tried to return, and continued his investigations throughout August as more names appeared. Another post office connection was made when George Veck, a former employee who now passed himself off as a clergyman, was arrested at Waterloo railway station. He was found to be in possession of some letters sent by Mr Algernon Allies, and Allies, who was questioned, revealed that he had previously had sexual relations with Lord Somerset, and had worked at Cleveland Street as a male prostitute.

Inspector Abberline pushed for the extradition of Hammond from France. The authorities, undoubtedly jittery about the well-to-do names already involved in the case, stalled. Abberline then set his sights on Lord Somerset, seeking any evidence he could to pursue the aristocrat who, by now, had also left the country.

Meanwhile, a trial date had been set for Newlove and Veck, and the pair's defence was arranged by Lord Somerset's own solicitor, Arthur Newton; still, they pleaded guilty to indecency and received sentences of four and nine months' hard labour respectively. The press remained strangely quiet on the matter until Newlove and Veck's trial, when they suddenly found their voices. The scandal went global and trails were numerous, but, despite his tenacious pursuit of the case, Abberline's progress was inhibited by those in authority. There were claims of a cover-up designed to protect certain important members of the Establishment, with unsubstantiated gossip naming the Prince of Wales as a client of the brothel. Hammond left France for the United States, whilst Lord Somerset remained in France, only to visit England on occasion.

Abberline, with his hands tied by those above him, was promoted to Chief Inspector (either out of gratitude or in an attempt to win his silence, depending on your viewpoint), and the matter faded from the public limelight almost as quickly as it had arrived.

NRAB

FURTHER READING

Hyde, H. M., *The Cleveland Street Scandal* (London: W. H. Allan, 1976)

Clouson, Jane Maria (1854–1871)

In the early hours of Wednesday, 26 April 1871, PC Donald Gunn was patrolling a footpath near Kidbrook Lane, on the edge of Eltham Common, when he came across the figure of a young woman on her hands and knees. She had suffered terrible injuries to her head, but she managed to plead with Gunn to hold her hand before crying out, 'Oh, let me die!' Soon afterwards she lost consciousness and, five days later, she died in Guy's Hospital. The victim was a seventeen-year-old servant, Jane Maria Clouson, who until two weeks before her death had been working for a Greenwich printer, Ebenezer Pook. He had two sons working in the family firm, the youngest of which was twenty-year-old Edmund, who, though secretly courting a Lewisham girl, was still living at home. Despite suffering severe epileptic episodes, Edmund enjoyed a lively lifestyle and would join his brother performing 'penny readings' in local music halls. According to a friend, Jane had said that she intended to meet Edmund on the night she was killed. He was therefore arrested but denied any involvement in the murder. An inquest established that Jane had been two months pregnant, although the foetus had died a fortnight before her own death. Her funeral at Brockley and Ladywell Cemetery on 8 May attracted huge crowds; the coffin was borne on a horse-drawn carriage and the pall-bearers were young women dressed as maids. A memorial stone, depicting a child kneeling in prayer, was commissioned by local residents; part of the inscription reads: *May God's great pity touch his heart and lead my murderer to confess his dreadful deed ...*

The trial of Edmund Walter Pook opened at the Old Bailey on 10 July before Lord Chief Justice Bovill, whose fractious disputes with leading counsel – the Solicitor General for the prosecution and Mr Huddleston for the defence – were criticised in the press. The police investigation also came under scrutiny: footprints at the scene were not investigated; a whistle found close to the body had been disregarded, although it had been established that Edmund Pook used a similar whistle to secretly communicate with his girlfriend in Lewisham. A locket, alleged to have been given to Jane by Edmund, was, in fact, a present from another of Pook's former servants. Two ironmongers gave conflicting evidence, but although one of them testified to selling a plasterer's hammer (similar to the one used by the killer), she was unable to identify Edmund as her customer. The purchaser of the hammer, she insisted, had been wearing light-coloured trousers, and these were not found amongst the clothing of the accused. Evidence was given that Edmund was seen near his girlfriend's house in Lewisham at 8.30 p.m., the estimated time of the assault on Jane (although her head injuries were so severe that she seems unlikely to have survived until 4.15 the next morning, when PC Gunn found her).

Jane's murderer, the court went on to hear, would have been drenched in blood during the hammer attack. Dr Henry Letheby, professor of chemistry at the London Hospital, found some small spots of blood on Edmund's clothes, but these could have been caused whilst biting his tongue during an epileptic seizure. Edmund Pook was acquitted on 15 July, but many who had followed the case in the newspapers felt that a guilty verdict should have been handed down. Soon after the trial, Ebenezer Pook issued a writ against the police for 'wilful and corrupt perjury', and Edmund brought a libel action against both the publisher and the author of a pamphlet entitled *The Eltham Tragedy Reviewed*, in which his guilt was (rather unambiguously) implied.

The reason the Pook family gave for dismissing Jane was that she was a lazy and slovenly girl, a description at odds with those of others who knew her. It is possible that she was dismissed over a clandestine association with Edmund – one which may have reached a crisis point when she announced that she was pregnant. Not only was the family reputation at stake, but a scandal might have ruined Edmund's chance of making a suitable marriage. It seems likely that, although the foetus had perished, Jane's attacker decided to silence her for good. As the annals of Victorian crime readily testify, it would not have been the first time that an amorous young man had resorted to murder to cover an inappropriate liaison.

KC

FURTHER READING

Smith-Hughes, J., *Unfair Comment upon Some Victorian Murder Trials* (London: Cassell, 1951)

Cooke, George Samuel (1865/6–1893)

Maud Merton, an eighteen-year-old prostitute, had only been working the theatre district around London's Strand for three or four weeks when, in June 1891, she came across a young police constable working the same area for E Division (Holborn): Constable 130E George Cooke. He was only twenty-five years of age himself at this time, and single. Whether this meeting was born out of Constable Cooke's professional duty or whether it was a more illicit encounter is not known. What *is* known is that the couple struck up a solid relationship, to the point where it was alleged that they moved in together at Merton's Lambeth address, where she told other residents that Cooke worked as a waiter and began to pass herself off as Mrs Cooke. Police regulations at the time were strict, and geared to protect the force's public image. The monitoring of constables was so thorough that they had to gain permission from their inspectors on matters such as where they could live and whom they could marry. It was clear to Constable Cooke that his seniors would not approve of his domestic arrangements, so, understandably, he kept it a secret from the senior officers at Bow Street Police Station, where he was based.

According to Merton, the relationship soon began to sour. Cooke began to beat her, and the beatings continued when the couple moved into new lodgings in College Street. In April 1893, Merton, claiming that she was sick of Cooke's harassment, walked into Bow Street Police Station and made a formal complaint against him. Inspector George Wood took her statement, and then interviewed Constable Cooke. Cooke admitted that he knew Merton, and that he often visited her at her lodgings, but denied that the pair were a couple, stating that he was ignorant of Merton's claim that they had taken lodgings together. Cooke also painted a picture of an obsessive Merton hell-bent on destroying his relationship with another woman whom he was planning to marry. Inspector Wood suspended him pending the Assistant Commissioner's inquiry into the matter, but only a week later Cooke was reinstated and immediately transferred to Notting Dale Police Station in X Division (Kilburn) – this was a clear attempt to separate the ill-starred couple. It was here that the matter took a dark turn.

On 6 June 1893, Constable 127X Samuel Rosewarne was on desk duty at Notting Dale Police Station when a woman arrived to ask whether Constable Cooke was on duty that day. Constable Rosewarne informed her that Cooke would be undertaking night patrol duty around Wormwood Scrubs Prison later that evening. At around 10.10 p.m., Constable 422X Joseph Harris was on beat outside the North Pole public house, near to Wormwood Scrubs, when he passed a constable patrolling the prison in the opposite direction. This was unusual, as Harris would often pass two constables at this point; however, it was not his responsibility to interfere with other officers' beat arrangements, so he carried on. Moments later, a young woman approached him, asking if he knew PC 365X. Harris did not know the constable personally but was aware that the constable she was asking about was the man who had just passed him, and so he pointed him out to her.

Constable 149X Alvan Kemp usually patrolled the perimeter of Wormwood Scrubs Prison with his new colleague from Bow Street, Constable 365X George Cooke. However, on the night of 6 June, Constable Kemp was detained by a report he had to complete, so he let Cooke go ahead without him with the intention of catching him up with him later.

Thomas Grimshaw worked as a chemist at Wormwood Scrubs, and he was returning to his home just outside the prison walls when he came across a couple having an argument outside his house. The man, dressed in police uniform, returned a 'Good evening' to Grimshaw before continuing his heated conversation with his female interlocutor in more hushed tones. Grimshaw, who had entered his home, was by now in the kitchen, which overlooked the spot where the couple were standing, and he heard the row continue in a muffled way. Suddenly, there was silence. Not long afterwards,

Constable Kemp caught up with Cooke outside Grimshaw's home, and the two constables continued their patrol in what Kemp would later describe as a 'jolly and jovial' atmosphere.

Harry Kimberley, a shepherd, kept his sheep on the Wormwood scrubland. At 5.00 a.m. on 7 June, he came across the body of a woman around 300 yards from Grimshaw's home. Her face was covered in blood and one side was horrifically deformed, as if she had been struck very severely. The woman was Maud Merton. X Division Police Surgeon Robert Jackson examined Merton's body and concluded that the causes of death were a fractured skull and haemorrhage of the brain, mostly likely caused by a blunt weapon such as a truncheon.

During that morning, policeman's wife Mrs Kate Robinson, with whom Cooke had taken up lodgings, spotted Cooke raking the earth in her back garden. She investigated the spot once the constable had left and unearthed the handle of a truncheon and a policeman's whistle. She informed her husband, who duly informed his inspector, who visited the Robinsons' home to take charge of the damning items in the garden (as well as a pair of Cooke's blood-splattered boots and blood-smeared trousers). PC Cooke was promptly arrested and sent for trial, during the course of which it emerged that Cooke and Merton had continued to see each other regularly, right up until her death.

Constable George Cooke was convicted of the murder of Maud Merton on 8 July 1893, sentenced to death and executed less than three weeks later. He remains the only serving Metropolitan Police officer charged with, and found guilty of, murder.

NRAB

Cotton, Mary Ann (1832–1873)

Durham-born Mary Ann Cotton was a nasty piece of work, a heartless woman without mercy who was quite prepared to administer arsenic to anyone – man, woman or child (her own included) – and to watch them die in agony. Her victims were those she considered dispensable, either when she wanted to trade in one husband for another or as a source of income from insurance claims. Though she was literate and had, at times, worked as a dressmaker, housekeeper or nurse, she soon realised that murder was a far more lucrative option.

Her first husband was colliery worker William Mowbray, whom she married in 1852 when she was nineteen. In search of pit work, they moved to the West Country and had, it is said, four or five children, of whom all but one – Isabella – died. Returning to the north-east in 1856, they had four more children, two of whom also died, as did Isabella (of gastric fever, or so it was said). When Mowbray himself died in 1865, Mary Ann claimed £35 – half a year's wages for a labourer – from the insurance company.

That same year she married her second husband, George Ward, freeing herself up for the union by transferring one of her two remaining children to her mother's care (the other, of course, died). Within a matter of months, Ward was no more, and again Mary Ann claimed the insurance. Before 1866 was over she had taken up with the man who would become her third husband – a widower and father of five, James Robinson; his youngest daughter, as Katherine Watson remarks mournfully, 'died within eight days' of Mary Ann's arrival in the family home. In 1867, Mary Ann's mother died shortly after a visit from her daughter, as did two more of Robinson's children, and William Mowbray's only remaining child (reclaimed by Mary Ann after the demise of her mother). Mary Ann then gave birth to yet another daughter who died soon after; a second child by Robinson survived, though it was later to be abandoned by its mother. Even this prolific schedule, with insurance payments rolling in on a frequent basis, could not keep her out of debt; when she failed to persuade Robinson to let her insure his life, the marriage came to an end and Mary Ann became destitute. Three years later, Mary Ann moved in with a thirty-nine-year-old pitman, Frederick Cotton, and bore him a son, Robert Robson Cotton. By September 1871, Frederick and his sister Margaret were both dead.

Mary Ann quickly returned to an ex-lover, thirty-five-year-old Joseph Nattrass, but when she spotted a more suitable proposition – a brewery excise man named John Quick-Manning, who hired her to aid his recovery from smallpox – it was time for Nattrass and the residue of the Cotton family to go. When one of Mary's stepsons (ten-year-old Frederick Cotton), her own child (fourteen-month-old Robert) and Joseph Nattrass all died, that left just Mary's other stepson, seven-year-old Charles Cotton, to off-load. At first Mary tried to get him admitted to the workhouse, but she was told by a local official, Thomas Riley, that she would have to be admitted as well, and so she declined, and resorted once again to murder.

By July 1872, the boy was dead, supposedly of a sudden gastric fever – an unexpected death that at last fuelled sufficient gossip to prompt the authorities to make enquiries. The insurance company also became suspicious and refused to honour Mary Ann's claim on the boy's life. Fortunately, the doctor who had attended Charles had taken samples and, applying the Reinsch Test, he proved the presence of arsenic. Mary Ann was arrested on 18 July 1872 and charged with Charles's murder. The doctor's findings led to the exhumation of the boy's body on 26 July and, later, those of his brother Frederick and little Robert – the remains of all three were found to contain arsenic. It is safe to say that, having gone undetected for so long, she may well have poisoned more than twenty victims over a period of twenty years. Prior to refrigeration, better nutrition, better healthcare and a more robust understanding of food hygiene, the child mortality rate was high, and many infant deaths were assumed to be the result of gastric fever. Many medical practitioners were far from vigilant, and were prepared to blithely accept a relative's version of events and to issue a certificate identifying natural causes of death.

The hazards of official incuriosity were already known, but society's safeguards were not keeping pace. In Essex, two decades earlier, Sarah Chesham had got away with a number of similar poisonings – including those of her two sons – committed with the express intent of making insurance claims upon the Prudential Insurance Company. Rebecca Smith, who killed at least seven of her children (though not for insurance claims), and Elizabeth Berry, who murdered her eleven-year-old daughter, Edith, and was suspected of dispatching other family members, were cut from a similar cloth and likewise operated freely for many years. They were eventually executed in 1849 and 1887 respectively, but in each case the widespread and tragic damage had already been done. Mary Ann Cotton, refining her method to take full advantage of the inaction of those with whom she came into contact, was further insulated from suspicion by the fact that she kept on the move, from one pit village to the next, ensuring that her neighbours were typically oblivious to the deaths that had occurred at her previous addresses.

Mary Ann was charged with four counts of murder – Frederick Cotton, junior, Robert Robson Cotton, Joseph Nattrass and Charles Cotton – but tried for that of Charles. The trial opened on 5 March 1873, at Durham Crown Court, before Sir Thomas Dickson Archibald. The prosecution was led by Charles Russell (see Adelaide Bartlett and Florence Maybrick). Mary Ann was defended by Mr Thomas Campbell Foster, who proposed that young Charles had died from inhaling poisonous fumes emanating from the arsenic used in processing the dye in the green wallpaper which decorated the Cottons' home. He admitted that his client kept a supply of arsenic (albeit only in the form of 'soft soap' to kill bedbugs), but, these legalistic imaginings notwithstanding, the indisputable facts were closing in upon Mary Ann. Surprisingly, the jury took as long as ninety minutes to return a guilty verdict; the sentence of death had to be postponed, however, until she had given birth to the baby she was carrying. During this time, the Home Secretary received petitions calling for a reprieve, all of which were rejected. She gave birth to Quick-Manning's child, a girl, at the gaol, and the baby was adopted. From the condemned cell, Mary Ann wrote a great many letters protesting her innocence, some of which are preserved in a private collection.

Distraught but unrepentant, Mary Ann Cotton was inexpertly dispatched by William Calcraft at eight o'clock on the morning of 24 March 1873 at Durham County Gaol As the rope was too short, she suffered for several minutes before being choked to death.

KC, MWO

FURTHER READING

Watson, K., *Poisoned Lives* (London: Hambledon and London, 2004)

C

Courvoisier, François (1816–1840)

François Courvoisier was a murderer whose crime provoked much anxiety about both the tension between the classes and the incomprehensible behaviour of foreigners. His hanging was attended by the great (Charles Dickens) and the good (Thackeray; see Execution).

Courvoisier, a Swiss national, worked in London in the service of the aristocratic Lord William Russell. In similar positions – for example, when working for Lady Lockwood at her house on Park Lane – he had attracted positive testimonials, extolling his 'kindheartedness, humanity, and inoffensiveness of disposition'. Upon reaching the household of Russell, however, some form of resentment began to take hold of him. He (privately) referred to his employer as a 'rum old chap', and, in the contemptuous diminutive, as 'old Billy'. This piqued the attention of Sarah Mansell, the live-in housemaid, but she saw no reason to think that it was anything other than a joke, perhaps mangled in the telling by Courvoisier's foreign tongue.

Russell's Mayfair home was regrettably separated from his club – Brooks's, on St James's Street – by a distance of about a mile, and his lordship, who was approaching his seventy-third birthday, sensibly employed a coachman to help him to and fro. On 5 May 1840, Russell instructed Courvoisier to tell the coachman to collect him from the club at five o'clock; according to Courvoisier, his master also issued a number of other instructions at the same time, and he – Courvoisier – had some difficulty keeping them all in his head. As it turned out, the overburdened Courvoisier omitted to deploy the coachman, and Russell was forced to return home, later than expected, in a hansom cab. Courvoisier thought that his lordship was 'angry', at least initially.

This little squall seems to have passed quickly, but for Courvoisier it may have been the final straw, assuming significance beyond its natural proportions. He had been the target of his lordship's ire once too often – perhaps there was fault on both sides – and, by the time Sarah Mansell began her duties at half past six the following morning, the house bore several new and unexpected characteristics. The ground floor appeared to have been broken into; Lord Russell was dead in his bed, with his throat cut 'so deep as to penetrate the vertebrae of his neck'; and Courvoisier, though apparently asleep when the body was discovered, seemed 'pale and agitated' upon being awoken. Sarah screamed and ran to fetch help; the cook and the coachman and a butler from a neighbouring household all sparked into action; Inspector Tedman of C Division and Henry Elsgood, a local doctor, arrived on the scene; and in the middle of all this activity, Courvoisier found himself a seat in the dining room, and said, to nobody in particular, 'Oh dear. They will think it is me, and I shall never get a place again.'

Before long, Courvoisier's remark came to seem like a feat of precognition, for the circumstances surrounding the murder failed to form a coherent picture. If the house had been broken into from the outside, why was the exterior of the property in its usual condition? There was no sign that anyone had scrabbled over the whitewashed garden wall, and no footprints disturbed a dusty lead roof which extended over the wall into the garden of the next house in the street. It was deduced that the burglary had been staged from inside the house, and, if there had been

François Courvoisier. (Authors' collection)

no intruders, the murderer must have been one of the domestic staff. The identity of the culprit was suggested by the eventual discovery that many of his lordship's valuables, supposedly lifted by the thieves, had in fact been concealed in the pantry where Courvoisier slept.

On Friday, 19 June 1840, the second day of Courvoisier's trial at the Old Bailey, Charlotte Piolaine, a last-minute witness, was hurried into the spotlight by the prosecution. She was the proprietor of the Hôtel Dieppe, on Leicester Square, and a distant acquaintance of Courvoisier. She had taken little interest in the murder of Lord William Russell, but when, on the morning of the trial's first day, her cousin arrived at the hotel with a French newspaper, she realised with a chill that she had, a few weeks before, agreed to look after a small package on behalf of London's most notorious defendant. Charlotte called for a lawyer and opened the parcel: a number of his lordship's trinkets (and 'a pair of dirty socks') peeped up at her. From this evidence – and plenty more – it became overwhelmingly clear that Courvoisier had, even before the murder, been systematically stealing from his master.

Courvoisier was convicted of murder and sentenced to death. There followed a confession, and then the literary spectacle of his execution. Over the years, it has been assumed that Courvoisier, whose attire was largely free from bloodstains, was naked when he cut Lord Russell's throat (apart, perhaps, from a pair of white cotton gloves, on which blood *was* found). This belief, though difficult to substantiate, was even articulated during the proceedings against William Herbert Wallace, who was found guilty of the murder of his wife – and then cleared on appeal – in 1931.

MWO

Cream, Thomas Neill (1850–1892)

In November 1872, Thomas Neill Cream, the Scottish-born son of a lumber merchant, made one of his earliest intrusions into the historical record when he registered as a medical student at McGill College, Canada. He graduated in 1876, and retained his licence to practise until 1881, when he was convicted of murder in Chicago. In addition to the homicide for which he was found guilty, he was suspected of as many as three more.

The facts were these: Cream was sentenced to life imprisonment in the Illinois State Penitentiary for the murder of Daniel Stott, who had died at home on 14 June 1881. Stott's wife, Julia, had visited Cream in the hope of obtaining a new medicine for her husband's epilepsy, but instead spouse and physician hit upon an alternative plan, the latter inserting strychnine into Stott's medication while taking on the former as his mistress. The relationship would be short-lived, however; upon her arrest, Julia quickly agreed to give evidence against Cream in order to avoid prison herself.

One senses that her decision was a judicious one, for Cream had begun to establish an unenviable track record. Over the previous two years, as well as being heavily suspected of offering illegal abortions, he had been variously involved in the investigations into the deaths of Kate Gardiner in Ontario in August 1879, Mary Ann Faulkner a year later in Chicago, and Ellen Stack, also in Chicago, in December 1880; it has been suggested since that he may also have been responsible for the death of Alice Montgomery, in Chicago, in April 1881. He was also known to have performed a botched abortion on his wife, Flora, whom he had married under protest in September 1876; the procedure may have contributed to her death a little under a year later. In the case of Stack, we see the start of a pattern of behaviour which would become typical of Cream, as he attempted to blackmail a local pharmacist upon whom he was keen to foist responsibility for her demise.

Despite his life sentence, Cream was released on 31 July 1891. On 1 October of the same year he sailed to England and, giving the name of 'Dr Neill', checked into Anderton's Hotel in London, a city to which he was not altogether a stranger.

Cream had previously undergone postgraduate training at St Thomas' Hospital, Lambeth, from 1876 to 1878, having left North America for Britain shortly after his coercive marriage. It has been suggested that Cream may have contracted syphilis in this period (freed as he was from his marital responsibilities) – certainly, he later seemed obsessed with the disease, and with the prostitutes by whose activities it was often spread. During the Stott case, Cream's lawyer had revealed his client's desire to 'get rid of women who were in a condition in which they were a menace to society'. Now he was back in town and frequenting London's most notorious locales.

On 6 October 1891, Cream met two women at a music hall. Three days later, now living in rented rooms in Lambeth, he wrote to one of them, arranging to meet. Both women watched out of a window for him to arrive and saw him speaking to someone else – Matilda Clover – as he approached. On 20 October, Clover was found dead.

A week earlier, another woman – Ellen Donworth – had died from poisoning, with her inquest delivering a verdict of murder 'by a person unknown'. Once again, Cream could not resist involving himself. In a letter signed 'A. O'Brien, Detective', he claimed he had information which could solve the case – available for the princely sum of £300,000. Under the name of W. H. Murray, he also distributed a leaflet at the Metropole Hotel, in Westminster,

Thomas Neill Cream. (Authors' collection)

claiming that Donworth's murderer was staying there. Adopting more false names, he attempted to blackmail several people over Clover's death, allegedly including Lady Russell, who received a letter claiming that her husband – his Lordship – had poisoned Clover with strychnine. Clover's death had (as ever) initially been considered natural, but the police now knew that someone, somewhere, possessed a suspiciously detailed knowledge of her real fate. A post-mortem confirmed that Clover had indeed been poisoned.

On 2 April 1892, having returned from a trip to Canada, Cream met another woman, Louisa Harris. He gave her pills, almost certainly saying that they were for the treatment of syphilis, but Harris had the good sense not to take them. Nine days later, he gave a bottle of stout each to Emma Marsh and Alice Shrivell in their flat in Lambeth. Both died after he left, due to the strychnine he had added to the bottles.

The police began surveillance on Cream, who was still going by the name of 'Dr Neill' – even during his subsequent trial, Cream would deny that Dr Cream and Dr Neill were one and the same. Nevertheless, once word of his previous conviction arrived from their counterparts in Chicago, the police were confident they had their man. His arrest followed shortly afterwards.

Cream was tried at the Old Bailey in October 1892, and on 15 November he was hanged inside Newgate Prison. Although his trial had officially only been concerned with the death of Clover, his likely culpability in the cases of Donworth, Marsh and Shrivell was also discussed, along with his meeting with the more fortunate Louisa Harris.

TNB

Further Reading

Teignmouth Shore, W. (ed.), *Trial of Thomas Neill Cream* (Edinburgh: William Hodge and Company, 1923)

Nash, J. R., *Murder America* (London: Rowman and Littlefield, 1980)

McLaren, A., *A Prescription for Murder* (Chicago: University of Chicago Press, 1995)

D

Dadd, Richard (1817–1886)

In August 1844, twenty-six-year-old Richard Dadd was listed as 'criminally insane', patient number 235, in the records of the Royal Bethlehem Hospital, the notorious mental institution then located in Southwark.

Just six years earlier, Kent-born Dadd had been considered a promising artist. His talent for sketching had been recognised during his teenage years, and at the age of twenty he was admitted to London's prestigious Royal Academy school. His lodgings in Great Queen Street became the hub of a progressive artistic movement now remembered under the moniker of 'The Clique', featuring such luminaries as William Frith and Augustus Egg. However, his career in the public eye was to be cut short by a tragic event – Dadd's murder of his father in 1843.

At 'Bedlam' he would have been a contemporary of attempted regicide Edward Oxford (see Assassination), as well as his own brother George – an early sign that a particularly virulent mental illness was affecting the family. In fact, George and Richard's sister Maria would shortly marry another Royal Academy artist, John Phillip, but the marriage was greatly affected by Maria's own mental struggles, which led eventually to the certification of a third Dadd sibling eleven years later.

The paperwork for Dadd's admission into the hospital is sparse, to say the least. He had been admitted from Maidstone Prison; he was a single man; and he was an artist. Seemingly important questions such as the nature of any previous episodes of insanity, details of any 'particular delusions', his propensity (or otherwise) to attempt suicide, his 'temper and disposition' and his 'habits of life or memory' are all left unanswered, the corresponding boxes on the form unfilled. Only one other detail is recorded – his 'state of bodily health' is recorded as being good.

Written a decade after his admission, in 1854, the following page of Dadd's record offers more detail. 'For some years after his admission,' it declares, 'he was considered a violent and dangerous patient for he would jump up and strike a violent blow without any aggravation, and then beg pardon for the deed.' In addition, when speaking of the murder of his father 'or any other [event] at all associated with it', he was said to become 'excited in his manner of speaking', rambling from the subject until becoming 'quite unintelligible'.

However, the writer also noted that Dadd was well educated, and 'thoroughly informed in all the particulars of his profession'. A later note, from January 1860, observes that 'he still employs himself daily with his brush, but he is slower in completing any work'. Aged forty-two by this time, the painter's spirit would seem to be diminishing. It is thought, however – as the earlier writer went on to add – that the young artist would have 'pre-eminently excelled' at his art, 'had circumstances not opposed'.

Those circumstances were these. In 1842, barrister and politician Sir Thomas Phillips engaged Dadd to accompany him on a trip through Europe and the Near East. By May of the following year, Phillips and an increasingly erratic Dadd had argued, and the latter was on his way back to England. There he renewed his acquaintance with Egg, who reportedly then visited Frith in great distress and declared that their mutual friend was, indeed, 'mad'.

Initially, Dadd's illness was optimistically considered to be merely the effects of sunstroke, and his family hoped that a period in the Kent countryside might help him recover. Instead, he would soon stab his father to death and then flee to the continent, by his own account with the intention of killing the Emperor of Austria.

In the event, another traveller fell prey to Dadd's increasingly violent delusions – attacked with a razor (in Dadd's own words, he had decided to 'operate' on the man). The victim survived, but Dadd was sentenced to twelve months' imprisonment in France. From there he was extradited back to Britain and sent to 'Bedlam' via Maidstone Gaol. Once installed in the hospital, Dadd would also claim that, while in Rome with Phillips, he had developed designs on killing the Pope. On searching his rooms in London, the police would discover a series of portraits of his friends – all portrayed with their throats cut.

This chilling image aside, the overall picture which emerges from a reading of the case notes is of a man who is alternately polite and violently unpredictable, clearly of unsound mind, and almost certainly – and quite understandably – depressed. Evidently troubled by the consequences of his crimes, today Dadd can appear as a rather pitiful figure.

Over fifty further entries follow the 1854 assessment, covering the next twenty years of Dadd's life in the hospital. The vast majority are perfunctory and repetitive – 'no change'. In July 1864, a warrant was granted for transfer to the newly built Broadmoor Criminal Lunatic Asylum, where he would have been amongst the first male admissions (the very earliest of whom had arrived in February).

Richard Dadd died in Broadmoor in 1886, aged sixty-eight. Today, his artistic reputation – largely founded on the extraordinary paintings he created during forty-two years of institutionalisation – has undergone a revival, and his works hang in galleries in London, Lancashire and beyond, as well as adorning the walls of the museum at the latest site of the Royal Bethlehem Hospital.

TNB

FURTHER READING

Tromans, N., *Richard Dadd: The Artist and the Asylum* (London: Tate Publishing, 2011)

Death in the Line of Duty

A total of 172 London policemen lost their lives whilst executing their duty during the reign of Queen Victoria, including the Metropolitan Police's Constable Ernest Thompson, the young bobby who found alleged Jack the Ripper victim Frances Coles and who was stabbed to death in a brawl in Whitechapel, and the City of London Police's Detective Sergeant Charles Thain, gunned down whilst transporting the criminal Christian Sattler back to

Great Britain. Whilst many succumbed to fatal accidents and misfortunes, a fair number were unlawfully killed.

One of the first constables to die in the Victorian era was Constable William Aldridge who, on the evening of 29 September 1839, attended a riotous scene outside the Navy Arms public house in Deptford. Two drinkers, brothers William and John Pine, were behaving rowdily, and upon the request of the landlady were told to leave the pub by Constable George Stevens. As Stevens escorted the pair off the premises and into the street, John Pine struck the constable who, in retaliation, drew his truncheon and struck Pine over the head before promptly arresting him. A gathering crowd had seen Constable Stevens's actions, deemed them unjustifiable, and proceeded to encircle the constable with the intention of freeing Pine. However, support was on its way for Stevens in the form of Constable William Aldridge.

As the two constables struggled with Pine, the crowd rapidly grew. Numbers were claimed to be near the 500 mark when stones and rocks began to hail down upon the two constables as they attempted to drag their man back to the station. Two more constables arrived to assist, only to find themselves caught up in the assault. Fearing for their lives, the four policemen decided to flee; however, as they ran, a large rock struck Constable Aldridge on the head, fracturing his skull. He died at 4.30 the following morning. The Pine brothers were eventually rearrested, and their trial for murder was heard at the Old Bailey where, along with their co-accused William Calvert and John Burke, they were convicted of the lesser charge of manslaughter. John Pine was transported to Australia for life, and Calvert for fifteen years. Burke and William Pine spent two years in prison for their part in the assault.

A mob assault also claimed the life of H Division's Constable James Carroll who, whilst attempting to make an arrest in Shoreditch on 3 October 1841, was relieved of his truncheon by yet another crowd trying to assist a prisoner in gaining his freedom. The truncheon was then turned on the forty-five-year-old constable: he suffered a brutal beating from which he never recovered.

Thomas Cooper was one of a dying breed of criminals – a highwayman. On 5 May 1842, he came across N Division's

Constable Timothy Daly at Highbury. Daly immediately recognised that the man was wanted for armed robbery and gave chase, but, as he fled, Cooper drew his pistol and shot the constable in cold blood. This act resulted in his execution outside Newgate Prison later that year.

Probably the most notorious murder of a police constable during the Victorian period occurred on the evening of 29 June 1846. Formerly based in H Division (Whitechapel), twenty-year-old Constable George Clark had found himself transferred to Dagenham, on the outer reaches of K Division's patch. At 9.00 p.m., Clark began his beat duty along a remote country lane in the Eastbrookend area, but by the time his shift ended at 6.00 a.m. there was no sign of the young constable. His mutilated body was found four days later in a corn field.

No one was convicted of Clark's murder, but suspects have not been in short supply. On the one hand, there were the fellow constables who lied about their sergeant's whereabouts on the night Clark went missing (it was stated that Clark and the sergeant's wife were having an affair); this scandalous perjury drew an unwanted spotlight upon the Metropolitan Police. On the other hand, there was the confession of a thief's wife, who stated that Clark was murdered by her husband and his friends after the constable had stumbled upon them stealing corn from a barn located on his beat.

The murder of serving officers was not merely an early Victorian phenomenon. In 1882, Constable George Cole's death (see Thomas Orrock) showed that crimes of this nature had the power to shock even in later years; and Inspector Thomas Simmons met an equally distressing fate in Rainham in 1885. Nor was this sort of offence the preserve of the industrialised quarters of the south-east. Similar outrages occurred across the country, and rural areas, in which poaching and moonlit larceny were not uncommon, were also likely to be peopled by men with guns. In 1844, in untouched Suffolk, Constable James McFadden spotted a clutch of robbers liberating corn from a barn (perhaps in anticipation of what was said to have occurred in George Clark's case) and 'crept along the ground until within a few paces of them'. One of the gang, whom McFadden, in his dying deposition, identified as William Howell, fired the contents of a rifle into the constable's thigh. Howell was hanged early in 1845, despite the protestations of over 1,000 local petitioners.

This is a small sample of Victorian policemen who paid the ultimate price whilst in uniform, an indication of the dangerous situations which could, if misfortune allowed, result in death in the line of duty.

NRAB

Deeming, Frederick Bailey (1853–1892)

Deeming continues to linger in the consciousness of crime historians, while other murderers with similar credentials have slipped into the background. This is largely because he is frequently given a run against the thoroughbreds in the Jack the Ripper stakes.

In 1891, at the height of summer, Deeming arrived in Rainhill, on Merseyside, full of vanity and bluster and hoping to leave behind him any traces of his extensive history of fraud and bigamy. This he attempted to effect by adopting the name of Albert Oliver Williams, and creating a backstory in which he had, in the course of an extensive military career, distinguished himself in several far-flung climes (fighting off Arab assassins here, and overcoming man-eating tigers there). The sudden appearance in the village of his wife, Marie, and their four young children, all of whom he had previously deserted, risked dissipating the fantasy; moreover, it threatened Deeming's engagement to the trusting Emily Mather – 'the girl in black, noiseless, subdued', as Edgar Wallace puts it. Miss Mather was potentially the heiress to her mother's stationery business; Deeming assiduously kept his family out of sight in a rented property called Dinham Villa, and explained them away as his sister, nephew and nieces whenever they were spotted by local tradespeople.

On the night of 2 August 1891, after spending the previous days digging a hole in the kitchen floor with the ostensible objective of improving the property through his own initiative and endeavours, Deeming cut his wife's throat, and annihilated the children. He concealed the bodies cautiously under layers of cement, and brought in a professional to finish the flooring to a good standard. Then, to Emily Mather's naïve delight, he announced that they would undertake a sojourn overseas. He married her in Prescot in September, and they sailed for the southern hemisphere on a German vessel in early November.

By the time the ship reached port in Melbourne, however, the gloss had come off the marriage. Emily was in a depressed condition, and Deeming was reserving his affection for a canary which he kept in a brass cage. Another new name was required – this time, Drewin was the appellation selected – and another suburban property was rented. Shortly before Christmas (or perhaps on Christmas Day itself), Deeming dispatched Emily in the manner to which he had now become accustomed, slitting her throat and situating her beneath the hearthstones of their little house in Windsor, just outside Melbourne. Kate Rounsvelle, whom Deeming met on the steamer from Melbourne to Sydney after giving up the house in which Emily's body was buried, was lucky not to come to the same end; his arrest interceded, having been prompted when the source of a terrible smell at Windsor was sought by the suspicious police. By this time, Deeming had appointed himself to the nobility and was calling himself 'Baron Swanston'.

News of the discovery of Emily Mather's body filtered back to England, as did confirmation of Deeming's identity with Albert Oliver Williams, found in some personal papers which he had only incompletely burned; an excavation at Rainhill revealed the ghastly truth of his months there. Deeming went to his death on the scaffold at Melbourne Gaol on the morning of 23 May 1892.

It was long believed that Deeming had been in South Africa, or otherwise in prison, at the time of the Ripper murders. Recent research, however, *very* cautiously suggests that he may indeed have been at large in England in 1888, and, as his subsequent history demonstrates, he was a man who could countenance brutality. Worse candidates for the title have been suggested, but still Deeming seems to have been a confidence trickster at heart, engaging and re-engaging with vulnerable women as if this aspect of his behaviour could not be controlled, but resorting to homicide only when he lost patience with them and could no longer tolerate the economic burden they (and their dependants) imposed upon him. This hardly makes him a nice man, which plainly he was not; but it may suggest that he did not share Jack the Ripper's brutal instincts.

MWO

Dickens, Charles John Huffam (1812–1870)

'Of all bad deeds that, under cover of the darkness, had been committed within wide London's bounds since night hung over it,' wrote the novelist Charles Dickens, sometime in 1838, 'that was the worst.'

The deed in question was the murder of Nancy, a practised thief and probable prostitute, at the hand (or, rather, by the butt of a pistol held in the hand) of her former lover, Bill Sikes. The bad deed occurs in chapter forty-seven of Dickens's second novel, *Oliver Twist*, or, to give it its full title, *Oliver Twist; or, The Parish Boy's Progress*. Dickens had good reason to be sympathetic to the plight of a 'parish boy'. Although he never suffered the indignity of life within a parish workhouse, he certainly came close.

A former naval employee, Dickens's father was imprisoned for debt for three months in 1824, during which time twelve-year-old Charles was forced to look after himself, his mother and younger siblings having also been sent to live with his father in Southwark's Marshalsea Prison. Charles lodged first in Camden and later close to the prison itself, and earned his keep by working in a factory packing shoe polish, a position he had taken the previous year, aged eleven (see Child Abuse).

Today, Charles Dickens is remembered almost universally as the greatest novelist of the Victorian period, as well as a startling chronicler of the era's social issues. What Dickens is rarely thought of as, however, is a writer of crime fiction.

It is the death of Nancy in *Oliver Twist* – a novel already replete with descriptions of thievery, kidnapping and deception – which best illustrates the fascination that true crime held for Dickens, who was also an enthusiastic supporter of the British police. Indeed, it has recently been suggested that a real-life killing was the inspiration behind the demise of Nancy. In 1838, although engaged (by all accounts, frenetically) in the writing of *Oliver Twist*, Dickens may have been aware of a sensational murder which took place just a short walk from his childhood lodgings in Southwark.

On 26 May 1838, the body of a woman was discovered in her room on the first floor of a house in Waterloo Road, Lambeth. The victim, who used the premises as a base for prostitution as well as a place to live, had been stabbed repeatedly; the cause of death would subsequently be given as blood loss from a severe throat wound. Some reports even suggested that her killer had attempted to decapitate her. The woman was identified as Eliza Grimwood, and the man who made the discovery, at least as far as his own account was concerned, was William Hubbard – her pimp, also variously described as her cousin and her lover.

A chronology of events soon emerged. An argument had been heard in Grimwood's room during the early hours of the morning, followed by hurried footsteps on the adjoining staircase. Some reporters claimed that it was Hubbard who heard the kerfuffle, whilst others stated that it was a fellow prostitute and her client (the two accounts being not necessarily mutually exclusive).

Interestingly, *Oliver Twist* is not the only parallel between Grimwood's death and Victorian literature: during the investigation, one clue which was considered important (and which contributed to suspicion against Hubbard) was that her apparently 'fierce' dog did not bark, suggesting that whoever had entered her room was not a stranger. Arthur Conan Doyle would employ this same device in the Sherlock Holmes story 'Silver Blaze', published in 1892.

Despite a thorough investigation, Eliza's murderer was never identified. Hubbard is said to have travelled to start a new life in America sometime afterwards. Other suspects included a client whom Grimwood had met on the night before her death, described as having the 'look of a foreigner'; the cab driver who had driven the pair from their meeting point to Waterloo Road; and a regular client, known by the amusing alias of 'Don Whiskerandoes', the apparent owner of a gaudy pair of gloves which were discovered at the murder scene. Later, the writer Barnard Gregory would publish his theory that the culprit had been the Duke of Brunswick, an assertion which landed Gregory himself in prison for libel.

Seven months after Grimwood was buried in an unmarked grave on the very same road where she had breathed her last, the demise of Nancy was first published. It remains the closest she has to a memorial, although echoes of her recur faintly in Dickens's later work. He would immortalise one of the detectives who investigated Grimwood's murder – Inspector Charles Field – in an 1850 article for *Household Words*, and Field is widely held to be the model for Inspector Bucket in *Bleak House*.

Charles Dickens died in 1870, aged fifty-eight, leaving his final work, *The Mystery of Edwin Drood*, six instalments short of completion. Dickens's first true foray into crime fiction, the novel revolved around the disappearance of the eponymous Edwin, but became possibly the greatest Victorian 'whodunit' of all, in which even the reader is left wondering what solution the author himself had in mind.

TNB

FURTHER READING

Collins P., *Dickens and Crime* (London: Macmillan, 1962)
Gowers, R., *The Twisted Heart* (Edinburgh: Canongate Books, 2009)

Dobell, Charles (1871–1889) and Gower, William (1870–1889)

On 12 November 1888, the honourable Louis Jennings MP took to his feet in the House of Commons and asked a question of his Conservative colleague, the Home Secretary, Henry Matthews. Would the government, Jennings wondered, be taking measures to address the spread of sensationalist publications – the popular 'penny dreadfuls' amongst them – which the MP asserted had led to a recent murder in Tunbridge Wells, along with 'so many other crimes'?

Today, Jennings's question is only rarely remembered, if ever, in treatises on Victorian popular literature. At the time, however, it was considered a serious point. Matthews assured Jennings that the government was prepared to 'take all the measures that the law permits' in order to address the issue.

The murder in Tunbridge Wells to which Jennings referred has also faded into obscurity. Given that Jennings was speaking just three days after the discovery of the body of Mary Jane Kelly, the most ghastly of the murders of Jack the Ripper, this is perhaps to be expected. Nevertheless, the story bears repeating.

Around 9.45 p.m. on 20 July 1888, a figure appeared at the door of 64 Tunnel Road, Tunbridge Wells. The house was home to Bensley Lawrence, his wife Maria, and the youngest three of their six children. Bensley was an engine driver at the town's Baltic Saw Mills, and the caller told him that the manager of the mills wished to meet him in a nearby public house.

Against the advice of his wife, Lawrence wandered off into the night. A little over an hour later a gunshot was heard. Two neighbours made their way to the mills' nearby timber yard, where they made a terrible discovery. Lawrence lay injured, with a single gunshot wound in his left temple. He declined a drink of water, but stated a desire to tell his wife what had happened. He was carried back to his house, still just about alive, and then eventually transported to the local hospital. He fell into a coma shortly afterwards and was pronounced dead the following afternoon.

Lawrence had been unable to identify his attacker, and witnesses were scarce. The only real clue seemed to come from two young men, Arthur Shoebridge and Frank Hemsley, who reported having seen two people standing in the timber yard shortly before 9.40 p.m., before one of them began to make his way towards Tunnel Road.

The trail quickly went cold despite a spirited police investigation and a reward of £100, put up by Lawrence's former employers; in the meantime, the news from London's East End began to dominate the popular imagination. On 27 September, however, a clue arrived in the form of a letter delivered to the offices of the *Tunbridge Wells Advertiser*.

It began obsequiously. 'Dear Sir – Two months having now passed, I venture to ask you to be kind enough to allow me a small space in your valuable paper for a few facts concerning the death of the late Mr Lawrence.' However, it quickly descended into a tone more reminiscent of the sensational literature that would soon occupy the mind of Louis Jennings. 'Bang! And once more Tunbridge Wells was startled by another mistery [*sic*] which is never likely to be found out.' The letter, which also displayed a curious concern with the minutiae of Maria Lawrence's inquest testimony, was signed 'Another Whitechapel Murderer'.

The police considered the letter to be a hoax, but the house of cards was falling and, a fortnight later, the author of the correspondence was identified. Two local teenagers – eighteen-year-old William Gower and seventeen-year-old Charles Dobell – had recently been in the habit of attending Salvation Army meetings, and on 11 October both 'approached the table' at the culmination of the service in order to offer their souls to God. Gower, however, in the words of the presiding captain, appeared to have something on his mind.

The following day, Gower visited the captain at home, and quickly confessed that he and Dobell had been responsible for the murder of Bensley Lawrence, in addition to a spate of recent arsons and at least one robbery in the town. There was also talk that they had begun planning a second murder.

The pair were arrested and, in December, a quick trial followed. Both Gower and Dobell pleaded not guilty, Gower's frank confession seemingly forgotten. Gower's mother and sister contributed the defence, such as it was, claiming that he had been in his bed at home by 10.00 p.m. Dobell was identified as the defendant behind the fatal shot: according to the captain, Gower had said that this role was allocated by either the tossing of a coin or the drawing of lots.

Dobell had also outed himself as the writer of the anonymous letter, as well as the caller at the door of 64 Tunnel Road, by continuing to complain about the accuracy of the evidence which Maria Lawrence had given at the inquest. The murder weapon had been located at Dobell's home, locked in a rabbit hutch in a shed.

A motive was finally identified for what had appeared a senseless crime. Gower, a colleague of Lawrence's at the Baltic Saw Mills, had grown angry at Lawrence for fines imposed for tardiness, which fell under the engine driver's remit. Somehow, he had convinced Dobell – his inseparable friend since childhood Sunday school meetings – that Lawrence was 'against the workers', and that revenge needed to be sought.

But why would Dobell agree to shoot a man against whom he held no grudge – in fact, a man whom he had never met? It was a question the captain had also asked. The answer, in the words of Gower, was that, 'He's my mate, and he's as true as steel.'

Despite pleas for mercy on account of their youth, both Gower and Dobell were sentenced to death following a jury deliberation which lasted all of twenty minutes. A subsequent petition to commute their sentences failed, although it attracted over 2,000 signatures, as well as the support of the aforementioned Salvation Army captain.

At 8.00 a.m. on 2 January 1889, Gower and Dobell were, in the legal phrase of the day, 'hanged by the neck until dead' at Maidstone Prison. Their executioner was James Berry – finally, they had met one of the notorious figures from the popular crime stories of late Victorian Britain.

He would not have known it at the time, of course, but Dobell himself would also in time pass into the history of true crime as the final person under the age of eighteen to be executed in the United Kingdom.

TNB

FURTHER READING

Ingleton, R., *Kent Murder and Mayhem* (Barnsley: Wharncliffe Books, 2008)

Johnson, W. H., *Kent Murder Casebook* (Newbury: Countryside Books, 1998)

Dorset Street

At one time the so-called 'Worst Street in London', Dorset Street's footprint is now lost under the city's shuffled architectural patterns. It remains enduringly famous for its association with Jack the Ripper, and in particular with his (conventionally) final victim, Mary Jane Kelly.

Kelly was murdered in her little room in Millers Court, which itself was a backyard slum accessible through a dark ginnel located between

26 and 27 Dorset Street (the street was numbered up-and-back, rather than odds-and-evens). There can hardly have been a more overlooked, neglected or disheartening place closer to the dynamic heart of the metropolis. And yet, perhaps, the common lodging houses – joyless night dwellings for the dispossessed – which had grown up along Dorset Street's forbidding axis were worse. Mary Jane Kelly ran up arrears on her room, omitting to pay her rent; but even this was a luxury. At Crossingham's, further down the road towards the City, the destitute of the East End packed themselves, disorderly and dirty, into a charmless sardine tin every night for fourpence, or were left outside to fend for themselves if fourpence was beyond them. Here Annie Chapman, discovered gnawing a potato in the kitchen quarters in the early hours of 8 September 1888, admitted that she was unable to pay her way. Nevertheless, she left with her optimism intact: 'Don't let the bed; I will be back soon.' She never returned, and encountered the Ripper at first light.

Criminality was the inevitable by-product of poverty and social pressure. In 1898, back in Millers Court – indeed, in the room directly above the one in which Mary Jane Kelly had been obliterated – Kate Marshall murdered her sister, Eliza Roberts, with a knife which, in calmer moments, she used in the making of whips. The weapon penetrated Eliza's chest between the first and second ribs, an inch to the right of the sternum, and pierced the lung. Drinking had led to quarrelling; Eliza's husband David was occupying the same room, as was their three-year-old son, whose distress and perplexity were voiced in newspaper reports: 'Where's Mummy? Is Mummy coming?'

In truth, all the preconditions for tragedy were already in place in the Marshall case. Alcohol misuse, domestic violence, transitory dwelling patterns, overcrowding, unsteady employment, previous convictions, the death and removal of children from the birth family, relational dysfunction: it reads like the list of contributory factors to a modern Serious Case Review. But Dorset Street must have been full of cases which could have ended similarly; perhaps the miracle is that more did not.

Dorset Street retained its gloomy reputation into the twentieth century. An early Edwardian murder – that of Mary Ann Austin – threw the spotlight on conditions in the lodging houses, but it was not until 1928 that the old buildings began to be torn down, ready for redevelopment. Even so, Millers Court, in particular, did not let go of its habits without a struggle. Kitty Roman was murdered there in 1909, in a room looking out and down upon the northern exterior of Mary Jane Kelly's room. And as late as 1926 Joseph Carson appeared at a police station in Bow, confessing to a murder in – as *The Times* erroneously put it – 'a court off Gossett Street, Spitalfields, opposite a church'. When Jane Williams's body was discovered in her room, it was realised that she had died of chronic myocarditis and interstitial nephritis, and Carson, unfit for the awful pantheon, was discharged to obscurity.

MWO

Further Reading

Oldridge, M. W., *Murder and Crime: Whitechapel and District* (Stroud: The History Press, 2011)

Drake, Sarah (*c.* 1815–1891)

Another tragic case of an impoverished, unmarried mother in service killing her child (see, for example, Eliza Boucher) was that of thirty-six-year-old Sarah Drake, who was tried at the Old Bailey on Thursday, 10 January 1850. The learned counsel had taken their places in the well of the court, the jury was assembled, and the two judges, resplendent in full wigs and scarlet robes, prepared to take their seats on the bench. The public gallery was packed with eager spectators waiting impatiently for the drama to begin. Sitting crouched down in the dock was a pathetically thin woman, her head lowered as she pressed a handkerchief to her face in an attempt to hide from public view. She was described in the press as 'a woman of middle height, very thin, almost emaciated', and one reporter unkindly observed that 'she could never have possessed even comely attractions'. She was charged with the wilful murder of her two-year-old son, Lewis.

An examination of Sarah Drake's life to this terrible point might help to explain her predicament, although the circumstances of her birth and upbringing in rural North Leverton, Nottinghamshire, are not known to have been especially remarkable. Even so, in the decade before her trial for the murder of Lewis there had been two shocking incidents, each apparently echoed by what followed. The first had been in 1842, when the body of an infant had been placed in a box and sent to a porter at the Union Workhouse at Knutsford, an attached note reading, 'You will do your wife a favour by burying this.' At the subsequent inquest into this child's death, a surgeon, after finding a thumb mark on the right side of the baby's neck and finger marks on the left side, concluded that the child had been born alive. Sarah was sent for trial at the Old Bailey on 9 May 1842, charged with infanticide, specifically the 'wilful murder of an illegitimate', but was found guilty of 'concealment of a birth' – which carried a maximum sentence of two years – and was imprisoned for six months.

Two years later, in 1844, the body of a new-born male had been sent to Sarah's family in North Leverton. At the inquest into this second infant death it transpired that the body had been sent anonymously from London's Euston railway station. The jury brought in a non-specific verdict, unable to say whether the child 'was alive before, at, or after its birth'.

The following year, Sarah went to live as a servant with Mrs Ramsay, in Oxfordshire, where she remained until she became pregnant by the French butler and was forced to leave. Lewis was born on 9 October 1847, and Sarah paid a Mrs Johnson, in Peckham, to care for him for 6s a week; but by the time she had started as a housekeeper for a Mrs Huth in Upper Harley Street, London, in 1850, Sarah was already in arrears. When Mrs Johnson received a letter from Sarah saying she was going abroad, she didn't believe a word of it and, on 28 November, hurried to Upper Harley Street with little Lewis in tow. She told Sarah that her husband had refused to let her keep the child. Sarah begged her to change her mind, but Mrs Johnson refused and left little Lewis with his mother. The following day Sarah sent a heavy box from Euston station, addressed to her family. When they saw that it contained the body of a child, they immediately handed it over to the police. The post-mortem findings indicated that blows to the head had been sufficient to cause death, and there was also evidence of strangulation by the handkerchief fastened around the child's neck.

The fact that Sarah Drake had been tried once before at the Old Bailey, in 1842, and imprisoned over the death of a baby – and that she had been *suspected* of being responsible but not tried or convicted for the death of another, in 1844 – was common knowledge by the time of her trial for Lewis's murder.

Throughout the proceedings Sarah sat in the dock compulsively rocking backwards and forwards, and at times 'her whole frame was convulsed with grief, but she never, even for a moment, raised her head or evinced the least curiosity as to what was going on around her'. After an arduous trial and a scrupulously fair summing-up by Mr Justice Patteson, the jurors found Sarah 'not guilty, on the ground of temporary insanity' and she was sentenced to be 'detained in safe custody during Her Majesty's pleasure'. There was slight applause in court but, having cheated the hangman, Sarah fainted. She was sent to the Royal Bethlehem Hospital and was recorded in the 1851 national census as a 'criminal lunatic' in residence, but the archives give up no further record of her during her incarceration.

It must be said that Sarah – who had been suspected of killing, if not proved to have killed, three of her children – was perhaps fortunate to receive an indeterminate sentence to be served in a hospital rather than a prison. Fellow servants had testified that she was a religious woman, regularly praying and reading her Bible. Bizarrely, she intimated that after killing her last two infants she had sent their bodies to her family in the country to ensure 'a decent burial'. By 1861, she was back in her village, aged forty-six, and, once more, living with her parents. She died in her seventies, in 1891.

KC

FURTHER READING

Clarke, K., *Bad Companions* (Stroud: The History Press, 2013)

Drouet, Bartholomew Peter (*c.* 1795–1849)

The Poor Law Amendment Act of 1834, and in particular its Bastardy Clause, caused the number of pauper children in parish workhouses to reach unmanageable proportions by the early Victorian period. To address the problem, many children were farmed out into institutions or asylums; although some of these gave adequate care, others were disgracefully negligent. On establishment falling into the latter category was Surrey Hall, in Tooting, south London.

Surrey Hall was run by Bartholomew Peter Drouet, who took in pauper children offloaded by a number of London workhouses, including the Holborn and St Pancras unions. Drouet charged the Poor Law Guardians 4s 6d a week for each child, and it was estimated that, in late 1847, about 850 children between the ages of six and fourteen were residing at Tooting. To comply with the expectations of the Poor Law Commissioners, it was understood that the children would receive a basic education; the boys would also be trained for employment in small workshops and the girls would be taught the skills necessary for work in domestic service. In truth, they were beaten, half-starved and humiliated. When first inspected by the St Pancras Guardians, the establishment was considered perfectly adequate; but, in May 1848 – by which time the number of children on the premises had risen to something like 1,400 – the Holborn Guardians made a further inspection (accompanied by the genial Drouet), during which they noticed that some of the boys looked sickly, and had scabies, thin limbs and distended stomachs. When asked whether they wished to complain about the manner in which they were being treated, a number of the boys had the temerity to raise their hands. Drouet's largesse swiftly evaporated: he called them 'liars and scoundrels' and threatened, in the presence of the Guardians, to flog them there and then. Reluctant to interfere in case Drouet retaliated by returning the children to the workhouse, the Guardians departed, and a timidly satisfactory report on the Tooting establishment was issued.

In January 1849, an outbreak of cholera forced the Guardians to take action. Most of the 155 sick children whom they moved to the Royal Free Hospital survived, but an emaciated seven-year-old,

James Andrews, died the following day. Malnutrition, gross overcrowding and the lack of basic hygiene had rendered the children susceptible to infection, and those left behind soon perished. Dr Richard Grainger, a Board of Health inspector, was sent to Surrey Hall. His report made horrific reading. Children suffering from cholera were crammed into cold, evil-smelling, ill-lit rooms without adequate ventilation; one room housed 150 children next to a filthy yard where livestock, including cows and pigs, were kept; nearby were open ditches filled with toxic effluent. The sick children were given only the most rudimentary nursing care, some of which was provided by older pauper children who were yet free of the disease. When questioned, Drouet insisted that the cause of the outbreak was a fog hanging over the area – it was a commonly held belief that cholera was caused by inhaling 'bad' air – but, although there was cholera in other parts of London, Tooting was, at the time, clear of the disease.

Several inquests into the children's deaths were initiated by Thomas Wakley, the Coroner for Middlesex and editor of *The Lancet*. His findings detailed the extent of the deprivation and exploitation of the pauper children. On 13 April 1849, Drouet was tried at the Old Bailey on a sample charge of 'feloniously killing' the little boy, James Andrews; three other similar charges were held in reserve. The clear evidence of criminal negligence was rejected by the Recorder, Mr Baron Platt, who argued that it could not be proved that James and the other children had died due to any ill-treatment on the part of Drouet; once infected with cholera, he thought, they would have died anyway. Peter Drouet was acquitted and died three months later, on 19 July, of heart disease and dropsy, aged 55.

Predictably, the press dubbed the story 'the Massacre of the Innocents'. Accusatory articles in *The Examiner* (probably penned anonymously by Charles Dickens, always vociferous in matters of poverty and inequality) stated that the cholera epidemic had occurred because Drouet's 'farm for children' was 'brutally conducted, vilely kept, preposterously inspected, dishonestly defended, a disgrace to a Christian community and a stain upon a civilised land'. Dickens's novel *Bleak House*, which was serialised in 1852 and 1853, featured a young maidservant called Guster who was 'farmed or contracted for during her growing time by an amiable benefactor of his species resident at Tooting'.

Efforts to prevent malpractice in institutions such as Drouet's continued, meeting with varying degrees of success. Ernest Hart, the editor of the *British Medical Journal*, led a long campaign against child cruelty (concentrating mainly on the widespread practice of 'domestic' baby farming); but it was not until 1870, when the undercover investigations of a police officer at Scotland Yard led to the exposure and prosecution of two Brixton baby farmers, Margaret Waters and Sarah Ellis, that the Infant Life Protection Society was formed. *The Spectator* commented:

> We must show by a rigid exercise of severity that baby farmers are not to be allowed to traffic with infant life, and that murder, which is fearful enough when it springs from passion, is infinitely more loathsome and more criminal when it is reduced to a business.

Following the shocking case of Amelia Dyer in 1896, the Infant Protection Act was amended to give the authorities more power to supervise childcare establishments, both domestic and institutional. It proved impossible, however, to entirely stamp out these nefarious practices and, coupled with the high rate of infanticide, newborns, infants and even older children remained at risk. The National Society for the Prevention of Cruelty to Children, which received its Royal Charter in 1895, is still in operation to this day.

KC

Dyer, Amelia (1839–1896)

What does it take to strangle a baby? Certainly not strength, but a chilling degree of callousness – even at a time when the death of children was a commonplace occurrence in many families. Unwanted newborns were frequently dumped in canals, privies and alleyways, or buried under dung-heaps. Those mothers who could not bring themselves to kill their babies represented a lucrative business opportunity for ruthless baby farmers who viewed any unwanted infant as a disposable commodity. These women affected a veneer of kindliness, often posing as paragons of respectability, but one is almost bewildered by the number of children involved and the casual horror of their fates. In 1868, for example, Mrs Jagger of Tottenham, who advertised her services in the *Daily Telegraph*, was exposed in the *Pall Mall Gazette* after having starved to death between forty and sixty babies in the space of three years. In addition, diversification into abortion services was always a temptation: Mrs Martin of Dean Street in Soho was thought to have disposed of 555 babies and foetuses in ten months; and Mary Hall, in Brixton, ran a 'lying-in' establishment and was suspected of feeding aborted foetuses to neighbourhood cats. In 1865, Charlotte Winsor was convicted on a sample charge of killing an unwanted baby for a £5 fee.

One of the most notorious baby farmers was Amelia Dyer, dubbed 'the Angel Maker', who advertised her services as a foster nurse knowing that there would be a regular supply of desperate mothers knocking on her door, willing to hand over their illegitimate babies for a fee, usually between £5 and £10. Some may have genuinely believed Dyer's promise to find a family willing to adopt the child (and, by doing so, offer it a better chance in life); but others, though perhaps suspecting the nefarious nature of the deal, had no choice but to comply.

Having perfected her killing regime for years, getting away with it all the while, Amelia Dyer was finally apprehended through her own carelessness. In 1895, the bodies of three infants were dredged from the Thames. They were wrapped in paper parcels, and the white dressmaking tape used to strangle them still curled around their necks. The paper enveloping one of the tiny corpses bore an address which eventually led police to the home of Amelia Dyer, who, although she frequently used aliases and changed addresses to evade detection, was by then living at 45 Kensington Road, Reading. Fifty-seven years old, and a tall, bulky woman whose few remaining teeth were blackened stumps, she was arrested and, on 4 April, charged with the murder of a female infant.

Dyer's remand, awaiting her trial, merely precipitated a thorough investigation of her activities. One of several bodies subsequently found was identified as four-month-old Doris Marmon, and Dyer was now charged specifically with her murder. During a search of Dyer's house, piles of baby clothes – provided by the mothers – were found, ready to pawn, and Dyer had assiduously retained paperwork relating to hundreds of 'adoptions'. It was estimated that she had killed as many as 400 babies over a period of more than twenty years. Some had been so heavily drugged with Godfrey's Cordial, a laudanum-based opiate, that they had died of starvation, unable even to cry, whilst others were strangled within days of landing in Dyer's clutches. Dyer's daughter Mary Ann (known as Polly) and Polly's husband were also arrested, suspected of colluding in the gruesome crimes.

Amelia Dyer was tried at the Old Bailey on 21 and 22 May 1896, before Mr Justice Hawkins; the main prosecution witness was Polly, brought from Reading Gaol for the purpose. The deal Dyer had made with Doris Marmon's mother, Evelina, was made known and serves to illustrate a typical transaction, one repeated many times by baby farmers throughout the country. Evelina, who was unmarried and living in Cheltenham, had placed the following advertisement in *The Bristol Times and Mirror*:

> Wanted, respectable woman to take young child.

In the same paper appeared an advertisement placed by Amelia Dyer, using the name of Mrs Harding:

> Married couple with no family would adopt healthy child,
> nice country home. Terms, £10.

Evelina contacted 'Mrs Harding' and received a lengthy reply, part of which read:

> I should be glad to have a little baby girl, one I could bring up and call my own ... We are plain homely people, in fairly good circumstances. I don't want a child for money's sake, but for company and home comfort ... Myself and my husband are dearly fond of children. I have no child of my own. A child with me will have a good home and a mother's love.

Every word was a cruel lie, but Evelina, satisfied with these sentiments, arranged to entrust Doris to 'Mrs Harding'. It had been Evelina's intention for the arrangement to be a temporary one, but Dyer persuaded her to make a one-off payment of £10 and thereafter relinquish any claim to her daughter. Taking the child, Dyer headed for London and to the home of her daughter, Polly. Between them they strangled little Doris. The next day, 2 April, Dyer took charge of another child, Harry Simmons; but, as she had run out of dressmaking tape, she removed the piece from Doris's lifeless neck and used it to strangle the boy. That done, she parcelled up both bodies and took them by train to Reading in a carpet bag, weighted down with bricks. She then pushed it through the railings near Caversham Lock, to be swallowed up by the River Thames. Once this story had become apparent, Dyer was additionally charged with killing Simmons.

In court, Amelia Dyer pleaded not guilty to murder. Her defence counsel offered a plea of insanity on account of several periods of severe mental instability (for which she was detained in asylums) and frequent suicide attempts, possibly brought on by her addiction to alcohol and laudanum. The jury, who deliberated for less than five minutes, found her guilty in spite of the efforts of her lawyer, and she was sentenced to death. She was hanged by James Billington on 10 June 1896, having spent much of the previous day in Holloway Prison, whence she had been taken to ensure her absence while William Seaman, Albert Milsome and Henry Fowler were executed at Newgate. The newspapers recorded that 'on the receipt of a telegram forwarded after the graves of the murderers executed in the morning had been filled in and paved, she was taken back to Newgate. Before reaching her cell she had to walk over the newly made graves.' She retired to bed for the last time in a 'wretched and agitated state of mind'.

Polly and her husband continued to operate as baby farmers after her mother's execution. Dyer had insisted on the innocence of her daughter and son-in-law, and they were, in fact, lucky to be released through lack of evidence. But it was, and remains, impossible to believe that they were really oblivious to what was going on.

KC

FURTHER READING

Rattle, A. and Vale, A., *The Woman who Murdered Babies for Money* (London: Andre Deutsch, 2011)

Dymond, Charlotte (*c.* 1826–1844)

The victim of Cornwall's premier fatal assault, Charlotte Dymond was eighteen years old at the time of her death – although some sources have it as sixteen – and working as a maid at Penhale Farm, at the foot of Bodmin Moor. Posthumous assessments of her scintillating local profile probably overstate the case, but it is usually suggested that she was attractive, gleefully aware of it, and always pleased to receive attention from others.

Matthew Weeks was one of those who had fallen under Charlotte's spell. A twenty-two-year-old, smallpox-scarred, limping and illiterate farm servant, he was generally unsuited to competitive romancing and bedevilled by insecurities. When he reacted jealously and possessively to her teasing stories of widespread male appreciation, this augured badly, but it scarcely dimmed his ardour. For her part, Charlotte appeared to toy with Matthew's heart, radiating intimacy one day, and indifference the next.

On the afternoon of Sunday, 14 April 1844, Matthew and Charlotte left the farmhouse, heading out towards the moor, apparently going for a stroll despite the cloudy skies and rainy weather. Matthew's mood, too, had darkened: he had had an altercation with one Thomas Prout, who had lately (and quite openly) resolved to turn Charlotte's head; and he had been seen honing a razor, although his chin was covered in a beard of at least three weeks' growth.

Long after nightfall, Matthew returned to Penhale Farm. Charlotte did not. He spent the next few days deflecting the enquiries of the farm's other inhabitants, saying that Charlotte had gone to work in Blisland, on the other side of the moor. It was also noticed that his shirt was torn and missing a button. On 19 April, when a pig was to be slaughtered, he asked to undertake the task and did an uncharacteristically messy job, getting blood on his clothing. Two days later, amid intensifying local speculation, he left the farm, supposedly limping in the direction of his mother's house in Larrick.

Belatedly, it was decided to search the moor for Charlotte, of whom nothing further had been heard. Nine days after she had last been seen alive, her body was discovered in the channel of the River Alan, her throat nastily cut. Matthew Weeks was traced to his sister's house in Plymouth, his meandering route having doubled back upon itself and drifted across the Tamar into Devon. He was charged with murder and brought back to Cornwall.

His trial, before Sir John Patteson, was held at Bodmin on 2 August 1844. He pleaded not guilty, sotto voce in the high-ceilinged courtroom – he intrigued observers who could not decide whether his deportment was one of frozen terror or remorselessness. Gradually, the evidence against him, marshalled by the urbane Alexander Cockburn QC, coalesced into an irrefutable narrative. The case for the defence, urged reluctantly into shape by Frederick Slade (a barrister of little comparative repute), did not commence until nearly seven o'clock in the evening and, since Matthew had no witnesses to his version of events, it lasted – to within a couple of minutes either way – an hour. The judge was summing up before eight; the jury went out just before ten, and returned a little over half an hour later. Matthew was found guilty and sentenced to death; he was hanged at Bodmin Prison, apparently in front of a crowd of 20,000 people – nearly five times the population of the town – on 12 August 1844.

Charlotte Dymond's short life and lonely death are commemorated by a stone monument, erected on Roughtor within a few paces of the river course in which her body was discovered. Like others in this book, she survives as a ghost, 'walking in the wild marshes near the stream', according to James Turner, whose brief description of the case is rather sweetly written, but not altogether reliable. Pat Munn's monograph, originally published in the 1970s and since reprinted in memory of the author, remains the definitive account, although the conclusion she reaches is, by anybody's standards, an unlikely one.

MWO

FURTHER READING

Munn, P., *The Charlotte Dymond Murder* (Bodmin: Bodmin Books Limited, 1978; Bodmin Town Museum, 2010)

Turner, J., *Ghosts in the South West* (Newton Abbot: David & Charles, 1973)

E

Eastbourne Manslaughter, The (1860)

The Eastbourne Manslaughter was a cause célèbre of the mid-Victorian period. The victim, a fourteen-year-old student named Reginald Channell Cancellor, was thrashed to death by his schoolmaster, who had been taxed with the job of making him learn, in spite of himself.

Thomas Hopley, the schoolmaster in question, resided at Eastbourne, Sussex, and was in his spare time an agitator seeking to put an end to the horrifying conditions endured by children working in factories (see Child Abuse). When the deceased Reginald – who had a congenital learning disability, perhaps linked to hydrocephalus – was discovered to have left behind him a brutalised frame, extensively wounded after being beaten with 'a brass candlestick and other weapons', the newspapers felt free to comment on Hopley's shameless hypocrisy. *The Wells Journal* skimmed through one of Hopley's pamphlets, entitled *Wrongs which Cry for Redress*, alighting on this provocative passage:

> Now, reader, it is no use mincing words. Look upon this calmly; weigh the matter well; and have the manly or womanly honesty to call it by its right name; and what is it? *Wholesale murder* – murder for *Gold.*

'And what Thomas Hopley,' asked the newspaper, rhetorically, 'is beating a boy to death, because he would not or could not repeat the multiplication table? Call it by its right name; and what is it? ... If he would see a brute, he need not search for him in the manufactories of our land. All he need do is to look in the glass.'

Hopley's own behaviour had served to excite suspicions against him. He said that he had discovered Reginald's dead body in bed on the morning of 22 April 1860, but the servants in the house had overheard the assault, which had lasted from 'a quarter to ten to nearly half past eleven' the previous night. By the time Hopley announced Reginald's demise, the house was decorated with items of laundry which appeared to have been newly washed; even so, blood was visible on the carpet, and the candlestick, and the hearthstone, and the boy's underwear, and a bedsheet, and some pocket handkerchiefs, and a jacket. Hopley – too busy trying to clean up – had neglected to call a doctor in good time and delayed sending a telegram to the boy's father.

The trial took place at Lewes on Monday, 23 July. The courtroom was full long before proceedings began. Testimony of the most melancholy variety was given: according to Hopley, he had sought Reginald's father's permission to use corporal punishment, and the Reverend John Cancellor – who, brokenheartedly, had followed his son into the world beyond in June – had consented to the idea. The jury did not hesitate to find Hopley guilty of manslaughter, and he was sentenced to four years' imprisonment. Since Reginald's death had been caused by an educational strategy – however misguided and misused – it could not be described as murder.

In 1863, Hopley's wife began divorce proceedings, describing a pattern of mistreatment dating back almost to the beginning of her marriage (in 1855) and continuing through her pregnancies until Hopley's incarceration. She also accused him of inflicting violence upon their children. When their first child, Edward, was only about a fortnight old, Hopley beat him savagely; it may have been no coincidence that Edward grew into 'an idiot', as the Victorians expressed it. Hopley for his part identified two awkward lines of defence and ran them concurrently, saying, on the one hand, that he had not acted cruelly towards his wife, and, on the other, that she had colluded in any cruelty which had taken place. Remarkably, this worked for him, and the divorce action was thwarted. Today, he seems to be a textbook perpetrator of domestic abuse; a man whose 'fiendish temper', as one newspaper described it, was restrained, if at all, by only the most fragile threads; and very possibly animated by a personality disorder.

MWO

Edmunds, Christiana (1829–1907)

Christiana Edmunds was a highly strung, slightly eccentric, forty-three-year-old spinster, living with her widowed mother in Grand Parade, Brighton. Her life began to spiral out of control when, in 1870, she became infatuated with her married doctor, Charles Izard Beard. Whether or not her feelings were reciprocated is uncertain, but Christiana, on a social visit to his home, popped a poisoned chocolate into the mouth of the doctor's wife, Emily. Fortunately, she spat it out, but the situation took on a more sinister dimension when, hoping to deflect Dr Beard's suspicions, Christiana enlisted the help of some young boys to purchase bags of chocolate creams from Maynard's confectionary shop in West Street, Brighton. By using a false name and enlisting a random witness to her signature in the Sale of Poison book, she was also able to obtain supplies of arsenic and strychnine from a local chemist, citing the pretext of needing to get rid of feral cats. She then systematically laced some of the chocolates with poison and took them back to the shop, leaving them to be re-sold to unsuspecting customers. Tragically, a young boy from London on holiday with his family, four-year-old Sidney Barker, ate one of the chocolates and died. To disguise her part in the death, Christiana sent parcels of poisoned cakes and fruit to various prominent residents – even sending one to herself. Fortunately, those recipients who sampled the sweetmeats, though made very ill, nevertheless survived. However, suspicion soon fell on the deluded and lovesick woman, and she was charged with not only the murder of Sidney Barker but also with the attempted murder of three other people.

Such was the voracious regional interest in the case that, in the interests of impartiality, her murder trial was held at London's Old

Bailey; at the local courthouse in Lewes, every aspect of the events leading up to the poisoning spree had become common knowledge and a rich source of rumour and gossip. During the train journey from Lewes Prison to Newgate, Christiana began to exhibit bizarre behaviour. She screamed for Dr Beard and threatened to throw herself from the carriage window. Having reached Newgate, she complained bitterly about having to share a cell with a 'criminal'.

The trial was opened on Monday, 15 January 1872; the presiding judge was Lord Chief Justice Baron Martin, with Mr William Ballantine acting for the prosecution and Messrs Parry, Poland and Worsley for the defence. In the dock sat Christiana Edmunds, described as a 'slightly made and pale-faced woman' wearing 'a black velvet mantle with a small fur tippet around the neck; and the only noticeable peculiarity in her appearance was a large coronet of hair surmounting the smooth locks braided in a fashion now long out of date'. A large number of witnesses were called, among them several of the boys used by Christiana to acquire the chocolates for her to poison, and Mr John Maynard, the much-maligned owner of the sweet shop in West Street. Parry, for the defence, presented an impassioned plea of insanity, giving details of members of Christiana's family who were certified insane – evidence that was tearfully acknowledged by her elderly mother, Ann Edmunds, when she was brought before the court. Dr William Wood, at one time a physician at the Royal Bethlehem Hospital, described meeting Christiana at Newgate, concluding that he believed her quite incapable of understanding her position or of distinguishing right from wrong – one of the definitions of insanity listed in the M'Naghten Rules. Dr Lockhart Robertson, one of the Visitors of the Court of Chancery, considered her to be 'morally insane', an opinion endorsed by Dr Henry Maudsley.

Throughout Baron Martin's lengthy and scrupulously fair summing-up, Christiana sat in the dock 'unmoved and seemingly unconcerned'. It was noted that 'her hair was carefully and even coquettishly arranged in heavy folds across her head'. Whilst waiting for the jury to return a verdict, the judge was seen to be reading a copy of *The Times*, while other officials were heard discussing the charms of some of the female spectators gathered in the public gallery. The newspapers published descriptions of the dramatic scenes in court ad infinitum, especially when, having been found guilty and sentenced to death, Christiana announced that she was pregnant – a ploy adopted by many women facing execution, including Kate Webster. After ordering a panel of married women to examine her, this plea was rejected by the court, causing Christiana great distress.

Several petitions were presented to Queen Victoria via the Home Secretary, Mr Henry Bruce, pleading for a merciful reprieve. The judge, moved by her plight, persuaded Bruce to arrange for the eminent physician Dr William Gull and Dr William Orange, the medical officer at Broadmoor, to assess Christiana's mental state. After examining her, they came to the conclusion that she was, indeed, of unsound mind and therefore exempt from execution. Predictably, the reactions in the press were volatile, both for and against the judgement. Christiana was sent to Broadmoor, and on arrival Dr Orange noted that she was 'very vain', with rouged cheeks and quantities of false hair (it was subsequently discovered that Christiana, during her years of residence in the asylum, persuaded her sister, Mary, to smuggle in both clothing and bundles of hair). Records show that Christiana was generally well behaved and 'biddable', spending much of her time sewing, painting, playing croquet, or walking in the extensive grounds. In 1876, however, it was noted that she took great delight in 'ingeniously tormenting several of the more irritating patients' and then complaining to staff about their use of bad language. The following year it was observed that she affected 'a youthful appearance' and 'her manner and expression evidently lies towards sexual and amatory ideas'.

In 1880, after eight years in Broadmoor, Christiana wrote to the Home Office pleading for her release, but this appeal was rejected. Records show that by 1906 her sight was failing and she could barely walk – shortly before Christmas she was in the infirmary – but she was also heard to ask another patient whether her eyebrows looked all right. Reassured, she announced that at the Christmas ball she would get up and dance, declaring, 'I was a Venus before and I shall be a Venus again!' Did Christiana make it to the ball that year, heavily made-up and with her hair, false or otherwise, elaborately styled? And did she get up and dance to impress the less flamboyant patients and the male members of staff? She died nine months later, on 19 September 1907, aged seventy-eight.

KC

FURTHER READING

Clarke, K., *Fatal Affairs* (London: Mango Books, 2016)
Stevens, M., *Broadmoor Revealed* (Barnsley: Pen and Sword, 2013)
Appignanesi, L., *Trials of Passion* (New York: Pegasus Books, 2015)

Execution

At 3.00 a.m. on 6 July 1840, a man was awoken. He had intended to sleep for five hours, but his plans had been thwarted by a succession of interruptions. His own thoughts can hardly have helped. By the time he was roused, he estimated that he had slept for barely thirty minutes. After a disappointing breakfast of coffee and a portion of 'extraordinarily tough' chicken, he once again entered a carriage with his companions for the morning. They made their way through the City of London, passing on their way a number of policemen. The man imagined that the policemen glanced at them, aware of the purpose of their journey. Eventually, the group arrived outside Newgate Prison. They had come to watch a man die.

Newgate had succeeded Tyburn as London's primary site of public executions in 1783. Elsewhere in the country, executions were also often carried out outside major prisons. Previously, the infamous 'Bloody Code' had seen a staggering number of crimes punishable by death, but by the reign of Queen Victoria that number had been greatly reduced. Official figures show the extent of this reduction: between 1820 and 1830, 797 criminals were executed in England, at an average of around eighty a year, whereas between 1837 and 1840, only sixty-two executions were performed, an average of less than twenty a year. In London, where forty-three men and women had been put to death in 1820 alone, only five were to meet that fate during the first three years of Victoria's reign – the man due to die on that July morning, François Courvoisier, amongst them.

Perhaps this relative rarity contributed to the public's interest in such events. Famously, public executions in the Victorian era were a popular form of spectacle. However, even by the standards of the day, the death of Courvoisier was exceptionally well-attended – estimates converge around the figure of 40,000 people in attendance (equating to around two in every ten people living in London at the time). All sections of society were represented, including journalist and future novelist William Thackeray, he of the sleepless night and the unappetising breakfast. His friend Charles Dickens was also present.

Courvoisier had been condemned for the murder of his master, Lord Russell. As was customary, on the day before his appointed death he had attended a service in the prison chapel, a sombre affair during which he would have been in the presence of his own coffin. Also present would have been Edward Oxford, awaiting his delayed trial for an attempted assassination of Queen Victoria.

Subsequently, Courvoisier was instructed to sleep naked during his final night on earth – an inconvenience as well as an indignity to the former valet, who had planned to take his life during the night using a fragment of wood concealed within his clothing. Prisoners cheating the gallows had been a particular concern since 1828, when a convicted forger, Captain Charles Montgomery, had managed to swallow an ounce and a half of hydrogen cyanide just hours before his scheduled death.

Hanging may have lacked the visual impact of some former methods of execution, but reminders of the past remained – the Newgate gallows would be erected within visible distance of Smithfield, the site of numerous Tudor burnings; in order to reach the door, the condemned man or woman would also take a final walk through Newgate's former 'pressing yard'.

Typically, the prisoner would have their hands pinioned in front of their body. From 1856, post-Bousfield, their legs would also be held in place. They would be led to the gallows up a flight of steps, with encouragement from the hangman where necessary. After a few short words, a white hood would be placed over their head, a sure sign that the process was about to accelerate.

Many contemporary accounts talk of convulsions continuing for some time after the prisoner had reached the end of the rope, but in reality these were likely spasmodic movements taking place after unconsciousness had set in. Death could occur from many causes – fractures of the structures of the airway, dislocations between the cervical vertebrae, tearing of the spinal column, cardiac failure resulting from compression of the carotid arteries – but would only rarely have occurred solely from strangulation. Clinical death, confirmed by the absence of a heartbeat, occurred after the cessation of breathing, perhaps by as long as twenty-five minutes. The condemned would often urinate and defecate during the process, and males would sometimes experience priapism and ejaculation.

Several experiments were undertaken in an effort to understand the medical effects of hanging – in 1887, Newgate's medical officer recorded the pulses of three hanged men on carbon paper. One of his subjects was Israel Lipski. In all three cases, he recorded that clinical death was reached within twelve to fourteen-and-a-half minutes.

In 1872, the most significant development in the science of hanging was made by fifty-four-year-old former cobbler William Marwood, who devised the 'long drop', which used a formula based on the prisoner's height, weight and build to calculate the optimum rope length. Previously, estimated drops had, at times, led to flesh being torn from the faces of prisoners, or complete decapitations. Although Marwood's career as an executioner was relatively brief, variations on his work remain in use to this day in many countries.

One use of Marwood's formula took place in the town of Lewes on 29 November 1881. A journalist spoke of Marwood as a 'diminutive man', whom he at first mistook for a groom carrying horse-riding equipment – in fact, he discovered, this was the hangman himself, approaching the gallows carrying the leather straps used to bind the victim. Having identified himself, Marwood proceeded to show the writer his equipment with a clear sense of pride. Nearby, a grave had already been dug. The gallows itself was located within a small building – since 1868, scenes like those recorded at the death of Courvoisier had been no more, as all British executions were held in private.

The man soon to lie in the earth was Percy Lefroy Mapleton, convicted of murder five months previous. The writer concluded that 'the actual death was as merciful as it could well be', but remained concerned that Mapleton had suffered mental anguish in the preceding moments. Mapleton was subsequently buried in his pre-dug grave, but not until a jury of local men had been convened to confirm the cause of his death.

TNB

FURTHER READING

Grovier, K., *The Gaol: The Story of Newgate – London's Most Notorious Prison* (London: John Murray, 2009)

Thackeray, W. M., 'On Going to See a Man Hanged', *Fraser's Magazine* (1840)

Webb, S., *Execution: A History of Capital Punishment in Britain* (Stroud: The History Press, 2011)

F

Flanagan, Catherine (1829–1884) and Higgins, Margaret (1843–1884)

When they reached notoriety, fifty-five-year-old Catherine Flanagan and forty-one-year-old Margaret Higgins – otherwise known, not unfairly, as the Black Widows of Liverpool – were described as 'squalid' and 'ignorant', and exhibiting that 'brute-like sullenness' associated with life in the city's teeming tenements. They were charged with the murder of Margaret's husband, thirty-six-year-old hod-carrier Thomas Higgins; his ten-year-old daughter, Mary;

Flanagan's twenty-two-year old son, John; and a lodger, eighteen-year-old Maggie Jennings. Each had been poisoned with arsenic.

Both women were of short stature but relentless in their murderous ambitions, forged with the goal of claiming insurance payouts from various burial clubs. These organisations were intended to provide the poor – for payments of a few pence a week – with money to fund a 'decent' burial, and to provide some cushioning after the death of a spouse or breadwinner. It is estimated that in this way the sisters collected the equivalent of several thousands of pounds in today's currency. This was a lucrative business for those inclined to dispatch anyone they considered expendable in return for cash (see Sarah Chesham). However, it became clear during court proceedings that some agencies were woefully lax in their dealings, facilitating fraudulent claims and even allowing a person to insure the life of another without consent. Catherine Flanagan and Margaret Higgins took full advantage of the situation to secure five policies on the life of Thomas Higgins without his knowledge.

Their nemesis was his brother, Patrick Higgins, who, suspicious of Thomas's death in October 1883 – which a doctor had ascribed to dysentery – alerted the authorities; the funeral was halted. Margaret Higgins was arrested, but Flanagan remained on the run for ten days. After a post-mortem revealed the presence of arsenic in Thomas's body, attention turned to the earlier deaths of family members and the lodger, Maggie Jennings. Their bodies were exhumed and, on analysis of the viscera, arsenic was similarly found.

Amid great clamour, the Black Widows' trial began at Liverpool's St George's Hall on 14 February 1884, before Mr Justice Batt. Although the prosecution offered a plausible case against the two women, the evidence was purely circumstantial, despite the traces of arsenic found in the 'fluff and dust' in the pocket of Higgins's apron and the discovery of a bottle of contaminated liquid in the sisters' lodgings. Although they and others had tended the victims during their final illnesses, there was no proof that they had administered arsenic, and their defence counsel suggested that the arsenic in the bodies may have leeched in from the soil in the burial ground. Despite city analyst Dr Campbell Brown's startling experiment – related in court, and involving the soaking of fly-papers to extract arsenic – the prosecution was unable to prove that the women had ever purchased fly-papers (see Florence Maybrick). Crucially, the arsenic that had killed Thomas Higgins and the other victims had *not* been supplied by a chemist. Had it been legitimately purchased for killing vermin, it would have been coloured with soot or indigo – in accordance with the Arsenic Act of 1851 – to avoid accidental ingestion (see Christiana Edmunds). Arsenic extracted from fly-papers, however, would not have been coloured in this way. No trace of colouring was found during the post-mortems.

The jury found both women guilty of the murder of Thomas Higgins, but it was thought that they had been responsible for many deaths besides the four for which they had been indicted. The pair were so widely vilified that no petitions for a reprieve were presented, although public opinion *was* vociferous in its outrage against the lax practices of the burial clubs that had provided (to minds warped in such a way) a mercenary motive for murder. Flanagan tried to put the blame on her sister and insisted that there was a network of women involved – she even gave the police several names, but no other charges were brought. Whilst awaiting execution both women welcomed the ministrations of the Roman Catholic chaplain, but neither produced a written confession to her crimes. Bartholomew Binns was appointed as executioner, and, on the morning of 3 March 1884, at Kirkdale Prison, Flanagan and Higgins were hanged simultaneously by Binns and his assistant, and their bodies buried within the precincts of the prison.

KC

FURTHER READING

Brabin, A., *The Black Widows of Liverpool* (Lancaster: Palatine Books, 2003)

Forensics

At the root of the word 'forensic' is 'forum' – the setting for oratorical legal hearings in ancient Rome. To modern ears, however, the word invariably conjures a scientific image of laboratory coats and white paper overalls, of the delicate gathering of evidence rather than pure debate.

It is sometimes assumed that the use of forensic evidence was an original development during the Victorian era, but in reality many important steps had been taken in this direction during earlier centuries. Still, despite the acquisition of a certain amount of medico-legal knowledge, there remained no way of collating criminals' personal information into a record for easy reference. It was recognised that many crimes were committed by repeat offenders, and this awareness provoked the creation of the Habitual Criminals Register. Created by London's Metropolitan Police and housed at Scotland Yard, the register was initiated in the wake of the Habitual Criminals Act of 1869 – under the terms of which any person convicted of a felony and not sentenced to penal servitude was subjected to police supervision for seven years to ensure that he was making an honest living – and the Prevention of Crime Act of 1871, which decreed that all persons convicted of a crime in Great Britain must have their details registered. Accordingly, Scotland Yard began to note criminals' heights, weights, ages, and descriptions; years later, photographs also contributed to the records. The identification of reoffending criminals was made considerably easier: they could now be tracked down by use of the wanted poster and were sometimes identified by witnesses in their absence.

It was a Frenchman, Alphonse Bertillon, in the early 1880s, who took this advancement one step further. He created the world's first scientific system to be used by the police, with the intention of identifying criminals by the physical evidence they left at a crime scene. Bertillon was a copyist for the Prefecture of Police in Paris and the son of a statistician, so it seemed natural for him to begin keeping anthropometric records of criminals, choosing those housed at La Santé Prison as a place to start. Height, weight, gait length, foot size, head size, eye colouring, hair colouring and markings were all documented; photographs were routinely taken; and the record was filed by Bertillon at the Prefecture. At subsequent crime scenes, any evidence falling into the relevant categories was noted by police officials, and records were later trawled in order to identify the possible culprit or culprits.

The system, known as *Bertillonage*, was so successful that other police forces throughout the world also adopted it, and would often liaise with the Parisian police, keeping up to speed with any improvements made to it. Bertillon also studied the effects of ballistics at a crime scene, as well as the movements of a criminal and his victim, and even examined documents; in addition, he advanced the use of the camera as a tool for recording evidence. But the introduction of another forensic system in the late Victorian period rapidly superseded *Bertillonage*. Fingerprint identification would go on to be the forensic mainstay of the century to follow.

Fingerprints had been used as a form of identification since before Bertillon's time. In India, in the 1860s, Sir William Herschel, who worked for the Indian Administrative Service, introduced a system of fingerprinting rather than signing, contracts – it was his belief that, although an individual's signature could be forged by a third party (or impossible to reproduce in the case of illiterate signatories), each person's fingerprint was unique. At the time this was unproven, but the field developed swiftly. In 1892, a Croatian-Argentinian police official named Juan Vucetich successfully gained a conviction for murder by matching with his suspect a bloody handprint left at the scene of the crime. The Argentinian authorities immediately adopted fingerprinting as an official means of identification. Further support arrived in the same year, as Sir Francis Galton published a book claiming that fingerprints were 'an incomparably surer criterion of identity than any other bodily feature'.

Future Metropolitan Police Commissioner Sir Edward Henry also had been working on fingerprints whilst he was the Inspector General of Police in India during the early 1890s. He had liaised closely with Galton and produced the *Henry Classification System* in 1897, which placed fingerprints into three categories: loops, whorls and arches. This made it a lot easier to identify an individual's fingerprint, as all would fall into one of these three classifications. In July 1901, just six months after the end of the period covered by this book, Scotland Yard officially adopted the fingerprint system. And, whilst the discovery of the identifying properties of DNA has refined the identification of criminals to a high level of probability, the fingerprint system created during the late Victorian period is used as a forensic tool against crime to this day.

NRAB

Further Reading

McDermid, V., *Forensics: The Anatomy of Crime* (London: Profile Books, 2014)

Forgery and Fraud

The aspirational Victorian whose natural flair for legitimate business had been undermined by fate, social forces or some form of personal deficiency could always fall back upon forgery and fraud – supposing, that is, that he was willing to take the risk. From October 1837, under the terms of the Forgery Act, the most serious forgers could be punished by transportation for life; prison sentences were available for crimes of lesser magnitude. Even this represented a softening of the law. Previously, conviction for certain types of forgery – such as the forging of wills – could attract the death sentence (see Execution).

These legal conditions meant that careful innovation was by necessity at the heart of every self-respecting forger's nefarious plans. Harriet Brown and Sarah Wellfare were transported in 1853 after a series of frauds perpetrated in London's West End with counterfeit banknotes and improperly countersigned cheques. They had gone to some lengths to prepare their scheme, apparently managing to receive at least two forged notes – which carried the same serial number – by post, in envelopes with covering letters, from mysterious well-wishers in Birmingham. All seemed to be going well, with fraudulent transactions occurring at a draper's shop on Old Compton Street and a gold and silver refiner's shop on Hatton Garden, when human error brought the venture down. At his grocer's shop on the Strand, William Marshall looked closely at the banknote Brown had passed to him; after a little thinking time, he turned back to her, preparing to tell her that it was a forgery, and noticed that she already had in her hand the letter from the aforementioned well-wisher who had sent her the note in the first place. If she had passed the note innocently, without realising that it was a fake, then, Marshall reasoned, she ought not to have had the letter ready for him to inspect. Her thoughts had prematurely drifted onto the next part of her scheme – specifically, the contingency option, to be triggered only if the authenticity of the banknote was directly questioned. Marshall summoned a constable, and Australia beckoned.

At the other end of the scale, some frauds were the simple products of opportunism. In September 1845, Cornelius Strong happened upon his victim – a Malay sailor known only as Cashim – on board the *Eliza*, which was berthed at St Katherine's Dock. After a negotiation for Cashim's imports (which consisted of some silk handkerchiefs from China, three-dozen fans, and some cigars which Cashim preferred not to sell), Strong handed over four shillings and six worthless brass counters known rather grandly as Hanoverian medals, pretending that the latter were sovereigns. Perhaps the negotiation was not facilitated by its being conducted in rupees before conversion into sterling, but Cashim soon realised that he had been taken in, and his deceiver was sought for, arrested (subjecting the police officer to 'the most violent language'), and found guilty at the Old Bailey. Strong was a serial nuisance in the docklands and this was not his first conviction. He had been transported once before, and was now transported again.

Rare cases showed that one could, rather perversely, be accused of forgery – one of the most premeditated of crimes – while floridly insane. James Samuel Brown's faculties had been insecure ever since he was hit on the head by a brickbat at the age of nine; by twenty-two, he was suffering convulsive seizures and constant illnesses. His 1842 trial publicised his obscure behavioural repertoire: he would call his sister away from her domestic work, looking wildly at her and asking, '"Don't you think me very beautiful?" or "Don't you love me?" or something of that sort'. He kept a sword by his pillow, and he had taken to signing his name 'Colonel James Samuel Brown'. He varied between dressing the part of his military alter ego and dressing as King Charles II, as well as not dressing at all. He plunged his hands into a pot of boiling lead, saying, 'See, this will not burn me.' He swallowed poison; he lay in the rain for an hour; he claimed to have floated on the river. He had a seizure at the post office, gibbering in a mixture of French and English. He fed a shilling to his father's Newfoundland dog, deciding at the last moment not to feed it a sovereign, as, he asserted, 'the vagabond has got enough in his inside to last him a week'. He made a habit of sleeping surrounded by the family's pets, and attracted some attention when he dressed them with white ribbon on the occasion of his brother's wedding. He announced his own impending marriage to an imaginary countess of vast wealth. He lit a cigar with a £5 note (or, perhaps, threw the note into the fire when enraged with a child). The offence with which he was charged – for forging and uttering eight money orders with intent to defraud the Right Honourable Baron Lowther – hardly seems worth mentioning in comparison. He was found not guilty on grounds of insanity, and sent to an asylum.

MWO

Foster, Catherine (1829–1847)

It is often the case that when a young woman murders her husband she has already set her heart on his replacement. But sometimes there seems to be no such incentive, no promise of a passionate liaison waiting in the wings. One such case was that of seventeen-year-old Catherine Foster, who, on 17 November 1846, only three weeks after the wedding, poisoned her husband, John, by lacing his dumpling with arsenic. They were living in her mother's house in the village of Acton, near Sudbury, in Suffolk. Though later described as 'sullen and morose', Catherine was considered to be the belle of the village; she had been in service since leaving school at the age of fourteen, and John was a hard-working farm labourer, 'as happy as the day was long'.

Four days after she and John were married, Catherine travelled to Bury St Edmunds to stay with an aunt. On her return, she decided to poison her husband. Watched by her eight-year-old brother, Thomas, she prepared supper and, whilst they were eating their meal of dumplings and potatoes, she set aside a special dumpling for John to enjoy when he returned from the farm. He suffered terribly throughout the night and died in agony the next day. A number of neighbouring hens, scratching about in the communal yard, also dropped dead after eating the remaining scraps of John's dumpling, which seemed to point to Catherine's guilt. After her arrest, arsenic was detected in the muslin cloth she had wrapped around the suspect dumpling.

Catherine was tried for murder at the Shire Hall, Bury St Edmunds on Saturday, 27 March 1847, before Lord Chief Baron Pollock. *The Times* described her as 'somewhat good looking, but very simple', and, after a brief trial, Catherine was found guilty of murder and sentenced to death. Throughout it all she apparently remained remarkably 'calm and composed'. Whilst awaiting execution, however, she was subjected to the vigorous ministrations of the vicar of Acton and his fellow clerics, and she duly confessed to the crime. She was executed by William Calcraft outside Norwich Gaol on Sunday, 18 April, in front of a vast crowd of spectators. It was said that she 'walked up to the drop with the most extraordinary deliberation. Her youthful appearance created the most awful sensation amongst the assembled multitude …' Witnessing the girl's last struggle, some people in the crowd were heard to shout, 'Shame, shame; murder, murder.'

Catherine was unable to explain why she killed her husband. Perhaps her glimpse of another sort of life in Bury St Edmunds had changed her; at the time, it was a thriving market town with an abundance of shops, opportunities for entertainment, and, importantly, a newly-built railway connection to London and other big cities. Maybe the thought of returning to live out the rest of her life in a tiny cottage in Acton, enduring years of ill-paid drudgery and the company of a less-than-exciting husband proved too daunting a prospect.

It is disturbing to imagine the spectacle of a human being hanging from the gallows – even more tragic, perhaps, if the person, male or female, had been too young to resist the impulse to annihilate the cause of their frustration, as Catherine did that fateful day, by simply sprinkling a few deadly grains of arsenic into a mixing bowl.

KC

FURTHER READING

Clarke, K., 'A Dodgy Dumpling and a Clutch of Dead Hens' in Edwards, M. (ed.) *Truly Criminal* (Stroud: The History Press, 2015)

Hardy, S., *Arsenic in the Dumplings* (Stroud: The History Press, 2010)

G

Gallows Declamations

In reality, not all gallows declamations were as dramatic as those depicted in fiction – the altruistic last words of Sydney Carton (technically a guillotine declamation) penned by Charles Dickens, for example. From 1868, mainland executions were no longer carried out in public but in relative privacy within prison walls. Before that date, criminals were hanged before vast crowds of spectators, often reaching 20,000 or more if the crime had been particularly heinous or if the criminal had (for whatever reason) captured the interest of the mob. It was a horrifying spectacle, and for the condemned the ignominy was compounded by having to face hordes of jeering onlookers, hurling abuse and assorted projectiles including rotten eggs, vegetables and even cats and dogs. Pickpockets and sellers of broadsides describing the crime and execution had a field day as they mingled in the crowds. Reassuringly, some commentators (like Dickens) were appalled by the brutalising effect of those who revelled in such gruesome displays – though not all of these were opposed to capital punishment per se.

Yet the hideous spectacle of public execution allowed the condemned the opportunity to air their grievances and rail against their fate, justify their villainy or utter defiant diatribes against the Church, the state or, indeed, the whole world and its woes. Some chose to adopt the rhetoric of the pulpit in order to broadcast their innocence to the baying masses. If they were wealthy, they might choose to appear dressed in their finest clothes, playing to the crowd as though taking centre stage in a once-in-a-lifetime theatrical performance. Others, perversely, wore their foulest rags and in so doing cheated the hangman out of his concessionary right to claim their clothes after death. Some employed delaying tactics by making their gallows speeches last for as long as possible, much to the impatience of both the spectators and the hangman, who was always anxious to depart for fear of attack. Many must have prayed for a last-minute reprieve or harboured the hope that their friends or relatives might attempt to stage a rescue.

A surprising number mounted the steps of the scaffold with extraordinary stoicism, acknowledging the justice of their punishment and resigned to paying the ultimate penalty. Many remained deep in fervent prayer, whilst others were so distraught or paralysed with fear that they had to be dragged to the gallows, barely conscious and unable to utter any final words of either contrition or rage against their awful fate. At Carlisle, in 1886, James Berry conducted a triple hanging of members of a London gang (see Thomas Simmons). One of the men, James Baker, wrote a long letter to his girlfriend, Nellie, on the night before his execution, declaring his love for her and beseeching her to stay within the law. Just before the trapdoor opened, he shouted, 'Keep straight, Nellie!' One of the other gang members, Jack Martin, cleared his conscience by confessing to a murder for which an innocent man had been hanged. From the condemned cell, George Horton, who had killed one of his daughters in 1889, wrote heartfelt farewell letters to his children imploring them not to follow his example. The serial poisoner Catherine Wilson died still declaring her innocence; Kate Webster, by contrast, wrote a lengthy confession freely admitting her guilt. Mary Ann Britland, having mercilessly dispatched three victims, screamed in terror when faced with her own death, as did young Sarah Thomas. Mary Lefley, the so-called 'rice-pudding killer', screamed, 'Murder! Murder!' when approached by her executioner; but the brutal baby farmers Amelia Dyer and Margaret Waters faced death seemingly without remorse, as did the inveterate poisoner Sarah Chesham. Catherine

Foster confessed to killing her young husband but expressed the hope that they would spend eternity together.

In 1868, Priscilla Biggadike became the first woman to be hanged within the confines of a prison. Convicted of poisoning her husband, she was posthumously pardoned after her lodger, Thomas Proctor, made a deathbed confession. Now deprived of a platform for gallows speeches, convicts resorted to private confessions. These were often convoluted, self-serving statements extracted by prison chaplains (given the title of 'Ordinary' in Newgate), the task of the official being made simpler when his target was confined to a cell and awaiting death. Finding themselves in such a desperate plight, and under spiritual pressure, many reverted to the religious dogma learned in their youth, repenting their sins and begging the Almighty's forgiveness; others tried to justify their crimes by blaming the recklessness of youth, drunkenness, the influence of friends or the corrupting effect of poverty on their moral compass. As many criminals facing execution were illiterate, these confessions were often written out by the chaplain, parish priest or prison governor and then published in the contemporary press and penny dreadfuls; the commercially minded channelled them, in handy ballad form, for sale as broadsides. Some were used to inform the Ordinary's accounts, published as the *Newgate Calendar*, in the hope that others might be deterred from following the path trodden by those who had paid for their crimes with their lives.

KC

Good, Daniel (1792–1842)

He is an Irishman, aged about 46 years, 5 ft. 6 ins. high, very dark complexion, black hair, long features, and bald at the top of the head; walks upright; was dressed in a dark Great Coat, Drab Breeches and Gaiters, and Black Hat.

So reads an extract from the wanted poster of murderer Daniel Good, whose crime was the catalyst for the creation of the world-famous Metropolitan Police's Detective Department.

Good's offence was brutal and horrific. However, the chain of events that led to his hanging began in almost trivial circumstances. On 7 April 1842, Good, a coachman working for a Putney-based family, pulled his pony chaise to the door of Columbine's Pawnbrokers in Wandsworth High Street, London. He asked to look at a pair of knee breeches, which were promptly handed over to him. Good haggled with Columbine, and the pair reached an agreement. As Good was known to the pawnbroker, payment was agreed to be deferred; however, as he left, Good picked up another pair of trousers and hid them under his greatcoat, an act seen by Columbine's shop boy. The boy raised the alarm, and Columbine exited the shop in pursuit of the coachman, who had by now climbed aboard his chaise, preparing to leave. Columbine challenged Good but, rather than opening his coat to prove that the lad was lying, he simply denied the accusation and drove off.

The incident was reported to PC V279 William Gardiner of Wandsworth Division. Once Constable Gardiner had obtained Columbine's side of the story, he, along with the boy and another shop lad from the neighbouring grocery, made his way to a farming property in Roehampton Lane, owned by a Mr Shiell. Initial enquires at the Shiell residence showed that Good was not there; the three adventurers moved diligently on to examine the next building on the property, a farmhouse. So as not to alarm Good, Constable Gardiner instructed Speed, the grocer's boy, to ring the bell whilst he stood back in the shadows and watched. Speed did this, and the door was opened by the farmhouse's occupant. Speed asked to speak to Good; the man announced that he was Good; and Constable Gardiner stepped forward and explained his reason for being there. Good denied stealing the pair of trousers and stated that he would accompany the constable to the pawnbrokers where they could sort the matter out. Gardiner agreed but, on the lookout for the incriminating evidence, he told Good that he must examine his chaise first.

The four men then made their way over to the coach house where the chaise was stored. Gardiner found nothing of worth. Unperturbed, the constable moved to the next set of stables to continue his search. However, as he reached the stable door, Good immediately jumped between the threshold and Gardiner and exclaimed, 'We had better get to Wandsworth, and get the matter settled.' It was at this stage that Mr Sheill's bailiff, a Mr Oughton, who lived near to the stables, came out to see what the fuss was about. The constable apprised Oughton of the situation, and, despite expressing his surprise that Good would do such a thing, Oughton agreed that a search of the stables was in order. So the constable entered the stable, instructing all to remain beside Good before he did so, adding that they should be prepared to seize the coachman if required.

As they entered the stable with Gardiner leading, Good became more and more agitated, and was constantly expressing his desire to go to Wandsworth in order for the matter to be satisfied. Unhesitatingly – and no doubt sensing that he was on to something – the constable continued his search of the stable, furrowing through the loose hay as he did so. Suddenly, in alarm, Gardiner exclaimed, 'My God! What's this?' Initially, he thought he had come across the carcass of a goose, then a dead pig; as Gardiner and the rest of the group tried to make sense of what they were seeing, Good broke free, ran to the stable door, closed it and, locking all inside, made his escape. The trapped men tried unsuccessfully to force the door open with a pitchfork, and then turned back to the macabre discovery. It was Columbine's shop lad who made the correct identification, exclaiming, 'Oh my God – it's a human being.'

In fact, what they had found was the mutilated trunk of Jane Jones, a woman who sometimes passed herself off as Mrs Jane Good. A hunt for her murderer followed – a hunt that exposed the poor communication and coordination of the nascent police force. Wanted posters were issued for the 'Putney Murderer', but still Good continued to evade detection; with six divisions working upon the case (as well as constabularies outside the Met's jurisdiction), leads and positive enquiries were rapidly lost in the heaps of information being fed into Scotland Yard. The confusion and inefficiency underlined the case for the recruitment of specialist investigative policemen, which resulted in the formation of the Metropolitan Police's Detective Department a few years later.

As for Good, he was eventually tracked to Tonbridge. A former local constable, aware that Good was a wanted man, recognised the murderer in the town and informed his one-time colleagues.

Good was arrested, sent for trial, found guilty of murder and sentenced to hang. His execution took place before a large crowd outside Newgate Prison on 23 May 1842.

NRAB

Gull, Sir William Withey (1816–1890)

In other universes not far from this one, nobody has heard of Sir William Withey Gull. This is not to say that he was not a man of some importance in his day. Appointed as Physician-in-Ordinary to Queen Victoria in 1887, he had long been cherished by the monarch, whose son – later Edward VII – he had saved from typhoid in 1871. But there were several Physicians-in-Ordinary, and appointments ran concurrently. Who remembers Sir Henry Marsh and Sir David Davies?

During his life, Gull's interactions with the world of crime were infrequent. In 1876, he was called to attend rising solicitor Charles Bravo, but Bravo had swallowed a dose of antimony so large that he could hardly have hoped to survive, irrespective of the stylishness of the choice of physician; Gull was powerless to prevent the victim's demise. Tending to the medical issues of the wealthy was generally to be preferred to involving oneself with the Victorian era's common brutality: the Bravo affair simply happened to occur in the mysterious liminal zone where murder and high society crossed over – in Balham (see The Balham Mystery).

Gull's criminal career flourished only after his death. In the 1970s, when all things seemed possible, it was decided that Jack the Ripper had been Prince Albert Victor, the Heir Presumptive to the British throne. In early versions of this tale, Gull was innocent of any murders but had participated in a cover-up, certifying the wayward prince and condemning him to an asylum (from which he subsequently escaped to kill again – it is that sort of story). Later iterations shuffled the cast: the knife was wrested from the grasp of Prince Albert Victor and placed, instead, in Gull's hand. Around the edges of the frame, other characters appeared, joining the conspiracy: the painter Walter Sickert; a coachman named John Netley; and the Freemasons, who featured among their number several senior figures from the worlds of politics and law enforcement. It was soon objected that Gull's own health was in terminal decline by 1888 – the year of the Ripper murders – making him an unlikely candidate to embark upon a vigorous murder spree.

Little though there was to recommend all of this, Gull remains in the popular consciousness as the personification of the supposed abuses and secrecy of the Victorian establishment. He is largely gone from serious Ripperology but continues to chalk up victims in Ripper fiction – and beyond. In 2013, Alison Rattle published *The Quietness*, a novel for teenagers which she based loosely on the baby farming case of Margaret Waters. In it, she depicted the emotionally cauterised, upper-class household of young Ellen, whose father, 'the eminent anatomist Dr William Walter Swift', knows people 'from the inside out'.

MWO

Further Reading

Rattle, A., *The Quietness* (London: Hot Key Books, 2013)

H

Homosexuality

By the start of the Victorian era, male homosexuality, or more correctly the consummation of homosexual relationships through anal penetration, had been a capital offence in England for over three hundred years. This had been reiterated by the Offences Against the Person Act (1828) without any significant changes, although one consequence was that sexual intercourse between two men was now listed alongside rape, the performance of illegal abortions, and various classes of intentional wounding.

Further legislation, in 1841, removed the threat of execution for those convicted of rape (including 'carnal knowledge' of a female of less than ten years of age), but not for those convicted of 'buggery', which would remain a capital offence until 1861 – meaning that for twenty years in Britain it was possible for a man to be hanged for engaging in consensual sex but not for rape or child abuse.

In practice, the final executions for acting 'feloniously, wickedly, diabolically, and against the order of nature' (to quote from their trial) in this way had been those of James Pratt and John Smith, who were put to death in 1835 (Charles Dickens visited Newgate Prison whilst Pratt and Smith were being held there and described their demeanour in 'A Visit to Newgate'). This did not prevent the death sentence from being passed in some later cases. In 1857, Henry Holding was 'indicted for an unnatural offence' and tried without legal representation at the Old Bailey. He was sentenced to death but, the case notes say, 'in consequence of the result of some inquiries made by the officer in the case, the prosecutor (a boy of fifteen) was shown to have made certain false statements upon his examination'. Holding was hurried back into court ('an interval of two or three hours having elapsed since the original finding, and another case having been tried') to be found not guilty and released.

In 1861, the maximum penalty for buggery was reduced from death to life imprisonment. However, this was followed twenty-four years later by the so-called 'Labouchere Amendment' (more properly, section 11 of the 1895 Criminal Law Amendment Act), which greatly enhanced the potential for the prosecution of homosexual males by the creation of the offence of 'gross misconduct'. This carried a maximum sentence of two years' imprisonment, with or without hard labour, and, when compared to the thresholds for buggery, significantly reduced the amount of evidence required to bring a charge. Although it has been shown that overall conviction rates did not significantly increase, several men were charged and convicted of this new offence. They do not deserve to have their names listed in a book about crime.

One notable case does hold interest for the scholar of Victorian criminology. Francis Tumblety, by his own account a suspect for the Jack the Ripper murders, was arrested for gross indecency on 7 November 1888, but fled the country before he could be tried. It has variously been suggested that Tumblety's alleged offences represented an attempt by the police to concoct a reason to detain him in order to investigate him in relation to the Ripper crimes, or that he had been the victim of a blackmail campaign. Indeed, the Labouchere Amendment has often been referred to as a 'blackmailer's charter' because it created a landscape in which such activity could flourish.

For the Victorian period's foremost example of criminalised homosexuality, see – of course – Oscar Wilde.

TNB

FURTHER READING

Robb, G., *Strangers: Homosexual Love in the Nineteenth Century* (London: Picador, 2003)

I

Infanticide

Infanticide during the nineteenth century was so widespread, so clandestine and, in most cases, so typically unreported that it would be impossible to estimate the numbers truly involved. Aimed at shaming unmarried mothers and punishing them for producing illegitimate offspring, the Bastardy Clause in the Poor Law Amendment Act of 1834 had left them demonised as feckless and morally defective, and solely responsible for their illegitimate children until the age of sixteen (although this was amended in 1872 to extend a measure of responsibility once more to the putative fathers). Methods of contraception used by the poor were primitive and ineffective, and women burdened by unwanted pregnancies had to resort to attempts at abortion using homespun remedies such as the knitting needle or the gin-bath.

When these methods failed, there were few options: if unmarried or unsupported by family, the workhouse loomed; there a mother would be separated from her child (see Eliza Adkins) and, when the numbers in the workhouse became unmanageable, the child could be farmed out to disreputable institutions such as that run by Bartholomew Peter Drouet in Tooting.

Many young women became pregnant whilst working as live-in maidservants, and their predicament normally incurred instant dismissal (see Sarah Drake). If unable or unwilling through religious conviction to abort the unborn child, they often tried to hide their pregnancy – even from fellow servants – and gave birth unattended in attic rooms, outhouses or basements. A woman desperate to keep her job might resort to farming out the infant to a genuine child-nurse such as Nelly Gentle (a figure in the Louise Masset case), although at the periphery of this practice lurked the baby farmers (see for example Amelia Dyer and Margaret Waters). These women advertised in newspapers using coded messages perfectly understood by most readers to indicate that they were willing to 'dispose' of an unwanted child for a fee and with no questions asked. In addition, advertisements for 'lying-in' accommodation also frequently masked a covert abortion and disposal service. Some of these transactions may have been naïvely entered into by vulnerable young women, but many must have been knowingly complicit in this form of infant murder. Some mothers resorted to leaving a newborn on the doorstep of a kindly neighbour or outside a Foundling Hospital or similar charitable establishment – though many of these would only accept 'lawfully begotten' children. Even so, these orphanages were often little more than a stepping stone to the workhouse, where if pauper children survived long enough they would be sent out to work from a young age as apprentices, labourers or maids in service.

The only other option was infanticide. Though the definition has always been compromised by law and public opinion, it is generally accepted that the crime constitutes the killing of an infant under a year old by its mother. Many women must have prayed for a stillbirth or decided that, if the newborn drew breath, it would be put aside and ignored in the hope that without attention it would soon die – as in the case of Eliza Boucher. If the infant survived against all the odds, it could easily be strangled or suffocated and then disposed of, hidden in dung heaps, ash-piles and privies, or thrown into canals or rivers; some were simply wrapped in rags or paper and left on the street. In the 1860s, Mary Anne Baines, a campaigner against the phenomenon, wrote that the police 'think no more of finding the dead body of a child in the street than of picking up a dead cat or dog'.

The law was capricious in its dealings with mothers charged with infanticide. Perhaps surprisingly, more often than not the all-male judges and jurors were lenient in their judgement when trying a case of infanticide, which was widely considered less heinous than other murders; but it was not until the Infanticide Acts of 1922 and 1938 that the death penalty for infanticide was abolished.

In the three decades prior to Queen Victoria's accession, only nineteen women were publicly hanged for 'killing a bastard child' – the last being in 1834. The charge was often commuted to one of 'concealment of a birth', which carried a maximum sentence of two years' imprisonment. In practice, most women served three months or less (in 1860, Sarah Gough served just one month in Newgate for killing her newborn). In some instances, the woman was deemed to be suffering from 'puerperal psychosis' or 'temporary insanity' and detained in a lunatic asylum (see Sarah Drake). When, however, the death of a child was registered and swiftly followed by a parent or family member's claim on the insurance – offered by one of the many 'burial clubs' that proliferated during the Victorian era – mercenary infanticide was often suspected, and the law reacted more harshly. In some cases, the latest addition to the family was considered expendable, as the insurance money would provide for the sustenance of its siblings. These clubs would insure a child's life – though some, as the rate of child mortality at birth was so high, not until the age of three months – at a rate of a penny or less a week. This practice, coupled with the easy availability of arsenic for domestic use, contributed to the public paranoia surrounding a spate of deaths by poison in the 1850s, particularly those of apparently surplus children (see Sarah Chesham).

Thomas Wakley (again, see Bartholomew Peter Drouet) and Dr Edwin Lankester (Wakley's successor as coroner for Central Middlesex) were vociferous in their attempts to address the problem of infanticide and baby farming by campaigning for the extension of the powers of the enforcers of the law; adding their voices to the choir were Dr William Burke Ryan, Dr John Curgenven, Ernest Hart, and many others. Eventually these efforts culminated in the Infant Life Protection Act of 1872, which sought to oversee and regulate institutions housing abandoned children.

KC

FURTHER READING

Clarke, K., *Deadly Dilemmas* (London: Mango Books, forthcoming)
Clarke, K., *Bad Companions* (Stroud: The History Press, 2013)
Rose, L., *Massacre of the Innocents: Infanticide in Great Britain, 1800–1939* (London: Routledge and Kegan Paul, 1986)

Insanity

For most of the Victorian period, the rules governing crime and insanity were fairly easy to understand. Following the influential decisions in the case of Daniel M'Naghten, legal insanity was established and was to be identified by an almost aphoristic test of the defendant's capacity to know what he or she was doing, and to know whether what he or she was doing was wrong. Those who could not hit the mark in either one or both of these categories were criminally insane and not accountable for their actions. Only the intercession of Queen Victoria could muddy the waters – and this she proceeded to do. Fed up of being the target of would-be regicides who were later acquitted by the courts on grounds of insanity (see Assassination), she invented a new and illogical verdict – guilty but insane. This trampled on the established legal principle that guilt implied a secure and rational foreknowledge of one's actions.

Even so, for those who reached the courts the protocols surrounding insanity appeared straightforward. If you were mad when you committed the offence with which you were charged, you were expected to show some common sense and say so right at the beginning. The burden of proof would then switch to the defence, and experts and lay witnesses could be called to prove that you were not in full control. If this was proved, however, an indefinite spell in a lunatic asylum was bound to follow, with recovery a condition of release, and many defendants, fearing that they would *never* get out, preferred not to take this risk. Accordingly, it was not unheard of for defendants, especially in murder cases, to subvert the system, pleading not guilty, testing the evidence of the prosecution against whatever evidence they had compiled in their defence, and then, if they were convicted, appealing against the statutory death sentence by saying that they had been insane at the time of the offence. This sparked the Home Office into reluctant life – they would send their experts to assess the prisoner, and there was the chance of a commutation, swapping imminent physical death for the otherwise undesirable half-life of incarceration in an asylum. In 1890, Mary Pearcey tried exactly this tactic, and the Home Secretary, Henry Matthews, grumpily annotated her file to show that, in his view, it was becoming 'too common'.

No doubt Matthews was right, but this was only one of the ways in which the criminal behaviour of the insane troubled the Victorians. It was sometimes possible for mentally deranged people to act in ways which betrayed a good deal of internal consistency. Richard Dadd and Christiana Edmunds were both floridly insane, but Dadd's paintings – evocative fairy worlds – were characterised by all the things by which sane people's paintings were also characterised: unity of composition, structure, perspective. Edmunds, for her part, had acquired poison under a false name because she wished to avoid detection. These people were behaving in ways which were irrational in the main, but composed of parts which were, individually examined, apparently rather sane. The comprehensiveness of their delusions accounted for the paradox, but one senses that Victoria's disenchantment with the precise legal implications of insanity must have been shared by others. Can the parents of Sidney Barker – Edmunds's child-victim – have felt that justice had been done by her admission to Broadmoor? She had testified at Sidney's inquest, presenting herself as another target of the anonymous, indiscriminate (and, at that time, unidentified) Brighton poisoner, and this made it seem as if, having deprived the family of the four-year-old boy, she also wished to deprive them of a proper explanation of his death. Was it sufficient to say that this person was not guilty on grounds of insanity? Some of those directly affected by the actions of the insane must have found this dispassionate, detached conclusion difficult to bear.

Then there were those whose conduct was so outrageous that it seemed hard to believe that they were *not* mad. Could the repeated murders of Amelia Dyer, the century's most famous baby farmer, have been the actions of someone of sane mind? The concept of personality disorders – life-long conditions, not to be confused with acute and treatable mental health crises – was still some way off, but it seems perfectly unnatural to countenance so neutrally such widespread destruction. Dyer was hanged and largely unmourned, but today her mentality would be better understood.

Perhaps the truth is that the true scope of insanity in Victorian society remains impossible to evaluate. Society itself was, directly or otherwise, the cause of generalised abuse, with disenfranchised and under-represented groups, particularly women and children, being particularly vulnerable to psychological trauma. As the victim of considerable domestic abuse (physical, emotional, and so on), Florence Maybrick might, if her case came to court today, plead diminished responsibility and accept treatment, but at the time there was little moral compunction about the mistreatment of wives by their husbands, and there was no mitigation for poor Florence. It should be remembered that judicial corporal punishment was not removed from the statute books until the late 1940s; the death penalty was last used in 1964; marital rape was not made illegal in England and Wales until the 1990s. In a society which makes traumatic experience an aspect of everyday life, nobody can be surprised when a subset of the population retreats, whether by design or by default, to an inner world.

MWO

J

Jack the Ripper (1888–1891)

The Central News Agency, a news distributor based in London's press district, dealt with the sensational. Tabloid journalism was just starting to take its first steps, with a new publication, the *Star*, leading the way. During the late summer and early autumn of 1888, this newspaper had reported on a series of murders in the run-down East End quarters of Whitechapel and Spitalfields, where a few women had been brutally murdered. This distressing news was swiftly pounced upon by the reporters of the *Star*, which, with its anti-establishment undercurrent, sought to make political martyrs of the victims and to point an accusatory finger at Whitehall, feeding its readership a mixture of shocking accounts of the murders and fervid political opinion. There was no shortage of the latter flowing from the journalists' pens; however, the former had to be sought from elsewhere, most commonly the Central News Agency.

On 27 September 1888, a letter was received by the Central News Agency that found its way to the desk of one of its reporters, Tom Bulling. Bulling noted the letter but discarded it as a joke; it was not until news broke of two more murders – occurring within the space of an hour, and separated by only a short distance – that Bulling paid more attention. 'Dear Boss,' it began, in a spider-like, red-inked scrawl:

I keep on hearing the police have caught me. but they wont fix me just yet. I have laughed when they look so clever and talk about being on the right track. That joke about Leather Apron gave me real fits. I am down on whores and I shant quit ripping them till I do get buckled. Grand work the last job was. I gave the lady no time to squeal How can they catch me now. I love my work and want to start again. You will soon hear of me with my funny little games. I saved some of the proper red stuff in a ginger beer bottle over the last job to write with but it went thick like glue and I cant use it. Red ink is fit enough I hope ha. ha. The next job I do I shall clip the

ladys ears off and send to the police officers just for jolly wouldnt
you. Keep this letter back till I do a bit more work. then give it out
straight. My knife's so nice and sharp I want to get to work right
away if I get a chance. Good luck.

In the letter's signature a dubious legend was born. It simply read,
'Yours truly, Jack the Ripper.'

The murders of this serial killer began, according to the official
police files on the crimes, in April 1888, when a prostitute named
Emma Smith died in Whitechapel's London Hospital. By her own
account, she had been set upon by a gang of youths not far from
her lodgings, and had made the final yards of her trip home in
agony. She was immediately rushed to hospital for treatment, but
sadly succumbed to her injuries hours later. Why Smith is included
among the police files is not known, as her injuries do not match
those of any of the subsequent victims.

In early August 1888, Martha Tabram was viciously stabbed to
death on the landing of George Yard Buildings, not far from where
Smith was assaulted some months before. As with any Victorian
murder investigation, the police began to seek forensic clues at the
scene: footprints, disturbed ground, any discarded weapon: they
found none. This murder, alarming though its characteristics were,
was only one of many crimes committed in the area patrolled by
the Metropolitan Police's overstretched H Division (Whitechapel).
After the murder and mutilation of Mary Ann Nichols at the end
of August, in neighbouring J Division (Bethnal Green), the police
hierarchy at Scotland Yard began to take note.

They sent the former head of H Division's CID, Inspector
Frederick Abberline, to aid the local detectives in their investigations.
No sooner had Abberline joined his old team than news broke of
yet another mutilated victim. Annie Chapman had been found
murdered in the yard of a house in Hanbury Street, Spitalfields.
This murder, occurring just one week after the murder of Nichols,
grabbed the attention of the press, who focused heavily upon
the police and their actions, as well as the communities involved
(who had, by now, formed themselves into vigilance committees
in an attempt to aid the local police constables). Scotland Yard
responded yet again, introducing one of their finest detectives,

Chief Inspector Donald Swanson, to coordinate the investigation and to act as the link between local CID and the Yard itself.

Though the press thought it impossible, 30 September 1888 brought even greater sensation, as two women were found murdered in one night. Swedish immigrant Elisabeth Stride was found at the entrance to a small yard in Berner Street, just off Whitechapel's Commercial Road. Unlike Nichols and Chapman, Stride had not been mutilated, and common opinion had it that her murderer had been disturbed. On the other hand, perhaps the killer was just varying his routine, since the second murder that night – that of Catherine Eddowes, in the City's Mitre Square – appeared to show that the Whitechapel Monster had departed from his usual patch.

Eddowes's murder meant that London's other police force, the City of London Police, became involved in the hunt for the killer now named as Jack the Ripper and, while extensive investigative sweeps were undertaken throughout the area, no further murders occurred in October 1888. As that month turned into November, life in Whitechapel and its surrounds seemed to have calmed a little. It was a false dawn. In a small rented room off the notorious Dorset Street, just a stone's throw away from Christ Church Spitalfields, the savagely mutilated remains of a young Irish prostitute named Mary Jane Kelly were found by an employee of her landlord. The date was 9 November, the day of the Lord Mayor's Show, and the police reinforcements for that event, who were being held at nearby Commercial Street Police Station, now found themselves rushing to a gruesome murder scene. The victim was described by Inspector Walter Beck, one of the first policemen on the scene, as having been 'simply cut to bits'.

Other murders occurred in following years. Alice McKenzie was found by a constable in Castle Alley in July 1889; and young Frances Coles was also found by a policeman in 1891, this time in a grubby railway arch known as Swallow Gardens. However, neither exhibited the ferocious mutilations of previous victims. As quietly as the murders had begun, they died down, leaving behind much myth and legend stoked by the memoirs and opinions of former police authorities, such as Abberline, Robert Anderson, Melville Macnaghten, and (albeit privately) Swanson.

And whilst investigations were wound down due to a lack of progress and funds in the mid-1890s, it is worth remembering that the case, like all unsolved murder cases, remains open to this day.

NRAB

FURTHER READING

Begg, P. and Bennett, J., *Jack the Ripper: CSI Whitechapel* (London: Andre Deutsch, 2012)

Evans, S. P. and Rumbelow, D., *Jack the Ripper: Scotland Yard Investigates* (Stroud: Sutton, 2006)

Sugden, P., *The Complete History of Jack the Ripper* (London: Robinson, 1994)

Begg, P., Fido, M. and Skinner, K., *The Complete Jack the Ripper A to Z* (London: John Blake Publishing, 2010)

Evans, S. P. and Skinner, K., *The Ultimate Jack the Ripper Sourcebook* (London: Robinson, 2000)

Ripperologist (bimonthly periodical); back issues and subscriptions available at www.ripperologist.biz

Jackson, Emma (c. 1835–1863)

In the late Victorian era, a number of scientific experiments in Italy and Germany were eagerly summarised in the international press. Fuelled by the relatively recent advent of photography, the reported results gave rise to one of the most pervasive myths of the Victorian era: the belief that the last image seen by a person before death would be recorded on their retina, and therefore (the supposition followed) could be revealed by photographing the victim's eyes. If the person had been murdered, perhaps the image of their killer could then be discovered. Would this prove to be the end of all those unsatisfying, unsolved murder cases?

In the event, of course, it was not. A correspondent for the *Medical Times and Gazette*, in 1860, disparagingly referred to the originator of a suggestion that the technique should be trialled in relation to 'the mysterious murder near Frome' (presumably a reference to the murder of Samuel Kent by his sister, Constance Kent) as a 'wiseacre'.

Scorn and scientific fatuity, however, did little to discourage calls for the use of retinal photography to be renewed three years later, following the murder of Emma Jackson in a 'dirty, squalid room' in the notorious area of St Giles, London, on 9 April 1863.

Jackson's body was discovered lying on a bed in a lodging house in George Street; both victim and furniture were coated in blood. Twenty-eight years of age, Jackson had been living with her father, mother and brother in nearby Berwick Street, but would regularly leave their lodgings and venture elsewhere; her brother, John Jackson, would tell the subsequent inquest that he had last seen her alive four days previously and that she had been in the company of a group of men. She had last been in Berwick Street on the morning before her death. It is highly likely that Jackson was working as a prostitute, at least occasionally; her brother's insistence that she rarely drank alcohol also invited scepticism.

Jackson's injuries were described at the inquest by surgeon John Weekes, but his list appears to be incomplete. Weekes makes mention of five wounds but identifies only four: two to the back of the head, and two to the neck; the latter were considered sufficient to precipitate death. Jackson's body was dressed only in a chemise. It seems possible that the missing wound was targeted at the sexual organs, a detail not reported by the contemporary press owing to concerns regarding public decency.

A photographer, William H. Warner, wrote to the police suggesting that they employ him to photograph Jackson's eyes; he also wrote to the press advising them of his offer. This did not quite elicit the reaction he had hoped for. The police declined, although more on the basis of practicality rather than possibility (the reasons given were threefold: Jackson's eyes had been closed at the time of her death; it was considered that any image would only be recorded for a certain time period; and the body had already been buried).

The *Cincinnati Lancet and Observer* soon published a letter disparaging the whole idea: 'An absurd correspondence has being going round of the journals, and has been accepted in some quarters as conveying solemn truth of serious import.' The endeavour was described as 'an absurd impossibility', akin to an attempt to 'subtract the sound of flutes from a ton of coals'. The issue of timing was dismissed as a red herring, seeing as 'such a photograph taken more than twenty-four hours after death will succeed as if taken two minutes after'. In other words, it would not work at all.

During the latter decades of Victoria's reign, however, the idea that optography could help to detect murderers would every so often return to the popular consciousness, adding a soupçon of dubious modern science to tales of dark deeds in dingy places. In 1888, it was suggested, more than once, as a possible solution in the Jack the Ripper case – a proposal described by the police's own divisional surgeon as 'useless, especially in this case'. Earlier in the same year, the *New York Tribune* had supposedly stated that a successful application of the technique had led to a conviction in France, but it is difficult to trace the root of this claim.

More verifiable evidence was mounting on the opposing side of the debate. Back in 1866, experiments on the eyes of executed mass-murderer Anton Probst in Philadelphia had proved inconclusive. Experiments by the German police in 1877 had been similarly useless. The extraction of the eyeballs of an executed prisoner near the border between France and Germany in 1880 yielded interesting, but inconclusive, results. Perhaps most damningly, Professor Wilhelm Kühne, the pioneer of much of the research on which the theory was based, himself spoke out against the very suggestion that his work could be of any use in solving crimes.

Improved understanding of the physiology of the eye would eventually destroy any lingering belief in the detective benefits of retinal photography, and genuinely revolutionary new techniques in forensics would instead lead the fight against crime into the next century. Emma Jackson's murder remains unsolved, despite an all-too-familiar litany of charges and false confessions, including the arrest of a man in Cardiff, information about whom may have owed a large debt to the offer of a £100 reward. Jackson's murderer's lasting anonymity has likewise opened the door to recent suggestions that she died at the hands of Jack the Ripper, a quarter of a century prior to his more famous crimes (see also Harriet Buswell).

TNB

FURTHER READING

Boller, F., Finger, S. and Stiles, A. (eds.), *Literature, Neurology, and Neuroscience: Historical and Literary Connections* (Philadelphia: Elsevier, 2013)

K

Kelly, James (1860–1929)

James Kelly was a murderer whose offence, in other circumstances, might have been rather hastily forgotten. Two curious sequelae – one in the 1920s, and one in the 1980s – served to restore it to the consciousness of true crime historians.

The original murder was a comparatively compact affair. Kelly, a twenty-three-year-old Liverpudlian with syphilitic symptoms (which he attributed to an industrial disease, incurred at work: 'the upholsterer's itch', as he put it), married twenty-one-year-old Sarah Ann Brider at St Luke's Church, in Islington, London, on 4 June 1883. Within three weeks, Sarah was dead.

The star-crossed pair first met when Kelly began lodging with Sarah's parents at their double-fronted house in Cottage Lane, off the City Road, in 1882. One finds it difficult to be sure whether the marriage – which followed within the space of about a year – was really a love match: there are suggestions that Sarah had contracted syphilis; she may also have become pregnant, and James was in possession of certain paraphernalia which were (possibly) associated with procuring abortions. In addition, he had begun to feel a great deal of jealousy, believing that his wife had resorted to prostitution, and his equipoise was slipping. On 18 June, he picked up a knife during an argument, and was narrowly prevented from harming himself or somebody else. As he began to feel remorseful, he experienced a flicker of insight.

'I am mad,' he said.

'I think you are,' said his mother-in-law.

By 22 June, however, all the same anxieties had re-emerged. Sarah was late home; an argument brewed up; James called her a whore, denied doing so, sought her forgiveness. 'I can never forgive you,' she said, and he drove the blade of a knife into her neck, two inches below her left ear, such that it 'nearly divided the spinal cord', as the house surgeon at St Bartholomew's Hospital told it. Sarah died on the evening of 24 June, by which time her assailant had been taken unresistingly into police custody.

At his trial, on 1 August, Kelly contested the murder charge, but the evidence was all against him, and he was convicted and sentenced to death. Hedging his bets, he had also made sure to lay the foundations of an appeal, emphasising his mental disarrangement, not least in several eccentric letters written from his cell, in which he vaguely menaced his deceased wife's mother while referring to himself as her 'unfortunate and forgiving son-in-law'. The Home Secretary, persuaded of the case for commutation, consigned him to Broadmoor.

In January 1888, Kelly escaped, fed up of institution life. He had fashioned a key from a piece of metal which he had discovered in the kitchen garden, disappearing through locked doors and out-of-bounds areas before scaling the perimeter wall. The authorities, alarmed by this turn of events, nonetheless made a shabby job of recapturing him, and in the years to come Kelly would travel to France and America, and back to Britain, without undue trouble. Only in 1927 was he returned to the asylum, and this was because he had arrived at the main entrance asking to be readmitted. Even so, he was not initially believed and was stored at Wokingham police station until the relevant order arrived from the Home Office.

Kelly's reasoning was that he 'dreaded the idea of dying alone', and that, in the circumstances, life in Broadmoor was to be preferred to loneliness in perpetuity. Since 1988, and the publication of a suitably eccentric booklet under the title of *Jimmy Kelly's Year of Ripper Murders*, he has enjoyed the dubious pleasure of the company of hundreds of others – aristocrat and pauper alike – in the undesirable quarter of the next world reserved for those who might – *might* – have been Jack the Ripper. His candidacy, which was explored more comprehensively in a subsequent book by James Tully, has better credentials than those of some of the other contenders, but few are willing to appoint Kelly to the vacated title just yet.

MWO

FURTHER READING

Tully, J., *The Secret of Prisoner 1167* (London: Robinson, 1998)

Kent, Constance Emily (1844–1944)

It was late in the evening of Friday, 29 June 1860 by the time the inhabitants of Mr Samuel Saville Kent's large house in the West Country village of Road had gone to bed. Mr Kent, a self-important and libidinous sub-inspector of factories, and his second wife, former governess Mary Pratt – who was eight months pregnant – occupied one room with their five-year-old daughter, Amelia. The children's nurse, twenty-two-year-old Elizabeth Gough, shared a room with one-year-old Eveline and three-year-old Saville, a sturdy, curly haired toddler much favoured by the family. Elsewhere in the house were the four children of Samuel Kent's first marriage to Mary Windus: Mary Ann and Elizabeth, twenty-nine and twenty-eight respectively, sixteen-year-old Constance, and her brother, fourteen-year-old William. Mary herself had died, demeaned and in despair, in 1852.

The scene was set for the appalling drama that was to follow. At 7.15 on Saturday morning, Elizabeth Gough raised the alarm – young Saville was missing. He had been taken from his cot; the indentation of his body remained, but the covers showed no sign of disturbance. A frantic search was made of the house and grounds, and the child was found jammed against the soil-plate of the outside privy, his throat slashed almost to the point of decapitation; a puncture had been made in his chest by a sharp, pointed blade, and on his left hand there were two small cuts. The post-mortem evidence of pressure to the mouth suggested that the child had been smothered prior to mutilation, and the chest wound may have been caused by the assailant attempting to push the lifeless body past the soil-plate into the deep vault below.

When the local police failed to make any headway with their investigations, Scotland Yard deployed one of their men. This was Detective Inspector Jonathan Whicher, a highly regarded and experienced officer. Working against local resentment at his intervention – from the Kent family and suspicious natives alike – he soon established that one of Constance Kent's nightgowns had gone missing, and postulated that the garment and its owner held the key to the murder. Constance was a wilful and rebellious girl, who after her mother's death had been farmed out to a succession of boarding schools. She had developed a passionate resentment against the woman who had usurped the first Mrs Kent long before she became the second; but there was also some evidence to suggest that her emotions were more conflicted and less easily categorised. Her hatred for her stepmother, for instance, was tinged with guilt for the way she had initially contributed to her mother's shameful exclusion, and it did not extend to Saville or his two sisters.

Although Constance and later Elizabeth Gough were subsequently brought before magistrates at Trowbridge charged with Saville's murder, they were both released through lack of evidence, and Jonathan Whicher returned, defeated and castigated, to his duties in London. Constance, using the name Emilie, was packed off to a finishing school in Dinan, France, to avoid the notoriety heaped on her and her family. The newspapers were relentless in their coverage, informing readers of every aspect of the case and broadcasting intimate details about all the participants in the drama. Yet still the mystery remained – who had slaughtered the little boy in the early hours of Saturday, 30 June?

In July 1863, Constance entered St Mary's Home, a convent in Brighton, where she came under the spiritual influence of the curate of St Paul's Church, the Reverend Arthur Wagner. On 6 February 1865, Constance confessed her guilt and authorised Wagner to inform the Home Secretary, Sir George Grey. The following month, she travelled to Bow Street Magistrates' Court, where she again confessed to the murder of her stepbrother. Whether Constance divulged any further information in the confessional we cannot know: when the Reverend Wagner later testified in court, he refused to answer any questions concerning the private dialogue that passed between them. Predictably, legal commentators considered this to be an unwarrantable barrier to justice, and the matter was raised in parliament.

Constance was tried on 19 July, in Salisbury, before Mr Justice Willes. Ignoring the appeals of her defence team, she pleaded guilty and refused to apply for leniency on account of her age at the time. Nor was she willing to plead temporary insanity, although her mother and other family members had suffered from mental fragility, for fear that the stigma of madness would adversely affect her brother William's future career as a marine biologist. The trial, therefore, lasted but a few minutes, and the judge reluctantly passed a sentence of death. Numerous petitions were presented to the Home Secretary, and the sentence was eventually commuted to penal servitude for life. Despite frequent pleas for her release, Constance remained confined for the next twenty years, mainly in Millbank Prison. During her incarceration she became religiously motivated, compliant and reserved. She was released on 18 July 1885 and, a year later, joined William and their two step-sisters, Amelia and Eveline, in Australia. As Ruth Emilie Kaye, she worked as a nurse until she retired in 1932, aged eighty-eight. She died in Sydney on 10 April 1944, 100 years old.

Despite Constance's confession, theorists still speculate on whether she was assisted in murdering Saville that night. Some have suggested that her brother, William, may have helped her, though she always denied his involvement. Others have proposed that, when the child was carried away, Samuel Kent was in another room with the nursemaid, Elizabeth Gough; and that, on her return to the nursery, she found the cot empty. In this version, the distraught father discovered the body of his son jammed

Constance Kent. (Authors' collection)

inside the privy, immediately suspected Constance of suffocating the child, and, to make it appear the work of a crazed intruder, discreetly raised the window in the drawing room before slitting his beloved son's throat.

KC

Further Reading

Summerscale, K., *The Suspicions of Mr Whicher* (London: Bloomsbury, 2008)

Taylor, B., *Cruelly Murdered* (London: Souvenir Press, 1979)

L

Lamson, George Henry (1852–1882)

George Henry Lamson was a murderer whose star has long since waned. This is regrettable, since there is plenty to recommend him in his field.

Lamson was a doctor by profession and found himself readily able to obtain poisons from apothecaries, doing so in August 1881 at a shop in Hampshire, and then repeating the feat in Lombard Street, in the heart of London, in November. In both cases, his credentials made the transaction go smoothly, no questions asked. This unfettered access to toxic substances dovetailed nicely with the plans he had made to shore up his overstretched bank account.

Down at Wimbledon, Lamson's wheelchair-bound brother-in-law Percy John was looking forward to his twentieth birthday. He was a boarder at a school and apparently a young man of cheerful temperament, upon whom Lamson had always lavished attention, both personal and medical. He was also a ward of Chancery and expected to access his share of a legacy – a share being worth about £3,000 – upon reaching his majority. Percy's siblings (at least, those below the age of twenty-one) were awaiting their own dividends from the same fund, although, if any of them were to die before reaching adulthood, provision had been made to split the deceased's share between his married sisters. This had already happened once, in 1879, when Herbert John died. Lamson's wife, Kate (*née* John, one of the married sisters in question), inherited nearly £750 on this occasion, and she had entered into a settlement with her husband by which her money became his.

All that remained was for Lamson to find a way to ensure that Percy departed this world before claiming his money. This he managed on 3 December 1881, visiting the school, putting on an eccentric display of prestidigitation with some gelatine capsules and a bowl of sugar, and cutting a Dundee cake into precise portions, one of which Percy gratefully consumed. Within four hours, and having experienced excruciating gastric symptoms, poor Percy was dead.

Various medics proceeded to have a go at ascertaining exactly what had happened. Thomas Bond and Edward Little discovered no organic cause of death in the anatomy; but Thomas Stevenson enlisted the help of Auguste Dupré, a lecturer in chemistry from the Westminster Hospital, and together they subjected Percy's remains to a battery of chemical tests, eventually finding aconitine, a vegetable alkaloid and irritant rarely used in poisonings. They satisfied themselves of the deadly properties of the unusual toxin by collecting samples from Percy's body and injecting them into mice, which promptly died as Percy had; just to make sure, Stevenson also tasted Percy's residues, recording that they produced 'a burning tingling, a kind of numbness difficult to define' when placed on the tongue. Lamson, apparently in a state of grief, arrived at Scotland Yard on 8 December, hubristically seeking to rebuff the suspicion which had, by now, become attached to him – without further ado, he was arrested and sent for trial. After much wrangling over the medical facts, he was found guilty, and executed at Newgate on 28 April 1882.

One of the barristers defending Lamson was Montagu Williams, who described the case in his memoirs, *Leaves of a Life*. He noted the fidelity of Lamson's wife Kate, who, every evening at the conclusion of the court proceedings, 'would take the prisoner's hand and kiss it most affectionately'. After the trial, Williams realised that this gesture contained a great deal of hidden feeling. 'She full well knew her husband to be guilty,' he wrote. 'There can be little doubt that her other brother, Herbert, by whose death Lamson came into a considerable sum of money, was also murdered by him.' H. L. Adam, editing the trial transcript for the Notable English Trials series in the years before the First World War, thought otherwise, declaring Lamson not guilty of causing Herbert's death, but only on Lamson's own shaky word.

Unpicking the scene at the school is, even now, a tricky affair, but the theory of the prosecution was that the poison was contained in a raisin strategically positioned inside the cake, which Lamson himself cut up in full view of Percy's schoolmaster and several others. The fumbling with the sugar bowl and the gelatine capsules was a misdirecting sideshow, performed by Lamson before he moved seamlessly on to the next part of his operation, and wiped Percy mercilessly out of existence.

George Henry Lamson. (Authors' collection)

Following his hanging, it took three years for Lamson's probate to be settled. He left an estate of £15.

MWO

FURTHER READING

Williams, M., *Leaves of a Life* (London: Macmillan, 1896)
Adam, H. L. (ed.), *Trial of George Henry Lamson* (Edinburgh: William Hodge and Company, 1912)

Lee, John Henry George, *aka* John 'Babbacombe' Lee (1864–1945)

The most extraordinary aspect of the case of John 'Babbacombe' Lee was that, after being found guilty of murdering his elderly employer, Miss Emma Keyse, the executioner, James Berry, made three unsuccessful attempts to hang him. Twenty-year-old John Lee had been a wayward youth, but he was given a second chance by Miss Keyse, who employed him as an odd-job man at the Glen, her charming villa at Babbacombe Bay, near Torquay, Devon. Also living in the house were two elderly maids, sisters Eliza and Jane Neck, and John Lee's thirty-year-old half-sister, the cook, Elizabeth Harris. However, although seemingly settled and engaged to a local girl, he was not entirely happy about being rewarded for his labours with a bed-space in the pantry and very little pay.

On the night of Saturday, 15 November 1884, there was a disastrous fire, and the charred and lifeless body of Miss Keyse was discovered in the dining room. There were terrible injuries to her head and her throat had been slashed, cutting the flesh to the bone. Surrounding the body were piles of half-burned newspapers, and there was a strong smell of paraffin. The fire was eventually brought under control and – once the smoke had cleared – the police discovered a pool of congealed blood in the passage leading to the pantry. As there was no sign of a break-in, John Lee seemed the likely culprit – the Neck sisters were gentle souls of nearly seventy, and the cook, Elizabeth Harris, was pregnant. Lee was

John 'Babbacombe' Lee. (Authors' collection)

arrested and, such was the brutality of the crime, by the time he was brought to trial the publicity and speculation surrounding the case was rampant.

In February 1885, John Lee was tried for the murder of Miss Keyse before Mr Justice Manisty, who freely admitted that he had not studied the details of the case. Lee pleaded not guilty and sat through the proceedings affecting an air of nonchalance. Upon being sentenced to death, he told the judge, 'The reason, my Lord, why I am so calm and collected is because I trust in my Lord, and he knows that I am innocent.' Whilst awaiting execution, various petitions were forwarded to the Home Secretary, Sir William Harcourt, but these were rejected. John Lee was allowed visits from churchmen and family and, it was said, gave the names of two people who were involved in the murder of Miss Keyse. These were later to be revealed in the press as his half-sister, Elizabeth Harris, and her unnamed lover.

The execution was set for Monday, 23 February 1885; the executioner, James Berry, had travelled to Exeter Prison from his home in Bradford to prepare for what would be his nineteenth execution since his appointment the year before. Yet no amount of experience could have prepared him for the dramatic events that were to follow.

John Lee stood, hooded and with the noose around his neck, but, as Berry withdrew the lever, there was only a slight grating noise, and the trap remained closed – even when two warders were ordered to stamp on it. The hood and rope were removed, and Lee, his legs still fettered, was shuffled forward a little so Berry could examine the apparatus. While the officials panicked, Lee stood quite still and his facial expression remained unchanged. For a second time he was placed over the drop, hooded; the noose was placed around his neck. The bolt was drawn once more, but the trap door remained firm, at which stage Berry was seen to be sweating. The hood and rope were again removed and Lee was taken to the back of the room where he was able to watch Berry's frantic efforts to rectify the faulty mechanism. When a third attempt to hang Lee also failed, he was removed to a cell, by which time the stress of his ordeal had begun to show.

News of the extraordinary occurrence spread rapidly, and Queen Victoria herself sent a telegram to the Home Secretary expressing her horror at 'the disgraceful scenes at Exeter' and suggesting that his death sentence should be commuted to one of life imprisonment. James Berry's account of the official inquiry into the failure of the gallows apparatus appeared in his memoir; elsewhere, rumours soon spread that on the night before the scheduled execution both Lee and his mother had dreamed that he would not hang. It was even suggested that Berry had been bribed to sabotage the equipment.

John Lee proved a truculent prisoner during his twenty-two years of confinement and was moved between prisons on account of his frequent angry outbursts and protestations of his innocence of the crime. He was finally released in December 1907 and became a folk-hero, mobbed by huge crowds, mainly consisting of women, wherever he went. He revelled in his notoriety, receiving hundreds of letters from well-wishers who followed his life story in *Lloyd's Weekly News*. Lee later worked as a barman in London and married in 1909, but three years later his wife and two young children were living in Lambeth Workhouse. Details of Lee's remaining years are uncertain but he is believed to have died on 19 March 1945, in Milwaukee, USA, aged eighty-one.

There is so much myth and folklore attached to the story of John 'Babbacombe' Lee that it lends itself to speculation, and investigative accounts continue to be published to this day. It was rumoured that, two years after the murder, Elizabeth Harris had made a death-bed confession, yet records show that the child she was expecting was born at the Union Workhouse in Newton Abbot in May 1885, and that Elizabeth subsequently settled in Australia, where she died in 1926. It was also suggested that her mystery lover was a young man from a well-connected local family who had died 'hopelessly insane'. The identity of the man was inferred in a recent book: in this reading, he was Reginald Gwynne Templer, the solicitor who bore the cost of Lee's defence during the inquest and magistrates' hearings before becoming of unsound mind prior to the murder trial. He had known Emma Keyse well and had been a frequent visitor to the Glen. He died in 1886, a year after Lee's conviction.

So what *might* have happened on the night that Miss Keyse was murdered? Awakened by noises, did she go downstairs to investigate, meeting her attacker in the passage leading to the pantry? Was he, perhaps, in the habit of visiting Elizabeth after Miss Keyse and the old maids had retired for the night? Knowing that he would be recognised, did he panic, frantically lashing out? Or were Lee, Elizabeth and her lover in the process of robbing Miss Keyse when she disturbed them? Lee's bitterness towards his half-sister was evident and he said all along that she and another person were involved in the murder. Yet at the time her lover was neither named nor required to explain his movements on the night of the murder. It would not be the first time that money and privilege had saved a young man from the gallows. John Lee, whether innocent or guilty, bore the ordeal of Berry's attempts to hang him with remarkable stoicism and, by beating the system, he certainly made his mark in criminal history. He will forever be remembered as the man they could not hang.

KC

FURTHER READING

Holgate, M., *The Secret of the Babbacombe Murder* (Devon: The Peninsular Press, 1995)

Berry, J., *My Experiences as an Executioner*, edited and with an introduction by Jonathan Goodman (London: David & Charles, 1972)

Lipski, Israel (*c.* 1866–1887)

As the Victorian era crept on, crimes characterised by purposelessness began to challenge popular notions of motive. Arguably, this began in France, with the dispassionate annihilation of the Kinck family by Jean-Baptiste Troppmann in 1870; if so, Lipski was one of England's earliest entries into this evolving field. Little more than a decade after Wainwright, whose case resonated with quintessentially Victorian melodrama, Lipski had transferred the action a few hundred yards to the south – to Batty Street, off the Commercial Road – and stripped the traditional narrative back to its rudiments. The machinery of homicide was exposed, unadorned by the usual trappings of its genre, and, in this way, Lipski's crime anticipated Modernism. Murderers would continue to operate in the old modes – working for gain, or for release from an intractable situation, or for love – but Lipski threw the spotlight on aspects of abstraction and futility which would be embraced by a generation whose outlook was eventually both shaped and epitomised by total war.

Israel Lipski lived in a little room on the second floor of the house at 16 Batty Street, and was one of millions of people displaced from Russia and Eastern Europe either as an immediate or secondary consequence of anti-Semitic pogroms. Two other recent immigrants, Isaac and Miriam Angel, a young couple expecting their first baby, lived on the floor below. Lipski's prospects seemed decent: he had recently thrown in his job at a nearby umbrella-stick factory and aimed to set up on his own, working from his room; and he was engaged to be married to a young woman named Kate Lyons.

On the morning of 28 June 1887, Miriam Angel was expected to visit her mother-in-law's house on Grove Street, but she failed to show up. Dinah Angel, the mother-in-law, became concerned, and went to Batty Street to see whether Miriam was ill. The door to Miriam's room was locked from the inside, but she could be seen through the weave of a muslin cloth which was draped across an internal window at the twist of the staircase to the second floor. She was motionless on the bed.

The door was broken down, and Miriam was found to be dead. An unpleasant froth bubbled from the corner of her mouth, and her chemise was burnt in pinprick spots, as if she had vomited or spat out a corrosive substance. She was naked from the waist down. A doctor was called, and he looked into her mouth, finding chemical damage to the soft tissues. Her right eye was dark and swollen where she had been assaulted.

Under the bed, a man was discovered. He, too, appeared to be unconscious; he had scratches on his forearms as if he had been engaged in a struggle; and his mouth exhibited a little damage – much less than Miriam's – where he had swallowed some of the acid which had been contained in a bottle found in the room. The man was Lipski. He was roused from his stupor without great difficulty, although he would not speak, and he was taken to the London Hospital to recover from his injuries. At length, he gave his side of events, in which he portrayed himself as the victim of violence at the hands of third parties, just the same as Miriam. The police's enquiries – which were nothing if not thorough – failed to substantiate any of Lipski's claims, and indeed there seemed to be many good reasons to believe that his account was simply untrue. All the circumstances suggested that he was the murderer, and he was charged with the offence, tried at the Old Bailey, found guilty in a matter of minutes, and then sentenced to death.

On the day before he was hanged, Lipski confessed, although his claim to have been motivated by robbery cannot be believed. Like the notorious W. T. Stead, who was splashing his lucrative dissent across the pages of the *Pall Mall Gazette*, Lipski was selfishly attempting to recast his actions in the classical style, fabricating a conventional rationale and endeavouring to force it into a familiar narrative structure. The truth was much less reassuring: that this apparently normal man, on an apparently normal morning, suddenly departed from normal social regulations and committed a ghastly crime. Lipski's biographer, Martin Friedland, is agnostic about the question of his guilt; his cautious conclusion and Stead's misplaced vehemence have both been influential, but a close reading of the surviving documentation leaves no space for doubt.

MWO

Further Reading

Friedland, M. L., *The Trials of Israel Lipski* (London: Macmillan, 1984)
Oldridge, M. W., *Murder and Crime: Whitechapel and District* (Stroud: The History Press, 2011)

Littlechild, John George (1847–1923)

I am a detective officer of Scotland Yard. On the evening of 31 December, I went with two other officers to watch 29 Marquis Road, Islington. About seven o'clock pm, I saw four men leave 29 Marquis Road. I knew but two of them: William Kurr was one; the other was a man named Stenning. They went into the Essex Road; I followed them about 200 or 300 yards. As I was drawing close they appeared to notice that they were followed; they hastened their speed and two of them turned into Canonbury Street, when I heard one of the men (who had hold of Kurr's arm on his left hand side) say, 'Now, run!' and Kurr started to run. I commenced to follow, but was stopped by the one who said, 'Now, run!' After freeing myself from him I gave chase to Kurr and overtook him. He faced round. I told him that I was an officer of police, and was going to arrest him on a charge of defrauding Madame de Goncourt. As he appeared to be about to take some action with roughness, I said, 'Don't be foolish, come quietly,' and he said, 'I will.' I thereupon took him to the station at Islington, where I searched him and found on him £4 1s 1d, some keys, some articles of jewellery, a six-chamber revolver loaded with ball, and a pocket knife. I read the warrant to him, and when I came to the name William Kurr, I said, 'That is your name, I suppose.' He said, 'Yes.' He made no reply to the charge.

So testified Detective John Littlechild, describing the singular event which, in 1877, catapulted him into the consciousness of the British public – the arrest of confidence trickster William Kurr. Kurr's Old Bailey trial, alongside fellow criminals Charles Bale, Frederick Kurr, Edwin Murray and the notorious Harry Benson, was the flutter of the butterfly's wing whose repercussions gradually exposed the corruption within the Metropolitan Police's Detective Department, culminating in what was to become known as the Trial of the Detectives. Although Littlechild was unaware of it at the time, the same sequence of events would lead to his own rise to the head of one of the most secret departments within Scotland Yard itself, Special Branch.

Littlechild joined the Metropolitan Police in 1867, and had established himself in the Detective Department by 1871. His arrest of Kurr, and the realisation, emerging from the subsequent investigation and trial, that prominent members of his own Detective Department had been on this criminal's payroll, helped Littlechild to establish himself as one of the most trusted detectives working in Scotland Yard. His diligent work during the restructuring of the discredited department into the Criminal Investigation Department (CID) saw him earn a promotion to Inspector in 1878; another – to Chief Inspector, in 1882 – came just months before his association with another major case of its day, the Phoenix Park Murders in Dublin.

It was due to his work in the latter case that Littlechild, in 1883, became one of the first members of the specialist department created to focus on crimes connected to the Irish quest for independence: the Irish Branch. Though technically headed by CID's overworked Chief Inspector Adolphus Williamson, Littlechild effectively ran the department. Because of the nature of its work, the Irish Branch, or Section B as it was known, was a secretive department even within the walls of Scotland Yard, with access to its offices available only with permission, and with information shared only on a strictly need-to-know basis.

A sister department to the Irish Branch – this being Special Branch (also known as Section D) – was formed soon afterwards. This department began to look into all criminal political activity which threatened to undermine the British government or to endanger the safety of politicians, public dignitaries and the populace alike (see Terrorism). This new department obviated the need for a specialist team focusing on one aspect of this class of crime, and Littlechild and his men were moved *en bloc* into Special Branch, with the Irish Branch being quietly closed down.

Littlechild remained in Special Branch for the next ten years, resigning to become a private detective in 1893. He was hired by prosecutors in 1895 to gather evidence against Oscar Wilde; served divorce papers on Arthur Reginald Baker three days prior to his murder by Kitty Byron in 1902; worked upon the murder case of architect Stanford White in America in 1906; and wrote a letter to journalist G. R. Sims in 1913, implicating a 'Dr T.' in the Jack the Ripper murders of 1888. Suggestions are that this was a reference to suspect Francis Tumblety.

Eventually, Littlechild settled in the Derbyshire spa town of Matlock, where on 2 January 1923 he passed away at Smedley's Hydrotherapy Complex; he is buried at the family plot at Putney Vale Cemetery, London.

NRAB

M

M'Naghten, Daniel (1813–1865)

Daniel M'Naghten was the eponymous anti-hero behind the influential insanity guidance, whose humane treatment contrasted sharply with the experiences of some of his forebears.

His story began with a shooting, in twilit Charing Cross, in January 1843. The victim, Edward Drummond, was the Private Secretary to the Prime Minister, Sir Robert Peel, and, by one of those occasional ripples in the historical fabric, Drummond was the one who was resident in Downing Street, with Peel preferring quarters in nearby Privy Gardens. Drummond's killer, Daniel M'Naghten, had been spotted in the vicinity of Downing Street several times since the turn of the year, hanging around on corners and, on one occasion, falsely claiming to be an undercover policeman. On 20 January 1843, he crept up behind Drummond, shot him through the abdomen, and was narrowly prevented from firing a second shot by the courageous intervention of a nearby constable.

On 25 January, the matter became a murder enquiry, with Drummond expiring in great pain, a hole extending through his body from back to front. It had rapidly become apparent that Peel had been M'Naghten's intended target, but the case seemed not to have the usual characteristics of a political assassination. The accused was not a political firebrand; rather, he chatted amiably with the police, and then calmly revealed in a statement the origins of his hostility towards Peel. 'The Tories in my native city,' he said, 'have driven me to this, and have followed me to France, Scotland, and other parts; I can get no sleep from the system they pursue towards me; I believe I am driven into a consumption by them; they wish to murder me. That is all I wish to say at present; they have completely disordered me, and I am quite a different man before they commenced this annoyance towards me.' M'Naghten was in the grip of a psychotic delusion. As his defence was patiently compiled, the extent of this delusion was discovered: the Tories were only the latest and most sinister of the conspirators against M'Naghten, having been preceded by the Catholic Church, the Jesuits, devils, and spies.

Examined from a distance, there is no doubt about M'Naghten's insanity, although it was noted at his trial that not all his acquaintances had spotted the symptoms. Occasionally the intrusive nature of his thoughts showed itself in his facial expressions; his sleep patterns were disrupted; he experienced mood instability; he had psychosomatic ailments and had been known, in the words of his defence counsel, to 'throw himself into the waters of the Clyde in order to seek some relief from the torturing fever by which his brain was consumed'. He had a paranoid metaphorical outlook, saying that 'everything was done by signs': in this vision, one of his persecutors, who appeared to him waving a few threads of straw, betokened a future of poverty, or alternatively incarceration in the subhuman conditions of an asylum. When he approached the Scottish civil authorities to complain about the harassment to which he was subjected, nobody was able to help him. Strictly speaking, the reason for this was that the entire thing was going on in M'Naghten's head; to him, it was confirmation of the complacent acquiescence of those in positions of power to the malevolent whims of his enemies.

M'Naghten was found not guilty on grounds of his insanity and removed to the Royal Bethlehem Hospital, and later to Broadmoor. Clearly, efforts had been made to avoid the rush to judgement which had followed the assassination of Prime Minister Spencer Perceval in 1812: Perceval's assassin, Henry Bellingham, had been hanged in a week, before those who knew him to be mad could arrive from Liverpool to argue in his favour. Nonetheless, the acquittal annoyed Queen Victoria, who was unable to shake the feeling that the M'Naghtens of this world were getting away with everything up to and including murder. In June 1843 the House of Lords consulted with the judges in order to clarify the limits of legal responsibility, and the results of this – the M'Naghten Rules – continue to steer judicial practice to this day. The most famous of the judges' responses to the Lords' enquiries held – and holds – that insanity was proved if it was established that 'the party accused was labouring under such a defect of reason, from disease of the mind, as not to know the nature and quality of the act he was doing; or, if he did know it, that he did not know he was doing what was wrong'. The details of M'Naghten's case fitted slightly uncomfortably into this framework, but his name – given here in the spelling used and popularised by the Lords, although alternatives are available – was propelled into immortality.

MWO

FURTHER READING

Keeton, G. W., *Guilty but Insane* (London: Macdonald & Co. Ltd., 1961)

Macnaghten, Sir Melville Leslie (1853–1921)

Bengal has always been a busy trading region of India. Its key location, with routes to Africa, the Far East and Europe, established it as a prime area of interest for the colonial British, who were similarly attracted by commodities including cotton, silk, indigo dye, salt, saltpetre, tea and opium. The British East India Company swiftly established dominance within the area, exerting itself in commerce, implementing a civil administration and, thanks to its own private army, pressing its military influence. One of the businesses established in Bengal – a tea plantation to be exact – was owned by the former chairman of the East India Company itself, Elliot Macnaghten. Busy working as a Justice of the Peace in the Supreme Court of Calcutta and the Council of India, Macnaghten left the day-to-day running of the plantation to his twenty-year-old son, Melville, in 1873.

There always had been sporadic outbreaks of violence in India during British rule. In 1881, that violence came to Melville Macnaghten's door. During a protest against land tax, Macnaghten was assaulted so badly by local workers that he was left 'senseless upon the plain'. It was during the investigation of this offence that Macnaghten came into contact with a man who not only shaped his later career but also became a very close friend: James Monro.

At this time, Monro was the Inspector-General of the Bengal Police and had worked closely with Macnaghten, trying to maintain order within the region around Macnaghten's plantation. By 1887, he had returned to Britain as Assistant Commissioner in charge of the Criminal Investigation Department of the Metropolitan Police. When his superior, Commissioner Warren, was in need of a Chief Constable in 1888, Monro put his friend Macnaghten up as a candidate, stating that he had seen 'his way of managing men' in India and had been 'struck by it'. However, the fact that Macnaghten had no police or military experience reinforced Warren's pre-existing belief that he was not the man for the job, and so he rejected Monro's suggestion. The relationship between Warren and Monro had never been cordial, and this clash, one of many between the two, was the final straw for the latter, who resigned. However, by the end of 1888 Monro was back in

Scotland Yard, this time replacing Warren as Commissioner; the following year he appointed Melville Macnaghten as his Assistant Chief Constable for CID. Macnaghten was, to use a modern phrase, very much a 'hands-on policeman', preferring to attend crime scenes than to sit in his office waiting to be briefed. By 1890, he had replaced the very popular Adolphus Williamson as Chief Constable of CID (the veteran Williamson had passed away).

Before long, the inquisitive Macnaghten stepped into a case into which he had originally had no input; it became the case with which he is most commonly associated. In 1894, *The Sun* newspaper published an article naming Thomas Cutbush as Jack the Ripper. Macnaghten, to refute the allegation, compiled a document which listed the details of the Jack the Ripper murders and, more sensationally, named three men more likely than Cutbush to have been the killer: Druitt, Kosminski and Ostrog. The document, known as the Macnaghten Memorandum, came in different drafts, with slight differences in each; however, the main argument remained the same in its various iterations. Some researchers question Macnaghten's conclusions as, correctly, they point out that he joined the Metropolitan Police after the case had peaked; others point out, again correctly, that his senior position enabled Macnaghten to view the case files, which were, at that stage, entire – or at least more complete than they are today. Wherever the truth lies, Macnaghten certainly provided an insight into the contemporary suspect list: one of the suspects he identifies in his memorandum – Kosminski – was apparently also named in writing by his colleague, Donald Swanson.

Another infamous case with which Macnaghten became involved was that of Mary Pearcey, who, in 1890, murdered her love rival and her child: he stated that he had 'never seen a woman with a stronger physique'. He also worked on several notable post-Victorian cases – that of Dr Crippen, for example, and the murder of Mr and Mrs Farrow in Deptford. Each of these, in its own way, was a forensic milestone: in the latter case, Macnaghten had laid the groundwork, contributing to the committee which brought fingerprinting into the police armoury.

Macnaghten was knighted in 1907 and retired from the police in 1913, with his health deteriorating. In 1914, he published his memoirs, *Days of my Years*; curiously, it is suggested that, by this time, he had already appeared in other people's books, showing up in G. R. Sims's *Dorcas Dene, Detective* stories as 'Mr Johnson' in 1897, and in Marie Belloc Lowndes's novel *The Lodger* (a tale inspired by the Jack the Ripper case) under the name of 'Sir John Burney'.

On 12 May 1921, Melville Macnaghten passed away at Queen Anne's Mansions, in Westminster. The great police chronicler, H. L. Adam, described him as 'somewhat reserved in manner, shrewdly preferring to listen to what you have to say to talking himself'.

NRAB

Maiden Tribute, The (1885)

'The Maiden Tribute', more formally the Maiden Tribute of Modern Babylon, was a term devised by the editor of the *Pall Mall Gazette*, W. T. Stead. In the grip of feelings of sexual guilt after he had lapsed into an extra-marital affair, Stead resolved to tear off the veil of innocence which obscured London's child prostitution racket (see Child Abuse). Even Howard Vincent, the former head of the Criminal Investigation Department at Scotland Yard, admitted to Stead that the problem had run out of control. An abused adolescent girl had no recourse to the law: 'Whom is she to prosecute? She does not know her assailant's name ... Even if she did, who would believe her? A woman who has lost her chastity is always a discredited witness.'

The appellation itself conflated its classical references in a most unfortunate way – the maiden tribute of Greek mythology had been paid by Athens to Knossos, and Babylon did not come into it – but, never one to engage in this sort of intellectual quibbling, Stead appointed himself Theseus and entered the labyrinth of Lisson Grove, in Marylebone, seeking his index case. This he found, on Derby Day 1885, and after a number of false starts, in one Eliza Armstrong, a thirteen-year-old, low-born, but apparently virtuous by the standards of the time. Operating via a proxy – Rebecca Jarrett, who had herself been a victim of early sexualisation but had latterly converted to the salvationist cause – Stead acquired Eliza from her mother, Elizabeth, for the sum of £5, the money to be split between the parent and a procuress who brokered the deal, with part of the payment 'upon liking': in this case, of course, the question of 'liking' was to be determined by an internal examination to check the veracity of Eliza's promised virginity.

Stead went as far as he could without requiring Eliza to be subjected to rape. In the Soho underworld, he exhibited her to a woman who casually confirmed that Eliza was 'pure'; introduced her to a brothel; ascertained that someone would be prepared to chloroform her if she was unwilling to comply with her awful fate; spirited her away again; had her untainted status confirmed by a qualified doctor; and then sent her overseas. This was not an uncommon destination for English girls, since the borders of Modern Babylon did not stop at the coast; but, instead of going to a foreign brothel, Eliza was taken to the headquarters of the Salvation Army in Paris, and from there sent into sympathetic domestic service in Loriol, in southern France. The thought of returning her to her mother – who, after all, had been willing to sell her in the first place – scarcely occurred.

Only when Stead wrote the whole thing up in his newspaper did Mrs Armstrong decide to raise an objection. The article, in which Eliza appeared pseudonymously as 'Lily', nonetheless contained clues to her true identity, and Mrs Armstrong saw that she herself had been depicted in unflattering (but perhaps not inaccurate) terms as 'poor, dissolute, and indifferent to everything but drink'. Popular opinion was polarised, and Stead's co-conspirators – figureheads of social reform such as Bramwell Booth, the Chief of Staff of the Salvation Army – began to find the pressure uncomfortable, even though they remained committed to Stead's radical vision. Before long, Eliza was on her way back to her homeland, and Stead, Booth and Jarrett stood among a small and notorious coterie in the dock at the Old Bailey, charged with abduction and indecent assault.

Much depended on Mrs Armstrong's understanding of what she had sold her daughter into, and here the intention of the exposé became blurred by the characteristics of the society in which it had taken place. Working-class girls were often 'sold' into domestic service, and it was not true to say that this social convention always masked a more harmful reality. Mrs Armstrong swore that she had thought that Eliza would be going into work at Croydon, but one wonders whether this distinction mattered to Stead. No attempt had made been made by Mrs Armstrong to establish the credentials of her daughter's would-be employers, and this could hardly be mistaken for responsible parenting. Moreover, the personal consequences of his plot were, to his mind, obviated by their social impact: to introduce another classical allusion, Eliza was Iphigenia at Aulis, sacrificed by the custodians of power in the interest of their overarching ambition.

Stead and his collaborators were found guilty, which only served to give his cause more oxygen. The Criminal Law Amendment Act of 1885 – demanded in the aftermath of these events – raised the age of heterosexual consent to sixteen, and brought many more vulnerable young people under the protection of the law. Later in life, Eliza herself was said to have written 'a grateful letter to Stead, telling him that she had married a good man and was the mother of six children'.

MWO

FURTHER READING

Pearson, M., *The Age of Consent* (Newton Abbot: David & Charles, 1972)
Plowden, A., *The Case of Eliza Armstrong* (London: BBC, 1974)

Manning, Frederick (*c.* 1819–1849) and Maria (*c.* 1821–1849)

Frederick and Maria Manning were seminal south London murderers whose creativity under pressure was articulated in their escape routes: in Maria's case, by train to Edinburgh, under the name of Smith; and in Frederick's, by boat to Jersey, under the name of Jennings. Neither, however, was destined to remain at liberty for very long.

The Mannings had married in 1847. She was Swiss by birth, and had been a maid in the house of the Duchess of Sutherland; he was a worker on the railways and readily tempted into small-time criminal enterprises, petty thefts, and so on. As a couple, they seemed like a bad fit, and Maria, the more restless of the two, went fairly frequently to visit Patrick O'Connor at his house just off the Mile End Road. She had been acquainted with O'Connor since her single days; he seems to have had little to recommend him except for – rather surprisingly – a nest-egg of shares in some French railway companies. Frederick, whom H. M. Walbrook describes as a '*mari complaisant*', was increasingly immersed in drink, and either unable or unwilling to object to his wife's extra-marital activities.

Nonetheless, when money ran short, the Mannings concocted a scheme in which O'Connor was its chosen victim. At their house on Miniver Place, Bermondsey, they hosted a lodger, William Massey, who was studying at Guy's Hospital. Frederick approached William, asking him to recommend a compliance drug, enough to induce its recipient to put pen to paper. However, if the original plan had been to defraud an intoxicated O'Connor of his shares, this was quickly superseded by something more drastic. Returning to William, Frederick wondered about the part of the head that was most susceptible to blunt force trauma. William never seems to have speculated about the significance of all these questions, and, when the Mannings told him that they were leaving town, and that his tenancy was therefore at an end, he obediently moved out. By Thursday, 9 August 1849, the Mannings were alone in

Frederick and Maria Manning. (Authors' collection)

their house, with a crowbar, a barrel of quicklime, a ripping chisel, and a loaded gun.

Clearly, the missing element was O'Connor, who was accordingly invited to dinner, dispatched (and overkilled, being shot *and* horribly beaten about the head), and swiftly concealed beneath the kitchen flagstones. Maria Manning, whose presence was familiar to O'Connor's landlady, visited his lodgings the same evening, explaining that he had missed a dinner appointment and that she wished to wait for him in his sitting-room: the landlady closed the door, and Maria helped herself to O'Connor's share certificates. Within a few days, O'Connor's absence from work had been noticed, and the police, following what leads they had, visited the Mannings. Maria was the soul of concern, as bewildered by O'Connor's sudden disappearance as everybody else; the police, persuaded by this performance, went to look elsewhere.

Then Maria fled northwards; Frederick fled southwards; the police returned to Miniver Place, and the flagstones in the kitchen were pulled up, exposing a corpse which, by its distinctive set of false teeth, was easily proved to be O'Connor's. All that remained was to track down the culprits, and, once this had been achieved (partly through the use of the telegraph, which was then announcing its utility in the detection of crime), it turned out that each blamed the other. Frederick's protestations are certainly worth remembering, and it is hard not to sympathise: 'She left home with £1,500 on her,' he complained; 'I came away with twelve!' The conspiracy was collapsing, and they remained estranged through the duration of their trial, indeed until 13 November, the day of their execution at Horsemonger Lane, when, to borrow Richard Altick's phrase, they 'kissed and made up'.

The hanging itself was attended by a huge crowd, studded with literary luminaries: Charles Dickens, John Leech, John Forster, Herman Melville. Judith Flanders sees reason to suppose that Maria's infamous black satin attire interfered with Thomas Hardy's personal memories of the hanging of Elizabeth Martha Brown. It was once believed that Maria's notorious association with this particular fabric provoked no little disruption in the fashion world, but this no longer seems to be the case (perhaps proving that there is no such thing as bad publicity).

MWO

FURTHER READING

Flanders, J., *The Invention of Murder* (London: HarperPress, 2011)
Altick, R. D., *Victorian Studies in Scarlet* (New York: W. W. Norton, 1970)
Walbrook, H. M., *Murders and Murder Trials 1812–1912* (London: Constable, 1932)

Mapleton, Percy Lefroy (1860–1881)

Like William Bousfield, Percy Lefroy Mapleton resorted to murder as a contingency when he failed in his attempts to prosper in the competitive environment of the creative arts. In Mapleton's case, he thought he was a writer, but he was unsuited to the punishing lifestyle. Years of drudgery, angst and enervation – not to mention penury, frustration and ennui – were not for him. He wanted recognition, and found himself unable to accept the gloomy truth of it: an unwanted future – sweating blood for a breadline royalty, at best – must have appeared alarmingly imminent. He therefore resolved to do whatever he could to prevent himself from falling into this grim and hopeless trap. Such is the vanity of ambition; still, it is difficult not to sympathise with his predicament.

Frustrated though he may have been, there remained no excuse for the step he took next. On 27 June 1881, Mapleton boarded a mid-afternoon 'down' train from London Bridge to Brighton and, scanning through the first-class compartments, selected one in which Frederick Isaac Gold was already seated. Mr Gold, a sturdily built man in his early sixties, customarily travelled up to London twice a week for business purposes from his home in Preston Park – and even the most sentimental of Victorian novelists would have shied away from such brute nominative determinism if they had created him as a character in a story. For Mapleton's part, although he did not know Gold's name, one senses that, as he looked at him across the compartment, the elder man developed, to Mapleton's inner vision, a miraculous and unmistakeable lustre – much as avian characters in cartoons appear in the mental fantasies of their feline persecutors in their ideal final state, roasted and with a tantalising whiff rising hotly from the flesh.

By the time Mapleton spilled out of the compartment at Preston Park, where passengers' tickets were collected, he bore an insignificant wound to his head, about which the little blood which had crept from it had been rather theatrically smeared, and Gold was nowhere to be seen. Mapleton's recollection of what had happened was hazy, but he denounced a mysterious assailant who had assaulted him as the train hurtled into a tunnel. When the chain of a gold watch was seen poking out from the side of his shoe, he scarcely hesitated before announcing that it was his, and that it must have been placed there either by his attacker (in a fetishistic moment) or by himself in a half-conscious effort to protect his valuables. Mapleton was patched up and returned on an evening 'up' train in the company of two police officers who were detailed to ensure that he was all right. He induced them to allow him to leave the train a stop early – they had originally expected Mapleton to alight at Wallington, which is where he said he lived – and vanished into the distance. In the meantime, Gold's body – with its throat cut, and horribly injured where Mapleton had thrown it from the moving train – had been discovered in the Merstham Tunnel, but a telegram insisting upon Mapleton's detention failed to reach the sergeant travelling with him when the train passed through Three Bridges.

The whole thing had been a desperate bid for cash and other treasures, but Mapleton – now a notorious fugitive from justice – embarked upon a period of want more intense than any he had experienced before having recourse to murder. He managed to rent a room in Smith Street in east London, giving the name of Clark, but the world was looking out for him, and Gold's widow had publicised the serial number and the name of the maker of the watch, which Mapleton had, of course, stolen from his victim. This made the item unpawnable, and Gold had had nothing else about his person of any real value. The effect of his crime had been to condemn Mapleton to irremediable poverty – Gold had not been as lucrative as Mapleton had hoped – and when the police, led by Donald Swanson, finally located and arrested him, he was ill and half-starved.

Mapleton's trial was held at Maidstone, and all the evidence coalesced against him. He persistently averred that he was innocent, but this was nothing more than his usual arrogance. William Marwood performed the execution at Lewes Prison on 29 November 1881.

MWO

Further Reading

Arnold, R., 'The Murder of Mr. Gold' in Wallace, E., *et al*, *The Murder on Yarmouth Sands* (London: George Newnes, n.d.)

Marwood, William (*c.* 1818–1883)

Of all the executioners operating during the Victorian period, William Marwood was, perhaps, one of the more steady personalities. Few of his kind escaped the profession without several coatings of emotional trauma, but Marwood apparently retained much of his sanity for the duration. James Berry, who followed in his scurrying footsteps, described him as a 'quiet, unassuming man, kindly and almost benevolent in his manner, who was in no way ashamed of his calling, though very reticent about speaking of it, except to those whom he knew well'. No doubt this modest policy did much to insulate Marwood from the worst of the damage; even so, reports of his death implied that it had been hastened by drink.

Marwood's chief contribution to his discipline's fund of knowledge came when he realised that William Calcraft, the country's hangman of choice for decades, was doing it all wrong. Calcraft's 'short drop' induced death by strangulation; but Marwood, who 'had read a great deal on the subject' of judicial executions, 'including the work of doctors in Ireland', thought that a longer drop would be preferable. If the cervical vertebrae could be dislodged, insensibility and death would follow more or less instantly.

His 1872 appointment to hang William Horry, an uxoricide from Boston in Lincolnshire, gave Marwood (himself a Lincolnshire native) an opportunity to test the mechanics underpinning his theory. All passed off smoothly, and Horry was promptly interred in the keep of Lincoln Castle, having met his end without a struggle, and with his 'placid' features showing no 'special expression'. The results could hardly have been better, and Marwood kept it up until his death, ousting the ancient Calcraft in 1874 and polishing off many of the criminal luminaries of the late seventies and early eighties. The pickings were rich: Henry Wainwright, Kate Webster, Percy Lefroy Mapleton, George Henry Lamson and – not least – the infamous Charles Peace all vanished from this world at the end of Marwood's generous rope. 1875 brought about a curiosity, as Marwood presided over the public execution of Joseph le Brun in St Helier, Jersey. Hangings had been private affairs in the rest of the country since 1868, but, as the *Pall Mall Gazette* put it, the legislation which had brought about this change in procedure 'made no mention of the Channel Islands, and the authorities of Jersey believed they had not the power to make any alteration in the system of public hanging'.

In the early summer of 1883, Marwood travelled to Dublin to execute those convicted of the Phoenix Park Murders, apparently taking the precaution of making the journey garbed as a clergyman. Irish separatists had elevated the condemned to the status of martyrs, and Marwood – a cobbler by trade but, in this particular equation, the reluctant symbol of British authority – can hardly have avoided the feeling that he was under threat. Some reports suggested that he continued to receive menacing letters even after his return home to England. Then, the story went, he 'spent a convivial evening with a party of Irishmen', was taken ill and, on 4 September 1883, died.

The truth, at least as it was described at the inquest into Marwood's demise, was probably rather more pedestrian.

Marwood's widow said that he had 'never been well' since a visit to Lincoln on 24 August, but he denied that he had been poisoned and 'made light of the matter'. As far as she knew, he had not received any threatening letters 'since the one a year ago' – well before his Phoenix Park commission. 'He had,' she said, 'no fear or expectation of violence at the hands of the Irish.' The doctor who had attended him during his last fortnight and the surgeon who had performed the post-mortem agreed that Marwood had died of pneumonia, and he was buried without further fuss in the churchyard at Horncastle. His grave became a site of pilgrimage for those of a macabre turn of mind, and the stone soon had to be removed, having been disfigured a chip at a time by souvenir hunters.

Nevertheless, the impedimenta of his brief and notable career were visible throughout Lincolnshire for years to come, with one 1947 press report citing a 'case of relics' which had been taken from the Portland Arms at Lincoln to the Five Bells in Bassingham and then lost; and, in Horncastle, photographs, facsimile letters, a tobacco pipe (in the Ship Hotel), and 'a rope, formerly owned by the late Mr Charles Chicken, of Foundry Street', which was said to have been 'used by Marwood for six or seven executions, including a woman'. 'But even this,' the newspaper went on, 'is suspected by some people because it has a running noose, and Marwood is regarded as the first "scientific" executioner.'

MWO

FURTHER READING

Clark, R., *Capital Punishment in Britain* (Hersham: Ian Allan, 2009)

Masset, Louise (1863–1900)

In 1899, thirty-six-year-old Louise Masset was working as a peripatetic teacher of French in north London whilst living with her sister and her husband in Bethune Road, Stoke Newington. According to the judgemental mores of her family and the

Victorian society in which she lived, it was considered shameful when she became pregnant by her French lover. As she was not short of money, soon after Manfred was born in 1896 Louise arranged for him to be cared for by Nelly Gentle in Tottenham, though she visited him regularly for walks in the park. This nurse-child arrangement, favoured by the middle classes, worked well – until, that is, Louise announced that she would be taking the boy to live with his father's family in France.

At midday on Friday, 27 October 1899 she took him from Nelly's care and travelled to London Bridge railway station. Around 6.30 that evening, a child's body was found on the floor of the public lavatory at Dalston Junction station. The little boy had been stripped, stunned with a brick and then suffocated. On the following Monday, when Nelly read an account of the horrific murder in a newspaper, she went to the police and, deeply upset, identified the dead boy as her former charge, three-year-old Manfred Masset. Louise's movements were traced to a hotel in Brighton where she had spent the weekend with a young lover, Eudore Lucas, before returning to London on the Sunday evening and, apparently, carrying out her teaching duties the next day without any evident signs of grief or stress. A parcel containing some of Manfred's spare clothes had been found at Brighton station, sent back to London Bridge and identified by Nelly as those she'd given Louise to take to France. Nelly was also able to confirm that the child had been carrying some toy scales when she handed him over to his mother – these scales were found in a drawer in the hotel room that had been occupied by Louise and Lucas.

Louise Masset was arrested and charged with the murder of her son. Her trial opened at the Old Bailey on Wednesday, 13 December 1899, before Mr Justice Bruce; the prosecution was led by Mr Charles Matthews and Mr Richard Muir, with Lord Coleridge appearing for the defence. Public interest in the case was intense; each day huge crowds gathered outside the court and the newspaper coverage charted verbatim the testimony of the witnesses. Louise appeared in court each day, her fashionable outfit topped by a jaunty little hat – one newspaper commented on her 'attractive appearance', adding that 'at no time during the proceedings did she display the least nervous apprehension. She sat calmly listening to the whole of the evidence, only now and then conversing with her solicitor.'

By the time she was called to the witness box, Louise had decided to exploit the contemporary publicity surrounding several notorious baby farmers operating in the city, women who ruthlessly killed infants in their charge: women like the evil Amelia Dyer, who had been hanged at Newgate in 1896. She hoped, therefore, that the jurors would give some credence to the convoluted story she had concocted about handing over Manfred to two women called Browning, having paid them for a year's board and education at their newly-opened school in Chelsea. The implication was that they were baby farmers and had duped her into paying them money for the care of her son, only to murder him within hours, ready to repeat the scam with another desperate mother. Police investigations failed to find any evidence of either the mysterious Brownings or the school, although two members of the public later swore that they had seen two women and a child – who therefore resembled the Browning women and Manfred – aboard an omnibus on the afternoon he was killed. Both witnesses (if that is what they were) said that the boy seemed distressed and uneasy in their company.

A female attendant at one of the two waiting rooms at London Bridge station testified to having seen Louise and her son at about 2.30 that afternoon. When asked, Louise had said that she was not about to catch a train but was waiting for someone. An attendant in the other waiting room swore that she had spoken to Louise Masset shortly before seven o'clock that evening as she – Louise – was washing her hands in the cloakroom. She was alone. Once she had finished her ablutions, she hurried off to catch the 7.20 p.m. train to Brighton. It was little more than an hour earlier that the child's battered body had been found further up the line at Dalston Junction. Yet Louise swore that the attendant was mistaken, insisting that, after leaving Manfred with the Browning women, she had caught a much earlier train – the 4.02 p.m. from London Bridge to Brighton.

Lord Coleridge, Louise's defence counsel, chose not to disclose the contents of the letters she had recently written to the child's father, for the wording used made it clear that she was deeply upset, his affections having been usurped by another woman. Coleridge was of the opinion that the letters would have provided a strong motive for the killing; conversely, they could have worked in Louise's favour, eliciting the sympathy of the all-male jury – perhaps a more lenient verdict might have been forthcoming. As it was, Louise was found guilty and sentenced to death. Her solicitor, Arthur Newton, fought tirelessly to save her from the gallows, producing some last-minute evidence supporting Louise's version of events. A petition addressed to Queen Victoria was signed by 20,000 Frenchwomen and sent to the Home Secretary, Sir Matthew Ridley, by the editor of a women's publication, *La Fronde*. Several appeals were also made by Louise's relatives, quoting evidence of insanity in various family members – as in the case of Christiana Edmunds in 1871 – but to no avail. Louise Masset was hanged by James Billington within the walls of Newgate Prison on the morning of Tuesday, 9 January 1900. It was the first execution in England in the twentieth century. Her last words were ambiguous: she said, 'What I am about to suffer is just. And now my conscience is clear.'

Louise was buried within the confines of the prison. The following year, Queen Victoria's reign came to an end and she was granted her dearest wish: to be buried in the mausoleum at Frogmore, laid to rest for eternity beside her beloved Prince Albert.

As Louise Masset sat with young Manfred in the waiting room at London Bridge station that afternoon, was she steeling herself to carry out her plan to kill him? And did she decide to do it at the much smaller Dalston Junction station, where she stood far less chance of being observed? We can only guess at the reason behind this heartless and brutal murder of a young child. It was certainly not done in a sudden and uncontrollable fit of insanity, for it was premeditated – indeed, very carefully planned – and Louise seemed to have shown no remorse or anguish at what she had done. This in itself may suggest, if not insanity, an extreme personality disorder. We cannot know whether it was spite, revenge, some deep-seated resentment or madness that drove Louise Masset to murder her son and to further compound the atrocity by cruelly leaving his bloodied body on the floor of a public lavatory.

KC

Further Reading

Clarke, K., *Deadly Dilemmas* (London: Mango Books, forthcoming)
Eddleston, J. J., *A Century of London Murders and Executions* (Stroud: The History Press, 2008)

Maybrick, Florence Elizabeth (1862–1941)

Florence Chandler, from Alabama, would live to regret the day in July 1881 when, aged nineteen, she married forty-two-year-old James Maybrick. He was a successful cotton merchant from Liverpool and an active member of the city's business elite. Florence was yet to learn that her husband was a chronic hypochondriac, habitually dosing himself with toxic substances and using strychnine and arsenic as stimulants, or aphrodisiacs, or to ward off the symptoms of advanced neurosyphilis. In 1888, they settled in Battlecrease House in Aigburth, near Liverpool, and she soon learned that he was also an adulterer (he kept a mistress with whom he had five children). To the fashionable Liverpool set to which they belonged they seemed happy (at least at first), and their marriage had produced two children. Florence, however, failed to endear herself to James's brothers, especially Michael (alias Stephen Adams, a successful musician), and the servants took a dislike to her – in particular, the nanny Alice Yapp.

Not unnaturally, Florence became increasingly alienated and unhappy, accrued large debts and indulged in several romantic liaisons, including one with James's brother, Edwin, all whilst maintaining the façade of respectable family life. However, in March 1889 she spent three days in a London hotel with a wealthy local businessman, Alfred Brierley. This was recklessly indiscreet and resulted in a violent row during which James gave Florence a

Florence Maybrick. (Authors' collection)

black eye; the prospect of divorce, which would ruin Florence financially and socially, loomed into view.

In April that year, James Maybrick became unwell – he admitted to having taken a strong dose of strychnine – and in the early stages of his illness he was nursed by Florence, who supplied him with Valentine's meat juice, a common restorative given to invalids to which, she later testified, James had begged her to add some of his white powder – arsenic.

She admitted that, against her better judgement, she did as he asked, but she insisted that the adulterated contents had been spilled and not administered. Away from the sickbed, Florence wrote a letter to Brierley, informing him of her husband's illness; this was intercepted by Alice Yapp, and Florence's infidelity was exposed. On 11 May, James Maybrick died after suffering severe pain and vomiting, symptoms associated with death from an irritant poison.

Fuelled by the malicious gossip of servants and family friends, suspicion soon fell on Florence, and Michael Maybrick placed her under house arrest before removing the children. He then alerted the police, who arrested her on 14 May, charged with the murder of her husband. A search of the house revealed large quantities of arsenic and other toxins with no attempt at concealment. A post-mortem revealed a slight trace of arsenic in James's body, although this was insufficient to cause death. Hyoscine, strychnine, prussic acid and morphia were also found. Maybrick's body was buried and then impatiently exhumed, but further tests similarly failed to provide an incontrovertible indication of the cause of death.

Florence Maybrick stood trial for the murder of her husband at St George's Hall, Liverpool, on 31 July 1889, before Mr Justice James Fitzjames Stephen, two years before he was certified insane. The celebrated advocate Sir Charles Russell (see Adelaide Bartlett) led the defence, assisted by Mr Pickford, a local barrister, who five years before had been involved in the trial of the notorious 'flypaper murderers', Flanagan and Higgins. The Maybrick case fired the imagination of the press; newspapers reported every word and nuance of the trial, inciting outrage at Florence's infidelity (a stance, it was said, shared by that rigid advocate of the sanctity of marriage, Queen Victoria). The woman in the dock – young, attractive, foreign and an admitted adulterer – was on trial not for murder, but for immorality. Her predicament epitomised the dichotomy deeply ingrained in Victorian society: a man might take a mistress with impunity provided the arrangement remained discreet, but his wife must be above reproach. Any infringement of this contract was unacceptable, and a woman who succumbed to temptation risked being branded a whore.

Medical evidence was divided. Two expert witnesses, both Home Office analysts, gave opposing opinions: Dr Thomas Stevenson stated that death, despite the post-mortem findings, had been caused by arsenic, whereas Sir Charles Tidy suggested that gastroenteritis was to blame.

Prior to the Criminal Evidence Act of 1898, defendants were not permitted to offer any statement during the trial, but the judge granted Florence's own request to speak. This was considered unseemly and did her no favours. Had she sat sobbing in the dock, her face heavily veiled and her head lowered in abject contrition, she might have won the jurors' pity. Instead, she freely admitted that she had purchased flypapers which she had soaked to extract the arsenic to make a face-wash, following a recipe prescribed for her in America (cosmetic products containing arsenic were widely advertised). The court also learned that she had spoken to the family doctor expressing her concern at her husband's ingestion of so many potentially lethal substances.

The judge's summing-up took two days – it was blatantly biased in favour of a guilty verdict and contained many inconsistencies.

Florence was found guilty of murder and sentenced to death. The controversial verdict gave rise to fierce public debate, given full rein in the fickle press, and numerous petitions for leniency, signed by thousands of well-wishers, were presented to the Home Secretary. After much official handwringing, Florence's sentence was commuted to life imprisonment on a charge of attempting to murder her husband by administering arsenic – a crime for which she was never tried. Throughout Florence's fifteen years of detention, her mother, the Baroness von Roques, and many others – on both sides of the Atlantic – continued to campaign for her release, as did Lord Russell, who remained convinced of her innocence for the rest of his life.

Florence was finally released from Aylesbury Prison on 20 January 1904 and, a month later, returned to America. For a while, she gave talks about her ordeal and wrote a book entitled *My Fifteen Lost Years*. She died an impoverished recluse in Connecticut in 1941, living in a dilapidated cabin with only a colony of cats for company.

By a curious twist of fate, James Maybrick returned to public consciousness in the 1990s, recast as Jack the Ripper. The proposition was made possible by the discovery of a controversial diary, the text of which was in equal shares allusive and evasive. Numerous Ripperologists fell out with one another while the credentials of the document were vigorously explored, and the truth of the matter has never been definitely established, but the fact that the most recent monograph about the Maybrick case scrupulously refrains from making any reference to the diary perhaps shows (at least in a simplified way) where things stand today.

KC

FURTHER READING

Blake, V., *Crime Archive: Mrs Maybrick* (London: The National Archives, 2008)

Feldman, P. H., *Jack the Ripper: The Final Chapter* (London: Virgin Publishing, 1998)

Mignonette, The (1884)

The *Mignonette* was a yacht, unfit for oceangoing, whose sinking, in 1884, was the first act in the Victorian era's foremost cannibalism scandal.

Out in the South Atlantic, hundreds of miles from uncertain island harbours (and thousands from the coasts of South America and Africa), the *Mignonette* gave up the ghost and disappeared beneath tremendous waves, decanting its slender crew of four men into a thirteen-foot dinghy with no fresh water and only two cans of preserved turnips to sustain them. The men – Captain Tom Dudley, Edwin Stephens, Ned Brooks and seventeen-year-old orphan Richard Parker – now sought to survive against apparently insurmountable odds.

Early attempts to flourish on the fauna of the sea went badly: only one turtle was hauled aboard, and, since its blood was not considered fit for human consumption, this left only the unpleasant meat, which rapidly spoiled; the tinned turnips, meanwhile, lasted only a short time, despite the castaways' frugality. Thirst was a significant problem, and, like Coleridge's ancient mariner, they refrained from drinking the seawater by which they were surrounded, believing that madness would be the result.

Parker, an inexperienced seafarer, broke first, desperately guzzling down copious volumes of saltwater despite being cautioned not to do so. By day nineteen, he was ill, and thought likely to die. Emergency measures had already been discussed, and cannibalism had been considered; but, according to the Custom of the Sea, a code of ethics which could only be invoked in times of the most pressing urgency, this necessitated the drawing of lots. Now, this presented its own difficulties. There was not unanimous support for a lottery, and it had become increasingly obvious that the wrong result could require one of the more experienced seamen to die in order to give the diminishing Parker nothing more than an outside shot at life. Dudley and Stephens, in addition, had land-dwelling dependants who would miss them and whose economic prosperity would be affected by their deaths. The range of available options was narrowing down, and Brooks, an opponent of the lottery, came to realise that Parker would inevitably be sacrificed, discreetly averting his gaze when Dudley drove his penknife into Parker's neck. Still, all three surviving men drank the blood which issued from Parker's jugular vein, and then ate his innards. A few days later, full of human, they were collected by a passing German ship, full of humanity.

After the men had been returned to Falmouth and restored to health, a murder enquiry was launched. Dudley admitted freely that the Custom of the Sea had been dispensed with; Brooks – an unstable character – turned Queen's Evidence, and testified against Dudley and Stephens, before touring the country in castaway's rags for the entertainment of the paying public. At the trial, held at Exeter in November 1884, the judge, Baron Huddlestone, found himself in the unenviable position of having to respite judgement to the Queen's Bench Division, issuing the first so-called Special Verdict in an English court since 1785. In December, at a hearing in London, it was concluded that the defendants were guilty of murder, and both Dudley and Stephens were sentenced to death, with a strong recommendation to mercy. They served only six months in prison, and lived on, without eating anybody else, into the early years of the twentieth century.

The survivors' procedural lapse, nineteen days into their terrible ordeal in the middle of the unforgiving ocean, had been to forgo the lottery. This opened the way to a murder charge, but social sentiment had already shifted against the Custom of the Sea, since it was now considered improper to eat people, even at the risk of dying if one did not. Dudley, a man of strong principles, had considered the matter from a consequentialist perspective, weighing his actions against their likely results, and the advantages that he hoped would accrue to all left aboard after the sacrifice. Brooks drew a distinction between, on the one hand, the murderous act, which he saw from a categorical perspective, thinking it to be unconscionable, and, on the other, the consumption of Parker's flesh and blood, to which he was not so averse. *The Times*, covering the event in its columns, was not alone in considering the entire affair from a steadfastly categorical viewpoint; looked at this way, everything about the men's actions was inexcusable. These dissenting opinions are often revisited in legal and moral arguments, and the *Mignonette* case has received recent attention in

Professor Michael Sandel's popular and widely-broadcast lectures at Harvard University. For another example of consequentialism's influence upon the Victorian mentality, see The Maiden Tribute.

MWO

FURTHER READING

Hanson, N., *The Custom of the Sea* (London: Doubleday, 1999)

FURTHER VIEWING

www.justiceharvard.org – the *Mignonette* case is discussed in Episode 01

Millson, Sarah (*c.* 1812–1866)

The unsolved murder of Sarah Millson, a widow in her mid-fifties, proved to be one of the chief mysteries of its day, and the catalyst in a public reaction against the perceived incompetence of the police. One newspaper complained of their 'mental obliquity and professional incapacity' under the headline 'Police Intelligence at Fault'.

To begin at the end: a trial at the Old Bailey concluded on Thursday, 14 July 1866 with the acquittal of the only suspect in the murder of Mrs Millson, one William Smith. The defendant, delighted with the result, announced to the court that he was 'as innocent as a babe', and the judge, Baron Bramwell, concurred, saying, 'It is due to the prisoner for me to say I think so too. He is more than not guilty; he is innocent.'

The jury – who had not found it necessary to leave the room before making their decision, doing so simply by turning to one another in their seats – were of the same sentiment. 'We feel no doubt about it, my lord,' the foreman said. For the police, all this was deeply embarrassing.

Amid the madness, the identity of the victim had become rather forgotten. Even *The Era*, which had so strongly criticised the police's handling of the investigation, referred to her as 'Milsom' and 'Milson', both within the same article; and it is true to say that consensus about the spelling of her surname was never reached. Another journalist wrote that 'the unhappy woman ... was the heroine in one of those obscure dramas of real life which are called unreal and sensational when they appear in the pages of fiction. The staid, elderly matron ... had a life-story of her own not wanting in the elements of passion.' This sounded exciting, but the truth was that very little was known about Mrs Millson, and nothing that had been established in court gave any reason to suppose that she was really the heroine of a quixotic romance.

She left her mark, like so many others, only when she met her death. This occurred on Wednesday, 11 April 1866, in the warehouse building whose upper floors she occupied on Cannon Street, in the City of London. Elizabeth Lowes, a cook who lived with Mrs Millson – the unlikely pair were inexpensive security personnel, watching over the leather goods in the warehouse section below them – recalled the rainy evening. At ten minutes to nine, the doorbell rang, and Mrs Millson said that it was for her, and that she would go down to answer it. Nearly an hour and a half later, she had not returned; Ms Lowes knew that Mrs Millson enjoyed a doorstep chat and a gossip with visitors, but even she had begun to wonder what had happened. Descending carefully and by candlelight, she discovered Mrs Millson's body at the foot of the stairs. There was a woman at the front door – 'as I supposed, standing there for shelter' – but she would not come in to help, and quickly vanished. At last, a policeman passed and ran to fetch a doctor. But Mrs Millson was already dead, her skull smashed by a blunt instrument, and bearing other, dissimilar wounds made by something sharper. Much attention was given to a crowbar that was found nearby, but it was native to the warehouse and not covered, as the true weapon must have been, in blood and strands of hair.

Smith was eventually picked up in Eton. He was known to be involved in an operation to extort repayments from Mrs Millson, who had taken out bad loans for reasons which were not altogether clear. Smith's clothes were speckled with a dark substance with the appearance of blood, but it was soon found that it was shellac; Smith was a hatmaker by trade, and shellacking one's garments was an occupational hazard. The disappointed police nonetheless pressed on with their pursuit of Smith – Charles E. Pearce describes their tactics as 'unscrupulous, unfair and stupid'. At the trial, the defence took triumphant delight in calling witness after witness who could prove beyond any question that Smith was in Windsor on the evening of the crime.

There were two hints of something undiscovered. One, available before the trial, was the suggestion that the warehouse had been subject to repeated burglaries, with money and goods going missing. Could Mrs Millson have been connected in some way – either taking the money and the property herself, or enabling someone else to do so? Nothing of the sort was ever proved.

Perhaps the murder was more personal than it appeared. The second hint – published after the trial – depended on an understanding of Mrs Millson's history. 'It is known that Mrs Milson [*sic*] had been twice married,' read the aforementioned article in *The Era*:

> [T]he first husband, a dissolute, idle fellow, having soon deserted her, and as was supposed, emigrated to Australia. Years elapsing, and no news reaching his wife of his existence, it was taken for granted that he had died, and his supposed widow married Milsom [*sic*] … The first husband is now known *not* to have died, and is *more than suspected* to have returned to England.

In this interpretation, the prodigal husband may – who knows? – have been extorting money from his former wife, scaring her with the belated realisation that she was, de facto, a bigamist, and turning to murder when – owing to the trouble she had got into paying off the bad loan – there was no more money to take from her. The theory defies corroboration, but one wonders whether the approach of the newspaper, which at least tried to clarify Mrs Millson's blurry background, might have been a fruitful one if it had been adopted, long before the debacle, by the police.

MWO

FURTHER READING

Pearce, C. E., *Unsolved Murder Mysteries* (London: Stanley Paul, 1924)

Milsome, Albert (1863–1896) and Fowler, Henry (1865–1896)

The duo of Albert Milsome and Henry Fowler are known to grim posterity as 'Milsom and Fowler' – the *e* at the end of the surname of the former miscreant has been restored here, since it seems likely to reflect the spelling that Milsome himself would consider correct.

Like all the best partnerships, theirs arose from a shared interest, specifically in burglary and other crimes of a similar variety. Milsome had first appeared at the Old Bailey, understating his age presumably in an attempt to elicit the sympathy of the jury, in 1879; Fowler's path had caused him to meander in and out of custody for years, and by Christmas 1895 he was free, but on licence, and looking for ways of making ends meet. These were powerful bonds, but otherwise they were dissimilar, Fowler a 'callous brute' even in the words of his defence counsel, and 'stalwart, muscular ... a veritable Bill Sykes' in the words of one posthumous commentator, while Milsome was 'pusillanimous' with 'little brown eyes like those of a ferret'.

On the night of Thursday, 13 February 1896, Milsome and Fowler found themselves, quite by design, standing in the back garden of the sedate Muswell Hill property of elderly Henry Smith. Smith – whom popular rumour described as a miser – was believed to have a considerable sum of money squirrelled away, and Milsome and Fowler proposed to liberate it; by the light of a child's lantern they disabled Smith's mechanical burglar alarm, and they entered the house through a window.

Smith was awoken by this activity, and, by candlelight, he crept downstairs to see what

Albert Milsome and Henry Fowler. (Authors' collection)

was going on. By the time his gardener arrived for work at dawn, his body lay on the kitchen floor, growing colder, battered, bound, gagged, with cloth forced into the mouth; in the bedroom, his safe was open, and his money missing. It was not long before police shortlisting procedures delivered up the names of Milsome and Fowler, but it was not an easy task to establish the evidential links necessary to precipitate an arrest.

As it happened, the toy lantern proved to be the crucial clue – the murderers had left it in Smith's sink, and the police had retained it, hoping that it would shed some light on the mystery. Eventually it did: it was discovered that its previous owner had been Milsome's fifteen-year-old brother-in-law, who unhesitatingly recognised all the customisations he had made to it in order to improve its performance and the wear and tear it had sustained in the course of its use: '*this* is the lantern – *this* is the stuff I made the wick out of – *this* is the bit of penholder that I put on – *this* green glass is broken – *here* is where I used the sandpaper'. All that remained was to locate Milsome and Fowler, but they had ceased to frequent their usual locales, getting out of London and heading for Liverpool and, by their own declaration, heading for continents new.

Somehow the plan changed, and, with the Metropolitan Police in pursuit, they made their way through the provinces of England and Wales, eventually joining a travelling fair, in which Fowler performed as a strongman and Milsome shyly took the punters' money on the door. At length, this extemporary employment, which they had obtained under false names, took them to Bath, where, finally, they rested just long enough for the police to catch up with them.

Milsome was arrested without a struggle, but Fowler fought bitterly for his freedom, until at last it became necessary for a policeman to knock him unconscious with the butt end of a revolver. Again the conspirators' essential dissimilarities were underscored, and from this time, through police court hearings and a three-day trial at the Old Bailey, their alliance was utterly broken. Milsome, desperate to avoid the consequences of his actions, made a statement implicating Fowler alone; Fowler, learning of this betrayal, and feeling 'indifferent to the value of his own life', told the truth about what had happened, studiously recounting Milsome's part in it in addition to his own. He also admitted that the proceeds of the robbery had been disappointing, and that the local grapevine had exaggerated the extent of Henry Smith's wealth. Milsome's share – half the takings minus half of Fowler's expenses – had been '£53 and some shillings'. This was probably more than either man had ever seen, at least in the course of legitimate business, but it was hardly enough to risk execution for.

Towards the end of the trial, Fowler tried to strangle Milsome in the dock, and was only prevented from doing so by the intervention of an assortment of officials and police officers (at one point, this tremendously powerful man was apparently giving nine of them a very difficult time). Both defendants were found guilty and sentenced to be hanged at Newgate Prison. When the day arrived, Fowler's animus towards Milsome had given way to a general tranquillity (not to be confused with forgiveness), but even so a third condemned prisoner, William Seaman, was cautiously situated between the feuding pair on the scaffold, for fear of further incidents. A fourth candidate then seeing out her days in Newgate, Amelia Dyer, was removed to Holloway Prison while the triple execution occurred, and then hanged the next day.

MWO

FURTHER READING

Adam, H. L., *Old Days at the Old Bailey* (London: Sampson Low, Marston & Co. Ltd., 1932)

Abinger, E., *Forty Years at the Bar* (London: Hutchinson & Co., 1930)

Minor, William Chester (1834–1920)

William Chester Minor was a paranoiac and murderer whose enforced retirement, in the haunted rooms of Broadmoor, gave him enough time to develop a thoroughgoing interest in masochism. This he proceeded to express in two chief ways: on the one hand, by voluntarily detaching his own penis, eighteen years before his death; and, on the other, by contributing enthusiastically to the collection of citations for the first edition of the *Oxford English Dictionary*.

Like that of John 'Babbacombe' Lee, Minor's crime is therefore overshadowed by the action post-homicide, as it were. His erudition – particularly in the context of his undoubted insanity – challenges our preconceptions of those individuals who step out of shot, trailing away towards the indistinct edges of the usual human narrative; but it came with the characteristics of an infatuation or a displacement activity. Like the violin recitals put on by Charles Peace, Minor's cultural offerings continue to provoke curiosity (in the 1970s, K. M. Elisabeth Murray said that Minor's story had 'often been told'); but in 1872, three days after St Valentine's Day, there was an empty chair at somebody's table.

The offence itself was one of oddly cursory properties. Minor, whose mind had begun to unfurl in Reconstructionist America after a traumatic experience providing medical aid to the Union troops during the Civil War – or perhaps secondary to a venereal infection – was resident in Tenison Street, in Lambeth, south London. His landlady, Mrs Jane Fisher, became rapidly conscious of her lodger's pathological fear of the Irish (alongside other eccentricities), and implored her husband to go upstairs to talk to him. This Mr Fisher did, finding to his great satisfaction that Minor was 'extremely intelligent, and conversant with the works of many English and American authors'. Still, the newspapers – perhaps with perfect hindsight – later alleged that Minor's habit of carrying weaponry and surgical instruments whenever he went out had also caused consternation.

Simultaneously, the Metropolitan Police had also become aware of Minor's exaggerated aversions. Inspector 'Dolly' Williamson told the trial – held in Kingston, Surrey, on 4 April 1872 – that Minor had visited Scotland Yard to explain that 'he came to this country to avoid the Fenians [see Terrorism], and that they annoyed him in his bedroom, but were invisible'. Minor similarly expressed a fear of assassination, and thought that his persecutors (if they were successful in their occult scheme) would contrive to make his death look like a suicide, cheating him of justice even posthumously. This was far from being a police matter, but likewise nobody seems to have challenged Minor's florid delusions.

In the early hours of 17 February 1872, Minor was on the streets near his accommodation and in the throes of a paranoid storm. Now, his pursuers were everywhere, closing in on him, and when he spotted a man by the wall of the local lead manufactory, he realised that the time to act had arrived. He drew his gun, aiming it at his nemesis, and shot him through the neck as he was running away. The victim had, in fact, been walking to work, ready for his nightshift in the Red Lion brewery, unarmed, and, of course, knowing nothing of Minor. There had been no ceremony; there was no backstory created in Minor's fantasies; Minor himself made no move to escape from the scene. The trial lasted less than a day, since it was obvious that the defendant was insane. Edward Clarke, who attained great fame after his exploits in the trial of Adelaide Bartlett, represented Minor – but the case is not described in Derek Walker-Smith's biography, *The Life of Sir Edward Clarke*.

Had this dismal, fatalistic tale not finished in – of all things – lexicography, then it would probably have been forgotten many years ago. Minor was prowling the neighbourhood, psychotic, defending himself against nothing, and prepared to shoot – at nothing, or something; it hardly mattered which – if he thought it was necessary. Perhaps the Fishers, who were bringing up a brood of smaller Fishers in their modest home on Tenison Street, were fortunate: Minor could easily have mistaken them for the Fenians whom he so feared.

Simon Winchester, sympathetic to the sometimes uncomfortable paradoxes of Minor's case, dedicates his book, *The Professor and the Madman*, to 'the memory of G. M.' This was George Merrett, Minor's victim and, in Winchester's analysis, 'an absolutely unsung man'; or, perhaps better, one finally obscured by language.

MWO

Further Reading

Winchester, S., *The Professor and the Madman* (New York: HarperPerennial, 1999)

Monson, Alfred John (1860–?)

John Alfred Monson, the alleged murderer of Cecil Hambrough, gained his notoriety in a case which became popularised as the 'Ardlamont Mystery'. Monson appeared to think that the Scottish justice system, in which coroners were unknown, would be easier to defeat than its English counterpart.

An upper-crust background had not prevented Monson from falling upon hard times. Bankrupt by 1892 and with a wife and children in tow, he depended on the kindness – and carelessness – of strangers, mingling these strategies with an increasingly complex network of frauds. On one occasion, he torched a rented stately home, impatiently awaiting an insurance windfall that never came.

When it became clear that buildings were not guaranteed to pay out on their policies, Monson turned his attention to human beings. In particular, he managed to gain an appointment as tutor to Hambrough, a bulky and perhaps rather trusting young man, not far short of his majority, whose father had plans to send him into the army. By degrees, Monson engineered the departure of his family and his pupil to Ardlamont House, on the western fringes of the Scottish mainland, and here the main players arrived in 1893, in time for the shooting season. Before long, Hambrough was copiously insured.

Joining the party in early August was a man known (purely on an interim basis) as Mr Scott. Although 'Scott' claimed to be an asthmatic marine technician, interested in having a look at the misfiring engines of a local steam yacht, he was known socially as Edward Sweeney and professionally (as a bookmaker's runner) as Ted Davis. On the evening of Wednesday, 9 August, Monson and Hambrough put out to sea in a borrowed rowing boat, into the hull of which Scott had earlier introduced an untidy plug-hole. The boat, accordingly, went down; Monson – a good swimmer – rescued himself, and left Hambrough to it. The young man struggled to the shoreline (since the vessel had not gone far before it capsized), and, shortly afterwards and *sans* anything resembling recrimination, the adventurers dried off and turned in.

Thursday morning dawned, ready to illuminate the next attempt on Hambrough's life. This time, Monson, Scott and Hambrough went out to shoot rabbits – although Scott was unarmed – and, before long, something happened. A hole had been blown in Hambrough's skull, behind the ear, and Monson and Scott thought they remembered dragging him out of a ditch into which he had fallen, only to find that the signs of life were already extinguished. Scott, apparently sensitive to the shock and grief of his hosts, left Ardlamont the same day, quickly disappearing into anonymity.

Gradually, Monson's inability to stick to a coherent story, combined with his eagerness to claim Hambrough's insurance money, caused official suspicions to grow. Initially, it had seemed conceivable that Hambrough's fatal injuries were self-inflicted, but it was soon established that he had not been shot with his own gun – a twenty-bore piece – but with Monson's, a twelve-bore. The ditch into which he had supposedly fallen was overgrown, but none of the vegetation upon which Hambrough was said to have landed had been damaged, and the blood which had issued from his wound was pooled on the bank. No scorching was found around Hambrough's injury, which suggested that the shot had been fired from a distance beyond the reach of the victim; meanwhile, three trees which stood in a line beyond him were all marked by pellets, apparently consistent with the inferred angle of the fatal shot.

At Monson's Edinburgh trial, the relevant parts of the aforementioned trees, transported eastwards to give their noiseless evidence, made an appearance among hundreds of exhibits. For the defence, a number of exculpatory points were raised, challenging the scene depicted by the prosecution. Firearms experts testified, as William Roughead neatly summarised it, that 'with a gun, as with Providence, nothing is impossible'. Perhaps Hambrough had borrowed Monson's twelve-bore; perhaps he slipped, and, perhaps realising that he was destined to tumble (perhaps awkwardly) into the ditch, perhaps he threw the weapon away; perhaps it then discharged automatically; perhaps it was all a fearful accident. Perhaps Hambrough was worth more to Monson alive than he was dead; if so, perhaps there was no financial motive. No doubt, the attendance of Scott at the trial would have been helpful: he must have had a good deal to say about what had happened, but since he could not be located, his version of events could not be known. After proceedings lasting ten days, the jury reached a verdict of not proven in a little under an hour and a quarter.

The aftermath of all of this played out in an assortment of law courts. Everybody sued everybody else; Monson was awarded a desultory farthing in damages when Madame Tussaud displayed his effigy in wax. He eventually burned down another building and then became involved in an extortion scheme, in the course of which he and his associates may have commissioned a murder in Tangier (the actual attempt was bungled). His later years are largely obscure, although, in view of his general immunity to the workings of conscience, it seems fair to say that they may well have been colourful.

MWO

FURTHER READING

Roughead, W., 'The Ardlamont Mystery' in *Classic Crimes* (New York: New York Review Books, 2000)

Müller, Franz (1840–1864)

The railway age brought with it new possibilities for the aspiring criminal, and Franz Müller was the first person in Britain to realise the utility of trains as moving murder scenes. The compartments into which carriages were divided were private enough to make homicide a practicable option; and the distance between the stations allowed time for a murderer to act before alighting the train at the first opportunity and, with any luck, melting into a crowd. Later in the Victorian age, others would attempt to refine the formula (see, for example, Percy Lefroy Mapleton), but Müller – under other circumstances, a German tailor with little reason to be remembered – had first-mover's advantage in the discipline.

On the sultry summer's night of 9 July 1864, Thomas Briggs, a bank clerk working in the City of London, boarded the 9.50 train from Fenchurch Street Station, heading in the direction of Hackney and his well-appointed house at Clapton Square. His gold watch-chain was 'extremely visible', and, as he settled into his seat, Briggs may have been lapsing into sleep.

Then there are the lost minutes of the railway journey. By the time two passengers boarded at Hackney station and found themselves sitting, darkly, in a pool of fresh blood, Briggs had somehow exited the train; he was discovered lying unconscious and badly wounded between the tracks, two-thirds of the way along the line from Bow to Hackney Wick. The carriage itself presented mysteriously – besides the gore, a bloodstained walking stick, a leather bag, and a shabby hat (not Briggs's own) were all found. From Briggs's waistcoat, the gold watch-chain was missing. Remarkably, considering that he had been dispatched from a moving train, Briggs clung to the threads of life until the next day, but he could give no indication as to the identity of his murderer.

Müller was known by his acquaintances to have become disaffected with his day-to-day travails; he said that he was seeking a change, perhaps dreaming of America. There was little to tie him to Britain, with the possible exception of his relationship with one Mary Ann Eldred, and, since she was a prostitute, there may have been limited bonds even here. On the Monday after the murder, Müller visited a pawnbroker in Cheapside, exchanging a nice gold watch-chain, and carrying away another one in a box printed strikingly with the broker's name: Death. He gave the box to the daughter of a friend of his; the friend, Jonathan Matthews, noticed that Müller had dispensed with his usual hat and was wearing a rather better one. By the Wednesday, Müller had uptraded enough times to be able to cash in his possessions for a cheap transatlantic ticket on the *Victoria*, and he sailed on this vessel on the Friday – next stop, New York.

A little over a week after the murder, Matthews spotted a reward notice outside Paddington Station, and realised belatedly that Müller was a wanted man. The police had tracked the watch-chain to Death's shop, and Matthews produced the box given by Müller to his daughter. He also identified Müller's hat, which had been retrieved from the railway carriage (Müller, of course, had been sporting Briggs's hat, with apparent disregard for his chances of freedom). It was also discovered that the suspect had – equally carelessly – left the country under his own name and, with a view to catching him, Death, Matthews and two policemen (Inspector Richard Tanner and Sergeant George Clarke) all set off westwards. Somewhere en route, the pursuers' faster ship overtook Müller's chugging passenger craft; Müller was arrested upon his arrival in the States and his extradition was arranged. He passed the time on the journey back to Britain by reading, and apparently enjoying, *The Pickwick Papers* by Charles Dickens.

On 14 November 1864, Müller was hanged, publicly, outside Newgate. Kate Colquhoun, in her recent book about the case, appears to feel as if there is room for some doubt – or, if not doubt, then at least unease – about Müller's conviction. She identifies social forces such as xenophobia at play in the shadows, but it is difficult to see how phenomena of this sort could have affected, for

Franz Müller. (Authors' collection)

example, the exchange of hats, which was the product either of narcissism or of chance, and which pointed so clearly to Müller's culpability. Müller was not immune to cultural influences – indeed, he engaged, in his own innovative way, with the predominant social symbol of British technological advancement in the nineteenth century, namely the railway – but he does seem to have been, as far as anybody can tell, guilty as charged.

MWO

FURTHER READING

Colquhoun, K., *Mr Briggs' Hat* (London: Little, Brown, 2011)
Irving, H. B. (ed.), *Trial of Franz Müller* (Edinburgh: William Hodge and Company, 1911)

N

Newgate Prison

Newgate Prison: London's foremost paradox in stone. Despite its ineradicable presence in the imagined landscape of crime in Victorian Britain, Newgate Prison fell a few short years into the twentieth century, and had begun to appear anachronistic some time before that.

The work of Charles Dickens is, of course, partly responsible for the permanence of Newgate as a symbol of its age. Many will recall the scene depicted in *Great Expectations*, in which Pip is overwhelmed by feelings of contamination following a visit to the prison: 'I beat the prison dust off my feet as I sauntered to and fro, and I shook it out of my dress, and I exhaled its air from my lungs.' Likewise, the (earlier) vision of Fagin in the condemned cell, evocatively realised by Cruikshank, continues to haunt. Much space has been given over to discussions of the legality of Fagin's sentence – it seems that one could not be executed if one was found guilty of being an accessory to murder – but, this instance of poetic licence notwithstanding, the case otherwise bears some similarities to one that lies just outside the scope of this book, namely the prosecution of James Greenacre for the murder of Hannah Brown, and Sarah Gale for being an accessory after the fact. Here, the suspects in an appalling murder of certain transpontine properties were tried at the Old Bailey, sitting out their period of remand in Newgate: like Greenacre, Fagin swung outside the prison before a jubilant crowd; like Gale, however, he probably ought to have been transported to Australia.

Tableaux of this sort conflicted with the reality of Newgate's increasingly precarious existence. Newer penal facilities, typified perhaps by Manchester's elegant and fearful Strangeways Prison, had begun to highlight the extent to which Newgate had never outgrown its mediaeval origins. Refurbishments intended to preserve its utility simply sucked the capital out of overstretched coffers – the demolition of the interior of the north wing in 1856, for example, was undertaken with a view to installing a 'properly aired and ventilated' cellhouse, but already Newgate was in its last half-century and staring at the abyss. The Prison Commission recommended its closure in 1881; it stumbled on, but by 1894 it was no longer so much as a curiosity: 'Even those who are opposed to the dismantling of all buildings which can lay claim to antiquity can scarcely find memories of Newgate sufficiently pleasing to warrant its being handed down to posterity.' The end was inevitable, and the suburbanites of Pentonville, Holloway and Brixton realised with, presumably, something less than joy that the determined miscreants who once would have disappeared into the secretive, atavistic labyrinth in the heart of the city would now be luxuriating in the respectable placidity of the outskirts.

Along the way, Newgate had played host to many Victorian antiheroes. Countless ordinary individuals whose lives had led to a pitiable dead end (see, for example, William Bousfield) mingled invisibly with those whose deeds had made them lastingly famous: Henry Wainwright, François Courvoisier, William Palmer, Amelia Dyer. During decommissioning, in 1900, it was noted that the prison's graveyard – a discreet shortcut to the Central Criminal Court to the south – was to be lost, and with it the unsettling custom by which a man condemned to death at the Old Bailey would walk back to Newgate over the ground which would shortly obscure his body. 'The initials carved on the walls,' observed one newspaper, 'are those of murderers buried under the stones. At present they afford the short, sad memorials of a hundred and more crimes that make lurid the darker history of our modern Babylon.' These evocations of the past would, within months, be no more.

MWO

O

Orrock, Thomas (1863–1884)

Thomas Orrock was a criminal with a pleasingly Dickensian name, evocative of Orlick, a character in *Great Expectations*, who evinced a similarly murderous sensibility.

In October 1882, Thomas Orrock, an apprentice cabinet maker with a predilection for robbery, decided that the time had come to obtain a firearm. To this end, he responded to an advertisement in the *Exchange and Mart*, and bought a silver-plated pistol and twenty-five cartridges from a man in Tottenham, north London. He and two friends, Frederick Miles and Henry Mortimer, took the pistol onto the Tottenham Marshes to give it a whirl, and Orrock fired a bullet into the trunk of a tree.

On 1 December of the same year, a police constable, George Cole, was fatally wounded in Ashwin Street, Dalston, shot in the head; the bullet had penetrated his brain (see also Death in the Line of Duty). One other shot had missed its target, scarring the brickwork of a nearby building, and yet another had been absorbed by Cole's leather truncheon case. The fateful night had been a foggy one, and some ear-witnesses mistook the sound of the shots for fog signals on the railway track; another witness saw the flashes of light emitted by the gun when it was fired; and two saw Cole struggling with a young man in distinctively eclectic garb.

This young man was Orrock, who self-deprecatingly described his improvised outfit, compiled from second-hand throwaways, as causing him to look like 'a bloody parson'. He even had a soft felt hat to complete the effect. He had spent much of the evening of 1 December drinking with assorted others, before announcing that he wished to break into the Baptist chapel on Ashwin Street – at which he regularly worshipped – in order to steal the sacramental plate that he had, presumably, furtively coveted during services. Nobody bothered to deter him from doing so, and two of his chums – Miles and a fellow named Arthur Evans – waited in the Railway Tavern, at the junction with Dalston Lane, while Orrock staked out his target.

Then the shots rang out; Cole fell, and bled away; and Orrock vanished, failing to rendezvous with his colleagues in the Railway Tavern in the manner expected. In his panic, he had lost his hat, and his tools, including a wedge and two chisels, lay below the window through which he had intended to gain access to the chapel. All were retrieved by the police, but, beyond this, leads were unforthcoming. Orrock, realising that official suspicion had not immediately fallen upon him, asked both Evans and Miles to swear not to say anything to implicate him in the murder, to which they both agreed. Other acquaintances who asked Orrock about sudden changes to his presentation and circumstances – he was never again seen wearing his trademark hat, his trousers were mysteriously torn at the knees as if he had been in a scuffle, and he claimed that his new pistol was 'at the bottom of some river, I believe' – failed to report their concerns to the police. Orrock's confidence increased. He boasted about attending Cole's burial at Abney Park, and travelling to the cemetery in a tramcar containing Cole's grieving detective colleagues. Less than two months after the shooting, he got married (in St James' Church, in west Hackney – not in the chapel, as is often thought), and his bride, it was later observed, 'little thought, when she clasped the hand of her husband at the marriage ceremony, that she held the hand of a murderer, almost red with the blood of his victim'.

It took nearly two years for the whole story to come out. One of the chisels, it turned out, had been indistinctly scratched by a tool grinder to mark its ownership: the word 'Orrock' emerged under the microscope. Miles and Mortimer (who, like Evans, were now speaking up) took Sergeant Cobb to see the tree on Tottenham Marshes at which Orrock had shot; Cobb prised a bullet from the trunk, and a gunsmith noted that the three bullets which were now in the police's possession (the one from the tree, the one from the truncheon case, and the one which had been extracted from Cole's head at the post-mortem) were all of a similar type. Charles Nelson, the deacon of the chapel, pointed out the stupidity of it all. 'We use plated cups for the sacrament,' he told Orrock's trial in September 1884, 'which are brought there and taken away again; they are not kept at the chapel, but that was not known.'

Orrock was hanged at Newgate by James Berry on 6 October 1884.

MWO

FURTHER READING

Evans, S. P., *Executioner: The Chronicles of a Victorian Hangman* (Stroud: Sutton, 2004)

P, Q

Palmer, William (1824–1856)

An English poisoner of markedly indulgent habits, William Palmer squeezed a considerable amount into his not-quite-thirty-two years.

By the time the authorities caught up with Palmer – a doctor, albeit a lazy one, from Rugeley in Staffordshire – it was already too late for several former relatives, acquaintances and rivals. He had long had a mischievous spirit and found his way into medicine only after several false starts, all vitiated by his inability to regulate his urge to transgress. He had also taken an increasing interest in horse racing, and the loss of enormous sums of money did little to slake his thirst for betting.

To repair the self-inflicted damage, Palmer began to identify ways of bringing in an income, preferring those which did not require him to abandon the racecourse in favour of the surgery. Three murders followed – those of his mother-in-law, his wife, and his alcoholic brother – all occurring between 1849 and 1855, all poisoned, and all signed off by a compliant and trusting medical colleague as the unfortunate victims of natural circumstance. In the cases of his wife and his brother Palmer had made arrangements to insure their lives for excessive values, and neither lasted more than a few months once the paperwork was in place. The mother-in-law, by contrast, was thought to be good for an inheritance rather than an insurance dividend, but the principle was much the same.

One of the peculiarities of Palmer's history is that, if the rumours are to be believed, he was not animated solely by immediate financial gain. In the most recent book about him, *The Poisoner* by Stephen Bates, the author encourages his readers to dial back the sensationalism and, in particular, the exaggerated body count with which Palmer has become associated. Nonetheless, the gossip is too good to overlook entirely. Bates omits to mention Jane Mumford, but this individual – a difficult one to identify with certainty in the civil records of the time – was said to have been delivered of Palmer's illegitimate child, who later died mysteriously after seeing its father. Palmer's legitimate children did not survive *en bloc*: some have attributed this to their father's insatiable appetite for death, but Bates points to the infant mortality rates of the period and the possibility of congenital life-limiting conditions. Perhaps most intriguingly, Palmer is said to have goaded a love rival, George Abley, into an unhappy death by alcohol poisoning when he challenged him to a drinking contest. Palmer, it is said, 'fancied Abley's buxom wife'. It is possible to take a moderate view of this incident, too, but any of the popular stories with which Palmer was associated in the crescendo of his notoriety would suggest a homicidal instinct operating outside the conventional boundaries of monetary risk and reward.

Palmer's undoing came in 1855, when the death of his brother Walter began to provoke the scepticism of the insurance companies. He rapidly realised that he was tied up in debts here and as-yet-undiscovered forgeries there, and that he needed a change of fortune. As it happened, the man with all the luck was one John Parsons Cook, whose own gambling habits had brought him to the brink of ruin, with only his pecuniary interest in a (happily) fleet-footed and redoubtable beast named Polestar to cling to. Cook watched delightedly as Polestar swept home in the Shrewsbury Handicap, and found himself something in the region of £2,000 better off as a result. Palmer, who counted Cook among his acquaintances, took the lucky owner out for a drink, and Cook spent the night vomiting after swallowing an adulterated brandy and water. He even seemed to suspect that Palmer had poisoned him, but still the two men went together to Rugeley, where Cook continued to experience painful reactions to the food and drink he took, and Palmer, finally finding an outlet for his medical expertise, supervised the sick man's diet. On 21 November 1855, a little over a week after Polestar's triumph, Cook was dead, having suffered tetanic spasms of a sort much associated with the toxic effect of strychnine.

William Palmer. (Authors' collection)

No sooner had the death taken place than Palmer made arrangements to have the body buried; he also did what he could to get hold of Cook's windfall which, although far short of his gross debt, might have kept his creditors at bay for a while. This time, however, there was no way out, and investigation determined that, during the period of Cook's illness, Palmer had twice bought strychnine from a local pharmacist, and that the strychnine was now nowhere to be found. This led naturally to the assumption that it had made its way into Cook. Chemical analysis of the remains of the deceased did not reveal it, but this was believed to be a deficiency of the analytical process, which was not yet sufficiently refined – not fit for purpose. Palmer was convicted anyway, since all the circumstances showed what had happened, and he was executed at Stafford on 14 June 1856.

MWO

FURTHER READING

Bates, S., *The Poisoner* (London: Duckworth Overlook, 2015)
Knott, G. H., *Trial of William Palmer* (Edinburgh: William Hodge and Company, 1912)

Pay, Esther (1846–?)

It was on Tuesday, 20 December 1881 that young Georgina Moore went missing. That morning her mother, Mary, had taken her and her brother to the home of a friend in Westmoreland Street, Pimlico, and from there the children went off to school. They returned to the house at lunchtime, and shortly before two o'clock Georgina left to go back to school – and disappeared. When she failed to return that afternoon a frantic search was undertaken by friends and family (including the girl's father, Stephen), but without success. Newspapers reporting her disappearance described Georgina Moore as an attractive child, seven and a half years old and tall for her age, blue-eyed and with her fair hair worn in a fringe. When she was last seen she was wearing a dark blue dress, a coat with two rows of black buttons, a white straw hat trimmed with black velvet, dark blue knitted stockings and button boots.

There was, however, a reliable sighting – a young lad recalled seeing Georgina talking to a tall woman in a 'light ulster' that lunchtime and, moreover, he was able to pick out a local woman, Esther Pay, at a subsequent police identification parade. Local gossip soon revealed that the relationship between the girl's parents had been far from harmonious: Stephen Moore had often indulged in extra-marital affairs, one of which was with thirty-five-year-old Esther. She was living in the same street, knew Georgina well, and was known to wear a coat similar to that given in the young witness's description. Her illicit relationship with Moore had apparently ended only a few months before, although it was later proved that they were still in touch and on affectionate terms.

Mary Moore, provoked by these suggestive circumstances, confronted Esther at her house, asking her if she knew anything about Georgina's disappearance, but the distraught mother was given short shrift and shown the door. Inspector Henry Marshall from Scotland Yard, who was assigned to the case, also questioned Esther, but with the same negative result.

There things rested until 15 January 1882, when a child's white straw bonnet, similar to the one that Georgina was wearing when she disappeared, was found on the banks of the River Medway, near the railway station at Yalding, in Kent. Esther's parents lived in a cottage a short distance from the river, and it was her uncle, James Humphreys, who found the hat; but still there was no formal charge.

Six weeks after her disappearance, Georgina's body was finally hauled from the River Medway by a bargeman. The decomposing corpse was attached to a length of wire, wound several times around the chest, on the end of which was a heavy brick. The child's hands were clenched, the knees drawn up, and the injuries to the throat consistent with strangulation rather than drowning.

Inspector Marshall hurried to Yalding accompanied by Stephen Moore, who identified the body. They proceeded to the home of Esther's parents, having learned that Esther was staying there. Although she continued to deny any knowledge of the crime, she was arrested on suspicion of murdering Georgina Moore; turning angrily on Stephen Moore, she accused him of killing his daughter and then planting the body near her parents' cottage in a despicable attempt to implicate her.

Now the pace of events increased. Esther was returned to London by train and, on Wednesday, 1 February, she was brought before magistrates at Westminster Police Court to hear the case against her. That same afternoon, the inquest into the death of Georgina Moore was opened in Yalding, and adjourned to allow time for a post-mortem to take place. Georgina's burial followed on Saturday, 4 February, at Brompton Cemetery. Such was the hostility towards Stephen Moore that the mourners threatened to lynch him and, for his own protection, he was locked in the mortuary chapel until the interment was over and the crowds had dispersed.

Esther Pay's trial for the murder of Georgina Moore was held at the Lewes Assizes on Wednesday, 26 April, before Baron Pollock. Harry Poland led for the prosecution and Esther was defended by Edward Clarke QC (see Adelaide Bartlett). The defendant was described as 'a fine-looking, well-dressed woman' who calmly pleaded not guilty. When questioned, she said she had spent the day of Georgina's disappearance with two friends, both of whom denied seeing her that day.

As the trial progressed it became clear that the only evidence against Esther Pay was circumstantial. The testimony given by most of the prosecution witnesses was far from convincing and, although there were several accounts describing a woman and a child journeying between London and Spalding in the hours after Georgina's abduction, these were vague. None survived Clarke's scrutiny. In his closing speech, he reiterated the dubious nature of these sightings – made by witnesses walking along unlit towpaths or drinking in dingy ale-houses – with the goal of fostering the necessary doubt in the minds of the jurors. It worked, for the jury deliberated for less than twenty minutes before acquitting Esther Pay. It was another example of the astute advocacy of Edward Clarke, but it left the killer of Georgina Moore at large.

KC

FURTHER READING

Taylor, B. and Knight, S., *Perfect Murder* (London: Grafton, 1987)

Peace, Charles Frederick (1832–1879)

Once upon a time, Charley Peace, as he was fondly known, was the most famous and finest product of the Victorian criminal milieu. A prurient figure and simultaneously the subject of universal prurience, he could be described, not entirely insincerely, as 'our civic hero' by one Sheffield newspaper (admittedly, this remark was made at a safe remove, seventy years after Peace's execution in Armley Gaol, at the end of Marwood's unforgiving rope). Now, he finds himself in the shadow of others, his epochal symbolism usurped by Jack the Ripper and his story widely forgotten.

The merest outline can be given here. At heart, Peace was a prolific burglar, but one inclined to carry weapons; although his success in his chosen field must have been practically unparalleled (he frequently swept through entire suburbs, denuding the best houses of their best ornaments), occasional shootings helped him to escape from similarly occasional pickles. In the most notorious example, Peace shot and killed a policeman named Cock at Whalley Range, near Manchester, in 1876 (see Death in the Line of Duty). The authorities rapidly zeroed in on a suspect, but the one they selected – William Habron, an Irish labourer with a pre-existing grudge against Cock – was an innocent man. Peace sat in the public gallery at Habron's trial, watching as the defence case succumbed to circumstantial evidence. Habron was condemned to death but his sentence was later commuted to life imprisonment by the Home Secretary. Only when Peace's own race was run, three years later, did the true assailant admit his guilt in a half-literate confession: 'This man is inosenc. I have done my duty & leve the rest to you.'

Voyeuristic displays of this sort throw a little light on Peace's unusual character. He could be charming, affable, entertaining, ingenious, musical: he was always attracted by the curves of a violin, to the extent that at one point, it is said, he had so many stolen instruments in his possession that he ran out of room in his house and was compelled to ask his neighbour to look after some of them for him. He exhibited an apparently conventional passion for religion. He had a talent for changing his appearance, and claimed that he was able to go to Scotland Yard, peer at the wanted posters describing him, and walk out without attracting the suspicion of the duty officers. He took on a postmodern, meta-narratological role in his own story, present to his own illimitable satisfaction when the world around him believed him to be absent.

Gradually, Peace's obsessive appetites caught up with him. In Sheffield, he became enraptured with a married woman, Katherine Dyson, and shot her husband. He fled to London, adopted the name of Thompson, and reverted to burglary. When he was ambushed one evening while escaping from a property in Blackheath, he shot a police constable, and was lucky not to kill him. Apprehended and detained under the name of John Ward, Peace was convicted of as many counts as could be thought of, but none of his offences in the Blackheath incident was a capital crime. Life imprisonment therefore beckoned, and it was only when his identity as the murderer of Dyson was realised that he was transferred to Yorkshire for trial. On the way, despite being accompanied on the train by two policemen, Peace made a leap for freedom from the window of the carriage. He had induced his chaperones to turn their backs while he evacuated one of his lower abdominal organs – it hardly matters which one – into a paper bag. They recaptured him soon afterwards.

Charles Peace. (Authors' collection)

The Case of Charles Peace, a 1949 romp through this tale, is worth seeing – a film of good performances, very erratic accents and a rather confused moral vision, in which the supremacy of British justice is apparently meant to be the lesson, and throughout which the only truly interesting character is, paradoxically, Peace himself. It is hard not to feel that, with the death of the joyless Dyson, Michael Martin-Harvey's Charley did Chili Bouchier's Katherine something of a favour. Nor did death put an end to Peace's protean ability to assume new and dissimilar forms. It is told that, for a literary luncheon on the topic of crime, Miss Christine Foyle (of the family of booksellers) 'borrowed an effigy of Charles Peace from Madame Tussaud's and placed it next to the principal speaker. It was a great success, except that one woman went to the dummy and tried to shake hands with it under the impression that it was a Secretary of State for Scotland.'

MWO

FURTHER READING

Altick, R. D., *Victorian Studies in Scarlet* (New York: W. W. Norton, 1970)

Pearcey, Mary Eleanor (1866–1890)

In 1939, Mary Pearcey's case became entangled with that of Jack the Ripper. She, more than any other woman of her generation, seemed to the author William Stewart to have behaved with some of the Ripper's brutality. She was held up as a metropolitan example of feminine violence, a psychological study in awful passion, and Stewart invoked her as a means of demonstrating that – perhaps – the Whitechapel Murderer may have been a woman rather than a man. This, at least, was his awkward thesis.

Recent studies of Mary's crime tell a more nuanced story. In 1890, she was living in Priory Street, between Camden Road and Kentish Town Road, and across the city from the scene of the savagery of two years before. Mary had become enamoured with a young man by the unpromising name of Frank Hogg; Frank had not failed to reciprocate her affections, despite the fact that he had, at home in nearby Prince of Wales Road, a wife (Phoebe) and a baby daughter (named after her mother but nicknamed Tiggie). Mary's own romantic history was convoluted to say the least – she had been 'for years a woman of immoral life', as *The Times* expressed it – and she had a set of unconventional and generally unfulfilling relationships behind her, but with Frank something seemed different. She was literate enough to write syrupy letters to him but pragmatic and – arguably – liberated enough not to demand that he break off relations with Phoebe. She even nursed Phoebe, apparently diligently, during an illness.

By October 1890, however, the accumulated pressure was beginning to tell. Phoebe had become acutely suspicious of Frank and Mary; Mary was experiencing headaches which persisted for days. On 24 October, Mary sent a local boy to deliver a note inviting Phoebe to tea; for some reason, Phoebe accepted, and arrived at Priory Street, pushing Tiggie before her in a perambulator. There followed a sudden attack in the rear parlour, during the course of which Phoebe had the back of her head smashed in with a poker and then her throat cut. Mary bundled Phoebe's body into the perambulator – seemingly on top of Tiggie – and then left the house, heading for the railway arch at the end of the street, and then out into the darkening streets of north-west London.

It was later concluded that Tiggie had died either from smothering or from exposure; her body was found two days later, behind a hedge on the Finchley Road. Phoebe's remains, by contrast, had been discovered within hours of her death, abandoned without much attempt to hide them in Crossfield Road. Mary was quickly arrested and, on 3 December 1890, she was convicted of murder and sentenced to death. James Berry carried out the execution on 23 December.

In court, no witnesses for the defence were presented. Mary pleaded not guilty, and her barrister, Arthur Hutton, following this plea, made no attempt to mitigate for his client. She was tried as a sane individual, and convicted as one. Only after the conviction were doubts raised about her mental health. Mary's childhood was marked, it was said, by incomplete physical development and sickening head injuries, and these echoed through her adult life in the form of spasms of wild epilepsy, during some of which she would be gripped by violent compulsions. In addition, she had attempted suicide several times, by hanging, poisoning (twice) and drowning. Plainly, she was a fantasist, clinging obstinately to a groundless tale about an early marriage to an unnamed man of means in an apparently non-existent venue in Piccadilly. But in spite of it all – and even after rigorous assessments, conducted by the leading mad-doctors of the era – she was legally sane and accountable for her behaviour (see Insanity). Reading the detailed paperwork which survives in the archives is an unsettling experience – no injustice was done, but yet one is left with the uncomfortable feeling that Mary remained somehow misunderstood.

Mary has not quite vanished from the more shameless fringes of popular Ripperology. In 2011, J. E. Bennett self-published a short book, *The Ripper ... And Me*, which came on as if it were a sort of family reminiscence, and in which Mary was cast, inevitably, as the Whitechapel Murderer. This embellishment of William Stewart's original argument – in which Mary was a bit *like* the Whitechapel Murderer but not necessarily *the* Whitechapel Murderer – probably confirms that the ghost is not yet to be allowed to rest.

MWO

FURTHER READING

Hopton, S. B., *Woman at the Devil's Door* (London: Mango Books, forthcoming)

Peterson, Bertha (1853–1921)

The killing of John Whibley reads like a work of crime fiction. On Sunday, 5 February 1899, in the parish church in the tranquil village of Biddenden, Kent, the morning service was conducted by the curate, the Reverend Walter Raven. Amongst the congregation was a formidable forty-five-year-old spinster, Miss Bertha Peterson, who accompanied the hymn-singing on the harmonium. Her elderly father, the Reverend William Peterson, had once been rector there, and Bertha was paying a visit to her former home. Immediately after the service she hurried to a room in the nearby infants' school, where she had arranged to meet thirty-nine-year-old John Whibley, who was a shoemaker by trade, as well as an occasional reporter on local newspapers and a former Sunday school teacher. The object of the meeting, at which the Reverend Raven was also present, was the reconciliation of Bertha and Whibley, who had a long history of animosity. It was in 1893, against the backdrop of a malicious rumour – perhaps itself started by Bertha – that she had first accused Whibley of indecently assaulting a young girl; she was so incensed that she subjected him to a mock trial at the Rectory, and then sent libellous letters about him to various clerics, including the Archbishop of Canterbury. Now, six years later, a truce was promised. However, as Whibley dutifully gazed at a religious picture entitled *The Good Shepherd* that Bertha had fixed to the wall of the classroom, she drew a revolver and shot him in the back of the head. The bullet pierced his skull and he died instantly; Bertha made no attempt to escape and was soon arrested. On her way to Cranbrook Police Station she seemed unperturbed; she was far more concerned about having left her umbrella in the church, and ordered the police to 'see to it'.

Brought before magistrates and charged with murder under her full name – Bertha d'Spaen Haggerston Peterson – she cut an imperious figure. Her large hat was swathed in flamboyant black feathers and her shoulders were covered with a fur cloak. She carried a posy of violets and lilies-of-the-valley, and she peered through her pince-nez at the scandalised villagers gathered in court, smiling at them 'with the assured condescension of a local Lady Bountiful'. Evidence was given that Bertha was an extremely eccentric woman, prone to hysteria and known to hold fanatical religious views. Her pretty young lady friend, twenty-seven-year-old Miss Alice Gould, with whom she had once lived, spoke in her defence and was clearly devoted to Bertha. In the letters Bertha sent from Maidstone Gaol – where she was incarcerated in an unusual degree of comfort – she addressed Alice as 'My Own Darling Little One', among other equally saccharine endearments. Alice seemed to share the older woman's religious mania, and between them they had decided that John Whibley was the devil incarnate: in order to protect innocent children, he had to die. Bertha was so obsessed with this idea that she wrote, in a letter to a friend, 'It seems to me that the fate of Sodom and Gomorrah is hanging over Biddenden.' It was rumoured that she had sometimes been cruel to her elderly father whilst they were living in the Rectory, but when she was told of his death (in March, while she was still on remand), she became hysterical.

The murder trial was held at the Kent Assizes in Maidstone on 10 June 1899, before Mr Justice Mathews; predictably, the press coverage was extensive. Although there was abundant evidence that Bertha Peterson was mentally unstable (if not insane), she was deemed fit to stand trial. It was hinted that there was madness in the family; her mother had suffered a catastrophic epileptic fit, during which she fell into the fire and 'burned to a cinder'. For a brief period in 1898, Bertha had worked at Lady Somerset's Home for Inebriates, in Duxhurst, but the staff there expressed doubts about her sanity. Although Bertha admitted shooting John Whibley, she denied any responsibility. The killing, she argued, was God's will, not hers. It transpired, however, that a month before the murder she had bought the revolver from an Army and Navy Store for £2 7s 6d, and had been seen on a number of occasions, perfecting her shot.

The jury returned a verdict of guilty but insane and ordered Bertha to be detained indefinitely. She was sent to Broadmoor, where another eccentric and homicidal Victorian lady, Christiana Edmunds, was already in residence.

Bertha's trial almost coincided with that of a young maidservant, Mary Ann Ansell. Mary Ann was found guilty of poisoning her mentally defective sister and hanged at St Albans on 19 July. Her sanity had also been questioned and was the subject of debate in Parliament, but even a petition for mercy signed by a hundred MPs was rejected by the Home Secretary. Public opinion was divided as to whether justice had been served in either case: Silas Hocking – one voice among many – published a polemic in which he not only fiercely opposed capital punishment per se, but maintained that Bertha Peterson had escaped the gallows simply because she was a rector's daughter and had been born into a privileged layer of society. Mary Ann, by contrast, was merely a semi-literate scullery maid.

KC

Phoenix Park Murders, The (1882)

One of the foremost examples of political assassination in the Victorian epoch, the Phoenix Park Murders were merciless in their execution and extremely provocative in their fallout.

While strolling in Phoenix Park, Dublin, on the early evening of Saturday, 6 May 1882, Lord Frederick Cavendish and Thomas Henry Burke were ambushed by a gang of men, two of whom ran them through with surgeons' amputation knives. Cavendish was the newly appointed Chief Secretary for Ireland – the representative of the British government in its febrile Irish extremity – whose investiture had taken place at Dublin Castle earlier the same day. Now, he and Burke (the Permanent Under-Secretary at the Irish Office, and a man much resented by Fenian separatists, who inferred that he was personally sympathetic to governmental policy), were 'perforated in a shocking manner', as early reports put it. Both were dead long before assistance arrived.

It was quickly observed that the murderers had not waited for night to fall; this suggested a level of extremist zeal surpassing the moderate aspirations of the parliamentary Home Rule advocates, the most senior of whom – Charles Stewart Parnell – reacted to news of the assassination with anger and dismay. In fact, the assassins had emerged from a radicalised offshoot of the Fenian movement, three-dozen strong and unconnected to mainstream politics, who were calling themselves the Invincibles, and who accordingly imploded under the pressure of a police investigation, with several conspirators turning Queen's Evidence. Those convicted were idealised as martyrs; the 'traitors' – a relative term – who had brought the conspiracy down were despised, and one of them, James Carey, was murdered by Patrick O'Donnell on board the *Melrose*, then chugging between Cape Town and Natal, in July 1883.

O'Donnell followed the Phoenix Park murderers (Brady, Caffrey, Curley, Fagan and Kelly) to the scaffold, but the ripple effect continued. By the mid-1880s, with Gladstone's Liberal administration split by disagreements over the Home Rule Bill and insufficient in number to comfortably hold off the opposition of Lord Salisbury's Conservatives, Parnell's Irish Parliamentary Party had developed considerable influence. Elsewhere, however, the Fenians were impatient for progress, and dynamiting campaigns had begun (see Terrorism). In certain quarters, it was still being suggested that Parnell's sympathies really lay with the Fenians; if so, perhaps he was a liar, deceiving the electorate by pretending to be more moderate than he really was.

In April 1886, an ambitious young supporter of Irish independence, Edward Caulfield Houston, approached *The Times* with what he described as documentary proof of Parnell's clandestine radicalism. This took the form of a cache of incriminating letters, discoverable (for a fee) in France. The newspaper was then opposing the Home Rule Bill, and quickly spotted an opportunity to bring Parnell down and Gladstone into disrepute; accordingly, something in excess of £2,500 was paid to Houston who, taking with him a professor of moral philosophy as a guide, departed for Paris and a meeting with the dubious vendor of the explosive correspondence, Richard Pigott. The first letter to be published (in April 1887) was the most damaging, with its author apparently admitting that his outspoken denunciation of the tactics of the Phoenix Park murderers had been merely a strategic ploy, and that Burke, in particular, had 'got no more than his deserts'.

Parnell reacted calmly to this provocation, not allowing it to spoil his breakfast, but pointed out in parliament that the writing was not his, that the signature sloped the wrong way, and that the dot marking the abbreviation of his middle name in 'Chas. S Parnell' (as the letter styled it) had unaccountably been omitted, which was never his habit. *The Times* stubbornly stuck by its story, in spite of these very cogent objections. An inquiry, known as the Parnell Commission, lumbered into life, and eventually the elderly Pigott, an ex-journalist who had long since run out of legal ways of making a living, admitted to forging all the correspondence in the newspaper's possession. Thereafter he skipped the country for Spain and, when he realised that the police were catching up with him, he shot himself in the head with a revolver.

So it was that the Phoenix Park Murders continued to affect matters of life and death for years after the event. *The Times* made a *very* begrudging apology to Parnell, whose own ruin, when it arrived, was the result of an adulterous relationship, rather than his political convictions. W. T. Stead of the *Pall Mall Gazette* 'led the attack', as Kingsmill puts it, when news of the affair broke; by contrast, even Stead, whose instinct for a sensation never diminished, had turned down the forged correspondence which brought *The Times* such trouble.

MWO

FURTHER READING

Cole, J. A., *Prince of Spies: Henri le Caron* (London: Faber and Faber, 1984)

Kingsmill, H., 'The Phoenix Park Murders and the Sequel of the Pigott Forgeries' in Parrish, J. M. and Crossland, J. R. (eds.), *The Fifty Most Amazing Crimes of the Last 100 Years* (London: Odhams Press Ltd., 1936)

Pickpockets

The origins of Fagin – the mastermind of the Victorian period's most notorious (fictional) pickpocket gang – are more ambiguous than was once thought. The influence upon Charles Dickens of the highly publicised criminal travails of Ikey Solomon, a receiver of stolen goods and pickpocket whose golden years occurred before the reign of Victoria, has been regularly observed; less commonly recognised, but gaining ground, is an ingenious interpretation situating the source closer to home. Dickens's mother had a sister who had a husband who had a cousin by marriage – Henry Worms – who was transported to Australia in 1825 for receiving stolen goods.

Solomon, however, was the one who was supposedly known as a 'kidsman', obtaining his loot from a small army of juvenile pickpockets. This army, made up of street orphans and children whose parents could not support them (or did not care to), scarcely ran short of numbers and had advantages which adults no longer did. They could be nimble and agile; they could wriggle through small spaces; they would disappear rapidly into crowds; and often, no doubt, they were eager to learn. Two years before his transportation, Henry Worms had been acquitted of a similar charge at the Old Bailey, and his prosecutor, greengrocer Samuel Bye, whose stolen weights had been located in Worms's yard, told him that he 'ought to know better than to purchase such things of a boy'.

Nevertheless, the act of stealing items from a person's body without that person noticing was a refined version of common larceny, with a continuing appeal for men who did not wish to take the risk of personal violence and women who were up against the wage gap. One of the most successful female criminals of the era, Mary Anne Duignan, known as 'Chicago May', was additionally known throughout Great Britain, France and the United States as the Queen of Crooks, with pickpocketing being her particular speciality.

Many women operated alone, sometimes twinning pickpocketing with prostitution, and divesting gentlemen of their pocket books once they had divested themselves of their garments. Others would capitalise on their targets' conformity to gender-specific social expectations. Many an unsuspecting gentleman who helped a lady who had just 'stumbled' down the steps outside the local library would, shortly afterwards, discover that their pocket watch had mysteriously gone missing.

Unlike women, male pickpockets often operated in gangs and amongst crowds, with special events like horse-racing meetings being specifically targeted. The police would often send uniformed men to racetracks as a visual deterrent for pickpockets, and detectives appeared in disguise with the intention of capturing the offenders red-handed. The great Manchester detective Jerome Caminada tells a wonderful story of how, when dressed as a labourer, he managed to capture a pickpocket gang at a horse racing event; one of their victims had been his superior, the Chief Constable.

To counteract this social menace, the public took to placing some dangerous devices in their pockets, with mousetraps being the most favoured; this could result in nasty accidents when people forgot what they had in their own pockets. The fact that a pickpocket often worked blind, with the target often unknown in advance, meant that this type of theft could be a rather hit-and-miss affair, and therefore pickpockets would often commit multiple offences in one particular trawl. And whilst the frequency of pickpocketing has decreased since the Victorian age (as have the penalties for those convicted), it remains an offence commonly experienced by the public, an unwanted link back to the age of Fagin and Ikey.

NRAB

Prince, Richard Archer (1858–1937)

In the 1890s, few actors were more distinguished or celebrated than William Terriss. His glittering stage career had swept him through London's premier theatres, often in tandem with London's leading ladies. By the winter of 1897, he was appearing – at the peak of his fame – at the Adelphi Theatre, depicting Captain Thorne in William Gillette's *Secret Service*; appearing opposite him was Miss Jessie Millward, who was the principal female starlet of her day.

All this was apt to provoke professional jealousy in some quarters, and Terriss's particular antagonist was a Scottish actor named Richard Archer Prince. Compared with Terriss, however, Prince was a man of quite dissimilar characteristics: physically unprepossessing where Terriss was handsome and rugged; unconvincing where Terriss was plausible; unsuccessful and impoverished where Terriss was lauded and wealthy. The chief cause of their contrasting fortunes was easily understood – one was talented and desirable, and the other was not – but explanations of this sort did not appeal to Prince, who suspected that Terriss was secretly conspiring against him in a bid to protect his exalted status.

The truth could not have been more different. Prince's professional appointments were invariably unremarkable (bulking up crowd scenes, and so on), and his erratic behaviour ensured that producers rarely invited him back; the idea of undermining him can hardly have occurred to Terriss, to whom he was no threat at all. Indeed, Terriss was actually generous towards Prince. On Wednesday, 15 December 1897, Terriss bumped into him in the street and, as he often would, gave Prince a small amount of money. The star seemed genuinely aware of the often perilous financial circumstances of those who were failing to shine.

On this occasion, Prince spent the gratuity on a knife and, fixed on an illogical revenge, spent the early evening of Thursday, 16 December lurking outside Terriss's stage door. When he saw his imagined nemesis approaching, he struck, stabbing Terriss twice in the back and once in the chest; and then, with his victim expiring rapidly below him, he made no attempt to get away. From inside the theatre, Jessie Millward ran to the door to cradle her co-star, but he could not be saved, and a post-mortem examination determined that either of the injuries inflicted from behind would have proved fatal even if Prince's blade had not gone on to penetrate Terriss's heart.

Prince's trial at the Old Bailey was brief, and the defence presented by his barristers (to whom he was quite unhelpful) tested the limits of the defendant's competence. There was no doubt that Prince – who had become known in thespian circles as 'Mad Archer' – was an eccentric individual with an inflated sense of his own abilities. His mother, whose Scottish brogue Prince disinterestedly interpreted for the benefit of the jury, believed that he had been 'born mad'. He had previously conceived of other conspiracies against him, and had expressed the view that he was 'the Lord Jesus Christ' and his mother, by inference, 'the Virgin Mary'. Medical opinion held that he was insane, and no witness seemed to think that he was a good enough actor to be feigning madness with such verisimilitude. Prince was sent to Broadmoor, never to be released.

Shortly before her own (natural) demise, Jessie Millward gave a romanticised account of the murder, in which she 'dreamed of Mr Terriss's death three times in three weeks, before it occurred …

I told Mr Terriss about it. Little did either of us foresee its fulfilment.' Terriss's ghost splits its time between the Adelphi and, curiously, the nearby Covent Garden underground station, which was not opened until 1907. Sightings are apparently not as common as once they were.

MWO

Further Reading

Goodman, J., *Acts of Murder* (London: Futura, 1987)
Brandon, D. and Brooke, A., *Haunted London Underground* (Stroud: The History Press, 2008)

Pritchard, Edward William (1825–1865)

Nothing in the first nine-tenths (or so) of Dr Edward Pritchard's life could have persuaded anyone that he was destined for anything other than a sticky end. He takes his place with certain other notorious criminals of the world beyond living memory – men such as Samuel Herbert Dougal, George Chapman, and, to choose two examples from within the scope of this book, Henry Wainwright and Alfred John Monson – in the particular hall of mirrors that is dedicated to the memory of characters of markedly superficial desires and hubristic, conscienceless behaviour. Each of these men betrayed, to a greater or lesser degree, a selfish craving for the approval of the society around them, and none cared which of society's dearest precepts he would be required to break in order to obtain it.

Pritchard was a physician of seemingly unspectacular abilities, whose amorous and untruthful nature constantly undermined the trust of the communities who found themselves in the dubious penumbra of his care. By 1860, a peripatetic life had cast him ashore in Glasgow, married, with a number of children, and continually notarised by bank managers whose patience he had tested. In 1863, Pritchard's house at Berkeley Terrace mysteriously burned down; inside, the body of Elizabeth M'Girn, one of the Pritchards' servants, was discovered. There was some local suspicion about the circumstances of the case, but nothing could be proved; still, Pritchard's insurance company, to whom he sent an inflated claim on the loss and damage to the property, paid as little as they could. Pritchard did not challenge the decision, and he and his family moved to Royal Crescent, and then, in 1864, to Clarence Place, Sauchiehall Street.

By this time, Pritchard was immersed in – we would now say – an abusive relationship with his teenage housemaid, Mary M'Leod. She became pregnant by him, and he administered an abortifacient. Here was another complication to add to those which Pritchard was already facing. His financial situation remained intractable, but he managed to scrape together the pennies to begin curating a secret repository of antimony and aconite. In October 1864, Mrs Mary Jane Pritchard, the doctor's wife, began feeling unwell – vomiting, then cramps, then a debilitating asthenia.

As Mary Jane's symptoms progressed, Pritchard did what he thought the world around him would wish to see him do. He consulted with other doctors, he wrote to Mary Jane's brother (also a doctor), he dispatched her to Edinburgh to stay with her mother. The latter method did the trick – Mary Jane was much better, but she experienced a relapse when she returned to Glasgow. On 10 February 1865, Mrs Jane Taylor, Mary Jane's mother, seeing that her nursing did her daughter more good than anything else, came to stay with her in Glasgow.

Pritchard redoubled his efforts, and before the month was out Mrs Taylor had been seen off, 'dying,' as William Roughead puts it, 'under the influence of some powerful narcotic'. As was legal a century and a half ago, Pritchard signed the death certificate himself, attributing his mother-in-law's demise to paralysis and apoplexy. Mary Jane followed her mother into nothingness on 18 March, and Pritchard, again busy with the certificate, chalked it up to gastric fever.

For a few days it seemed as if this death, like the one before it, would pass without much remark, but a tipping point had been reached, and an anonymous letter awoke the senses of the authorities. The entire story emerged almost without defect, and the discovery of great quantities of poison in the bodies of the two deceased women merely underlined the extraordinarily heartless manner in which they had been murdered. Pritchard was convicted in Edinburgh after a five-day trial and hanged in Glasgow on 28 July, before a crowd of – perhaps – 100,000 unsympathetic souls.

As Roughead observes, the precise motive for Mary Jane's murder was never fully identified. Nobody believed that Pritchard really wanted to formalise his relationship with poor Mary M'Leod, and it was difficult to see how he could have gained financially from the loss of his wife: it was true that she was marked as the eventual recipient of two-thirds of her mother's estate (something in the region of £1,700), but he began poisoning Mary Jane long before he turned his attentions to Mrs Taylor, so the chronology was ostensibly incompatible with the motive of murder for profit. Perhaps it hardly mattered. Who knows how it is with these people? Their urges are not our urges, and abstract motivations – the desire for control, for example – can operate in abstract contexts, without the architecture of reason to prop them up.

MWO

FURTHER READING

Roughead, W. (ed.), *Trial of Dr. Pritchard* (Edinburgh: William Hodge and Company, 1906)

Prostitution

For many women, the alternative to a life of domestic drudgery – either in marriage or in employment as a domestic servant – was prostitution. This was especially true for those females raised in institutions and without family support, but, even taken from the general pool, some women were unable to find husbands to support them; others may have been unwilling to become chattels at the mercy of abusive husbands, or reluctant to risk their lives by multiple births. The number of prostitutes working in London in the nineteenth century was estimated in the many thousands, but by its nature the sex trade was clandestine, transitory and exploitative, and it was therefore impossible to arrive at a true figure. Those at the top of the pile paraded in their brightly-coloured clothing – but without hats – in the streets around the clubs and theatres in the Strand, Haymarket and Covent Garden (see Harriet Buswell); the Vauxhall Pleasure Gardens were also extremely popular for business. But many more women, those who were less favoured, were reduced to standing on street corners and wandering the dark alleys between the squalid tenements and courts in the poorer districts of the city – as in towns throughout the country – desperately plying their trade as best they could, and, as often as not, vulnerable to violent attack.

In 1885, in the *Pall Mall Gazette*, W. T. Stead dramatically drew attention to the procuring of young girls for sexual exploitation (see The Maiden Tribute). It was a shocking exposé, and its effects were far-reaching, even reaching the legislature – the Criminal Law Amendment Act, for example, raised the age of consent for girls from thirteen to sixteen. Even this was not enough to protect many young girls who, according to a report entitled *Inquiries Concerning Female Labour in the Metropolis* and issued by the National Vigilance Association in 1899, sometimes fell victim to agencies which lured them in with the promise of domestic employment, only to force them to work in one of the city's many brothels. The droves of naïve females drifting into London from the countryside or abroad were frequently preyed upon by procurers employed by the brothel keepers, and Christians of every persuasion attempted to address the problem. Midnight Mission meetings were arranged in premises in the Strand to coincide with prostitutes' leaving the theatres, music halls and taverns. In return for giving up their way of life, they were offered light refreshments, some intensive sermonising and a year's rehabilitation in a Lock Asylum, where they could learn to perfect their needlework and housewifery skills. It was noted by an observer at one of these meetings that this option was seldom met with any great enthusiasm. Many similar schemes were launched in London to rescue these girls: the Female Aid Society, for instance, provided three 'safe' houses but, with sanctimonious censure, graded the rescued women. The house in New Ormond Street, Bedford Row, catered for 'young, friendless servants of good character'; a second house in Southampton Row housed 'respectable servants out of a place'; and, thirdly, premises in White Lion Street offered sanctuary for 'the fallen'.

The proliferation of prostitutes in the Victorian era epitomised the dichotomy within the psyche of many in the male population, who were primed to view a woman either as the idealised image of 'the angel of the house' (sexually reticent and unsullied by impure thoughts) or as a prostitute, despised and demonised but pandering to their base instincts in exchange for money. The fascination of reformers and self-appointed guardians of morality for the plight of the 'unfortunates' – a favourite melodramatic theme in popular fiction – drove William Gladstone and others like him to make nightly forays through the city streets – in Liverpool this was undertaken by the campaigner, Mrs Josephine Butler – gathering up 'fallen women' in an attempt to save them from degradation and disease. For many of these women, however, prostitution was a perfectly viable enterprise, with flexible hours and a reliable market; and, although it could be dangerous, it was far less restrictive than the alternative – a lifetime of drudgery as a maidservant, working long hours for a pittance and sometimes being treated appallingly.

There was a whiff of prurient curiosity for a way of life conducted in the shadows, alleyways and street corners, far removed from the lush chaises longues and the warm glow of the traditional hearth. Many readers of lurid newspaper reports describing the murders of prostitutes – reaching a frenzy during the Jack the Ripper killings – though enthralled, must secretly have harboured a feeling that the victims had colluded in their own deaths by operating illegally, beneath the radar of police protection, and that they therefore deserved their grisly fate. The opposition to suffrage movements during the nineteenth century illustrates the conviction of many men – and, indeed, some women – that females were only qualified for child-bearing, housekeeping or providing sexually illicit services outside marriage ... until, that is, the outbreak of the First World War, when women found themselves needed in the munitions factories and on the land, and, having assumed a vital role in the defence of the realm, began finally to operate as political entities in civic society.

KC

FURTHER READING

Walkowitz, J. R., *City of Dreadful Delight*: *Narratives of Sexual Danger in Late-Victorian London* (London: Virago, 1992)
Ibid. *Prostitution and Victorian Society*: *Women, Class and the State* (Cambridge: Cambridge University Press, 1980)

R

Read, James Canham (1856–1894)

He thought about it for many years, but even so Robert Dowthwaite never knew what made him pay special attention to the couple who passed him in the lane. Perhaps it was simply that he had not expected to see anybody out for a stroll, arm in arm, at ten o'clock at night on the rural outskirts of Prittlewell, in Essex. He watched them until they turned into a field, disappearing down the slope towards a little brook.

The next day, Monday, 25 June 1894, Florence Dennis's body was spotted, crammed into a hedge and with a bullet penetrating her brain. This prompted a murder enquiry: Dowthwaite now realised that he was a witness to something. He had not seen the man's face, describing it as 'lowered and invisible', but his deportment, which was somehow irregular, had left an impression nevertheless. Other people who had also seen the ill-starred couple found themselves similarly struck by the mysterious gentleman, although none had a perfect view of him.

Before long, the suspect's name became known. He was James Canham Read, a respectable clerk at the London docks, who was variously and rather scandalously living as a family man with his wife and eight children in Stepney, or otherwise sleeping with twenty-three-year-old Florence (whom he had made pregnant), or, in a further iteration, sleeping with Florence's married sister Bertha (who had given birth to his illegitimate child). In the interval between Florence's disappearance and the discovery of her corpse, Bertha sent a telegram to Read at his workplace, demanding to know what he had done with her. He wrote back expressing ignorance but, realising that things were going to get rather hot for him, he took the precaution of stealing £160 from his employer's safe and vanishing into the distance. Gradually it was established that this busy individual had another woman, and another child, living at Mitcham under the name of Benson, and here Read was arrested by Essex Police Sergeant Alfred Marden, who earned himself a promotion for his diligence (see Thomas Simmons).

Read was charged with theft and murder and sent to stand trial at the Essex Assizes at Chelmsford, where he admitted the former offence but denied the latter. The case against him was a circumstantial one, but ostensibly compelling. Florence, *enceinte* and seeking financial reparations, had demanded a summit; he had wired back asking her to meet him off the train at Southend on the Saturday evening. The bullet in Florence's head matched those found at Read's Stepney address, and fitted a pistol which he was known to have possessed, and which was now unaccountably missing. Read had arrived at his workplace unshaven on the Monday morning, and looking like a man who had had a long walk; then he built a fire (in the middle of summer), began burning things in the grate, received Bertha's telegram, stole the money, remodelled his facial hair, and settled as best he could into an uncertain life in Mitcham, clipping articles about the Prittlewell murder out of the national newspapers in an almost obsessive manner.

Against all of this, certain objections were raised. Read may have been in Southend – of which Prittlewell was a satellite extension – on the Saturday, but nobody knew whom Florence had gone to meet on the Sunday. The witnesses who testified to seeing him were unified not only by their unwavering lack of doubt but also by the unpromising circumstances in which they undertook their observations, and the civilian witnesses, in particular, had all seen the papers before attending police identity parades, subsequently picking out the man who resembled the one described in the columns they had read. A police constable who spoke to a fellow tramping back to London from Essex in the early hours of Monday, 25 June had asked the lonesome traveller where he had come from. 'Southend,' came the unguarded answer, and was it likely that the murderer would admit such a thing to a policeman? Bertha – the prosecution's main witness – undermined the value of her evidence by lying before the magistrates; besides this, she had (arguably) a motive to want Florence out of the way, if she was jealous of her association with Read, and may also have hoped to punish Read himself for his inconstancy. Richard Storry Deans, writing about the case in the 1930s, considered the trial to have been 'not altogether satisfactory'. Too much, he thought, was made of Read's inability to establish an alibi for the night in question, or to disclose the whereabouts of his gun. As the defendant, Read was not obliged to prove his innocence; it was the duty of the prosecution to prove his guilt.

As it turned out, the jury did not experience similar uncertainties, and Read was found guilty, sentenced to death and executed at Chelmsford on 4 December 1894. His last words, supposedly uttered to the hangman, William Billington, are often thought to have been, 'Will it hurt?' In fact, he put this enquiry to the prison surgeon a few minutes before his hanging, and appeared greatly relieved to learn that his death would be 'expeditious and painless'. His last words to Billington, much less dramatically, were, 'Button my coat.'

MWO

FURTHER READING

Deans, R. S., *Notable Trials: Difficult Cases* (London: Chapman & Hall, 1932)

Wood, W., *Survivors' Tales of Famous Crimes* (London: Cassell, 1916)

Rush, James Blomfield (*c.* 1800–1849)

In his day, James Blomfield Rush was a murderer of surpassing infamy, sufficient to provoke the curiosity of Charles Dickens, who visited the scene of Rush's offence – Stanfield Hall – a little over a month after its commission. Dickens said that the property had 'a murderous look that seemed to invite such a crime'. Richard Altick, reviewing the case in his classic *Victorian Studies in Scarlet*, identified the source of the homicidal atmosphere in the Norfolk countryside, with its 'gloom and remoteness'.

There can be no doubt that, on the night in question, a thick fog (arriving as if by request) contributed to the general sense of menace; or that, in the moments after what would probably now be called a home invasion,

James Blomfield Rush. (Authors' collection)

two men lay dead, and two women were painfully injured. But what had brought Rush – the assailant – to this position?

As ever, the prelude to the case was extensive, and aspects of circumstance and personality showed up here and there. Even in his younger days, Rush was regarded by those who knew him as 'uncommonly tricky and not over-honest'; by the time middle age had set in, he had managed to accrue significant debts, and had apparently made recourse to a variety of illicit measures in an attempt to defray these (nobody knows for sure, but it seems possible that he shot his own father in order to expedite his inheritance). He had once had a serviceable relationship with Isaac Jermy, the owner of the land upon which Rush rented a farm, but, following the harvest of 1848, Jermy's patience was running short. Rush was struggling to meet his rent, and he now realised that he was facing eviction.

On 27 November 1848, Rush instructed a compliant and incurious boy to lay straw on the muddy footway leading from his lowly farmstead to Stanfield Hall (the Arts and Crafts building with the murderous look, and the home of the Jermy family). Between seven o'clock and eight o'clock, Rush's live-in partner, Emily Sandford, heard him go out, shutting the door behind him.

Shortly after eight o'clock, Isaac Jermy, who was taking the air on the porch of Stanfield Hall, was confronted and shot through the heart by an intruder; the gunman emerged out of the fog, with his face strategically concealed.

Next, the attacker entered the house. Isaac Jermy's son – the remarkably named Isaac Jermy Jermy – was moving towards the porch, having heard the first shot; he became the second victim, shot as his father was. The younger Jermy's wife left the drawing room, breaking down when she discovered the body of her husband in the hall; a servant, Eliza Chastney, went to attend her mistress; both women were shot, Mrs Jermy in the arm (which was later surgically amputated), and Ms Chastney in the leg. At this point, leaving his task in a state of incompleteness, the man with the gun vanished back into the fog.

As a nearby tenant, Rush was familiar enough to the other members of the household to cause him to be quickly suspected of the shootings; an uninjured butler, who had glimpsed the gunman, had not been fooled by the invisibility of his face. At his trial, which began on Thursday, 29 March 1849, Rush elected to defend himself, putting in a tour de force performance. Thrilling though this may have been to his prodigious ego, he would have been better advised to retain professional counsel. He was sentenced to death and executed before an enormous crowd at Norwich Castle on 21 April 1849 (just in time for Frederick and Maria Manning to begin their rise to popular celebrity: Victorian crime abhorred a vacuum).

A few last observations on this brutal case. A note which Rush dropped at the scene of his attack showed that he hoped to cast the blame for the events of the fatal night upon a disinherited offshoot of the Jermy family. Back at his farm, he had worked up a number of forged documents which he presumably expected, in the financial tangle which would result from the annihilation of the Jermys of Stanfield Hall, to be accepted as valid without scepticism. These cleared his debts – or would have done, if he had not been caught. His lethal blunderbuss, which was missing for some time, was eventually retrieved, after an official search of agonising inefficiency, from a dungheap.

MWO

FURTHER READING

Altick, R. D., *Victorian Studies in Scarlet* (New York: W. W. Norton, 1970)

Flanders, J., *The Invention of Murder* (London: HarperPress, 2011)

Teignmouth Shore, W. (ed.), *Trial of James Blomfield Rush* (Edinburgh: William Hodge and Company, 1928)

S

Sandyford Mystery, The (1862)

The Sandyford Mystery was a case of such unhappy precedent that the ordeal of Florence Maybrick would be made to seem trifling in comparison.

On Monday, 7 July 1862, rather suddenly, Jess M'Pherson was found chopped to death in her locked room at 17 Sandyford Place, Glasgow. She was one of the live-in servants of the Fleming family, and she had been especially deputed to stay behind in the property while almost everybody else in the household enjoyed a weekend out of the city. *Almost* everybody, because M'Pherson's particular duty, on this occasion, was to look after the elderly patriarch James Fleming, whose survival to a venerable age – he had been born just as George Washington was declaring American independence – was a blessing upon the family, and one tainted only by his boorish and unreconstructed personality. He was clearly a handy fellow to be leaving behind if one wished to actually enjoy oneself at the weekend.

Exactly what had happened to M'Pherson was unclear. Even the statements of Fleming, who had supposedly been alone with her in the house since Friday, seemed somehow unsuited to the circumstances. By his tale, he had gone to sleep on Friday night, and was awakened at four in the morning on Saturday by several loud shrieks; he had drifted off again, unconcerned; but then, when it was time for M'Pherson to bring him his breakfast, she failed to appear. He got up, went to her room, and found it locked and the key absent. He omitted to mention her disappearance to anybody, at first because he expected her to return, and then, well, just because.

The police, noticing that Fleming's tale was unsatisfactory, had him arrested and examined. Counterpunching, he threw the dull light of suspicion on one Jessie M'Lachlan – a former servant and still a friend of M'Pherson's. Closer inspection showed that Jessie M'Lachlan had indeed behaved rather unusually that weekend: she had stayed out all night, from Friday into Saturday; she had pawned some cheapish silverware that was missing from the Flemings' kitchen; she had sent her own clothes, and some belonging to the victim, by rail to imaginary recipients; and she had left her footprint, in blood, on the floorboards in M'Pherson's room. Asked to account for herself, she repeatedly stopped short of the truth. Inevitably, Fleming was released, and Jessie was tried for murder.

At the trial, the defence courageously took the line that the defendant was not guilty, because the guilty party was Fleming, now appearing, calculatedly airbrushed into the nineteenth century with flat-lens spectacles perched on his aquiline nose, as the principal witness for the prosecution. Time and again, Fleming's story failed to meet its forensic challenges, but the judge, Lord Deas, repeatedly intervened to dampen the sharper edges of the defence advocate's cross-examination. Fleming's character – nosy, interfering, threatening, and libidinous in spite of his years – was hushed up. A previous infraction, in which he had made a much younger woman pregnant in direct contravention of

Jessie M'Lachlan (see **The Sandyford Mystery**). (Authors' collection)

the teachings of his Church, was similarly glossed over. Shortly before her murder, Jess M'Pherson had encountered a friend to whom she described Fleming as 'actually an old wretch and an old devil', but she would not speak further about the matter owing to the inhibiting presence of her acquaintance's husband. Lord Deas, addressing the jury, turned the world on its head, and concluded that the deceased had meant that she planned to emigrate. But why say it in such terms?

Jessie M'Lachlan, with all stacked against her, was accordingly convicted of murder, and then, in a forty-minute statement which was read to the court by her representative, there followed what is normally held to be the true story of the death of the unfortunate M'Pherson.

Jessie *had* gone to the Flemings' house that night, but she popped out briefly to try to buy some whisky, and, when she came back, M'Pherson had been assaulted. She was bleeding heavily from severe head wounds, and Fleming said something to the effect that he had not meant to hurt her. Jessie stayed with her friend; Fleming started mopping the floors, and ended up clumsily drenching Jessie's boots, which she was obliged to remove – hence the footprint. When M'Pherson's condition deteriorated, Jessie insisted on fetching a doctor, but Fleming forbade it and, while Jessie searched frantically for a way out of the property, he took up a meat cleaver and finished M'Pherson off. 'I kent frae the first she couldna live,' he said. Jessie, fearing for her own life unless she complied with Fleming's wishes, allowed herself to be talked into an occult pact by which she pawned the silver to make the whole thing look like a robbery and did what she could to dispose of the bloodstained clothing.

Eventually, Jessie's execution was commuted, and she served fifteen patient years in prison for a murder that nobody thought she had committed. Fleming, having appeared for the prosecution at her trial, was conveniently placed beyond the reaches of Scottish law, but he had not long to live; as far as anybody knows, he did not bother to use the time remaining to him to perform any act of repentance.

MWO

FURTHER READING

Roughead, W., 'The Sandyford Mystery' in *Classic Crimes* (New York: New York Review Books, 2000)

House, J., *Square Mile of Murder* (London: Magnum Books, 1980)

Sattler, Christian (*c.* 1821–1858)

Christian Sattler was an incorrigible criminal. The Frenchman had a brief career in the German military, but preferred a life of thievery, offending across mainland Europe and continuing without interruption upon his arrival in England in the mid-1850s. It was while he was at Wisbech Gaol, on remand for petty theft, that Sattler drew attention to his murderous aspirations, some time before putting his ideas into practice.

Sattler was found guilty of theft and sentenced to imprisonment on 29 July 1857. The chief warder at Wisbech, Benjamin Eason, advised him to 'endeavour to obtain an honest livelihood' and averred that 'the good Christian people of England would not allow him to starve if he could not find any work'. Eason's words were wasted, however: freed after serving his sentence, the petty thief went straight back to his criminal lifestyle, and, on 2 November 1857, five days after his release, Sattler found himself sneaking into a room in the Golden Lion Hotel, St Ives, Huntingdonshire. He discovered on the floor a bag containing £234 in marked banknotes, and stole it, along with some clothes. The room's occupier, Mr Arthur Ballantine (a stock broker from the City of London), missing his property upon his return, notified the police, and a quick check of the hotel records showed that the last guest to have checked out was one Mr Christian Sattler. The chase was on.

The following day, Cambridge pawnbroker Robert Cole received an 11.00 a.m. call from a man who pledged 5s for a coat. The man returned at 1.00 p.m. and offered to buy a six-guinea watch with a £20 note. Cole, an experienced pawnbroker, was suspicious, but he dealt with the man, who handed over the money. Before giving change, Cole secretly sent his shop boy to the local bank to have the note examined. Whilst waiting, he pointed out that the man seemed to be carrying a large amount of cash, to which the reply was that he had received it from his father in Glasgow. The shop boy returned with the bank's all-clear, and, seeing no reason to detain the man any further, Cole completed the transaction and sent him on his way. However, he soon cursed his decision as news filtered through to him, via the local constabulary, of a theft at the Golden Lion Hotel in which a large amount of money in marked banknotes had been taken. Cole immediately told the police about his watch-purchasing customer, and they, in turn, notified the specialists in financial crime, the City of London Police.

The City Police put two detectives on the case, William Jarvis and Charles Thain. They traced Sattler to London after a chambermaid at lodgings in Gracechurch Street came across a shirt which Ballantine recognised as his. But Sattler had already fled the capital and was on his way to Hamburg, Germany. Thain set off in pursuit whilst his colleague, Jarvis, remained in London to continue the investigation. Eventually DS Thain caught up with his man in Germany, effected an arrest, and made plans to bring him back to England to face charges. He obtained a passage for both himself and his prisoner aboard the *Caledonia*, where the pair were to share a cabin for the trip back to England. Sattler, shackled in handcuffs, complained constantly, although according to the witness testimony of a few seamen he was well cared for by the detective. During the voyage, Thain explained that he would release Sattler from his bonds once he was safely in custody in England.

Just over a day into the journey, at around 4.00 p.m., three shots rang out from Thain's cabin. Mariner Stephen Robertson was the first on the scene, and, when the smoke cleared, he saw Sattler sitting astride a wooden trunk with Detective Thain standing over him, one hand upon his detainee, the other grasping at his own chest. 'The prisoner has shot me!' exclaimed Thain. Robertson seized Sattler and secured the pistol, which was Sattler's, and which Thain had locked in the trunk at the beginning of the voyage. Sattler had managed to break into the trunk, load the pistol and fire it – an impressive feat for a shackled man. Thain explained that he had locked the prisoner in the cabin in order to use the toilet, and returned to find Sattler armed and ready to shoot. As for Sattler, he claimed that Thain had broken a promise, refusing to free him from his handcuffs even though he was feeling unwell, and that he therefore felt justified in his act.

The crew were all for lynching Sattler, but sense was restored and the prisoner was secured in the forecabin while a very poorly Thain was nursed gently for the remainder of the journey. Once the *Caledonia* had berthed in London, Sattler was taken into custody at Bow Lane Station, and the ailing Thain was taken to Guy's Hospital, where he succumbed to his injuries on 4 December 1857.

Sattler was tried at the Old Bailey the following month and found guilty of murder. He was hanged before a small crowd at Newgate Prison on 8 February 1858, having been taken to the gallows weeping and pleading for mercy. One must recall Benjamin Eason's advice to Sattler, months before these events began, when he told him that the good Christian people of England would not allow him to starve. Sattler's unflinching response to Eason? 'It's not a Christian country, I will not ask for relief; if I cannot get employment, I will thieve, I will steal, and if anyone attempts to take or prevent me, I will shoot him like a dog.'

NRAB

Further Reading

Wade, S., *Square Mile Bobbies: The City of London Police 1839–1949* (Stroud: The History Press, 2008)

Simmons, Thomas (1844–1885)

In its day, the slaying of Thomas Simmons was notorious – a complicated 'Death in the Line of Duty' case characterised by brutality and heroism, cowardice and bravery, headlong flight and diligent pursuit. Few spicier ingredients were known to (or desired by) the readers of the Victorian crime columns.

The first act is perhaps the easiest to summarise. On 20 January 1885, three men were spotted alighting from a train in the pastoral climes of Rainham, Essex. It was rapidly inferred that they had not left London simply for recreation, and two local officers, Inspector Simmons and Police Constable Alfred Marden, resolved to detain them. When the gang noticed the policemen trundling towards them in a horse-drawn cart, they split, with one – the only one who had already been positively identified – heading through a hedge onto farmland, and the other two running off further up the Romford Road. Simmons spurred the horse on to new efforts, while Marden, dismounting, snagged the man in the field.

'What are you doing over here, David Dredge?' said Marden.

'You ——,' said Dredge, a known criminal. 'I will blow your —— brains out with this.' (In the retelling, the newspapers left the expletives to the imagination.) A revolver was aimed at Marden's head; and then there was the sound of a gunshot.

Marden, almost forgetting about the weapon trained upon him, looked round to see where the noise had come from, and picked out the figure of Simmons, no longer seated on the cart, upright but staggering backwards in the road. Facing Simmons, the taller of Dredge's companions stood, arm outstretched, holding a revolver with a cloud of smoke issuing from the muzzle. 'Come, they have shot me!' cried Simmons, and Marden went to him, supporting him while he regained his balance, and then, apparently with Simmons's encouragement, setting off across the fields in pursuit of the gang, who were making a rapid getaway. After a perilous chase, in the course of which the men hid behind a haystack and then, finally, disappeared across a small river, Marden returned to Simmons, who was, against the odds, struggling to keep up the pursuit. 'I think I'm done for this time,' said Simmons. 'Don't leave me anymore.' He clung to life for four days, but died of peritonitis caused by the destructive cross-sectional path which the bullet had taken through his large intestine; the projectile itself was discovered embedded in the vertebra at the base of the spine.

Now the curtain rose on the next movement in the drama: the hunt for the perpetrators. This occurred in a piecemeal fashion. Dredge managed to last out for two weeks before he was traced to Copperfield Road in east London and removed to Essex by Metropolitan Detective Sergeant William Rolfe, but the identities of his colleagues-in-arms remained frustratingly mysterious. Eventually, one – not the shooter – was discovered to be James

Manson, alias James Adams, alias James Lee, the most recent of whose alternative surnames had been adopted to commemorate the popular noose-cheating tale of John 'Babbacombe' Lee. Almost by chance, Lee was captured on Tuesday, 10 March in the act of attempting to pledge a revolver to a pawnbroker in Euston. Like Dredge, he was taken out to Essex, but local feeling, which was running hot, made it impossible for them to be tried at the county assizes, and their murder trial was reassigned to the Old Bailey. Here, on 27 April 1885, Lee was convicted and sentenced to death; Dredge was found not guilty, but rearrested immediately on the deferred charge of threatening to kill PC Marden. He served twelve months (with hard labour) for this offence, and was perhaps lucky to get off so lightly.

Still the murder of Thomas Simmons was not properly expiated: the man whose finger pulled the trigger had not been located. Lee's conviction (his execution followed on 18 May 1885) had turned the detective mind to the idea that the missing gunner was Jack Martin, a confrère of Lee's from the north London burglary rings. But Martin was absent from his usual cobwebby corners of the capital, and, although the remarkable Rolfe spotted him in the Commercial Road in August, Martin threatened to shoot him, and Rolfe could not effect an arrest.

The dénouement, like all the best of its kind, took the action out of London and out of the south-east, and transposed it to darkest Cumberland. On 28 October 1885, a jewellery robbery took place at Netherby, and the police established roadblocks in order to prevent the four-man gang from escaping. One – and surely not the least distinctive – of the team, 'One Armed Jimmy' Smith, had already elected to find his own way back to London by the time the three others – Jack Martin, Anthony Rudge and James Baker – stumbled into the police's trap, and from here the story unfurled in a way which did not seem to be without fearful precedent. Police Constable Joseph Byrnes was the unfortunate understudy for the role previously taken by Inspector Simmons, dying from a shot entering through the left eye and exiting behind the left ear; but, on this occasion, the thieves were taken, tried and, eventually, hanged by James Berry on 8 February 1886. Martin stubbornly declined to admit his part in the Simmons murder, but the general consensus was that his death put a long-awaited end to the affair.

Marden's courage was generally acknowledged and, after further distinguishing himself (see James Canham Read), he went on to become a senior figure in the Essex Constabulary. The psychological dynamics leading to his fall from grace in the early years of the twentieth century may never be thoroughly understood.

MWO

FURTHER READING

Rhodes, L. and Abnett, K., *The Romford Outrage* (Barnsley: Pen and Sword, 2009)

Smethurst, Thomas (*c.* 1807–1873)

The names of Victorian Britain's murderous doctors ought to trip off the tongue: William Palmer, Edward Pritchard, George Lamson, Thomas Neill Cream. Thomas Smethurst, however, is an outlier, refusing to conform to his professional stereotype. At the time, even serious publications found themselves on the horns of an illogical proposition, one which confronted the empirical basis of scientific practice. 'Is the prisoner guilty?' the *Medical Times and Gazette* asked itself, when considering Smethurst's case. 'We believe he is. Was he *proved* guilty? Certainly not.' The solution to this conundrum has become no clearer over the years.

Smethurst was a hydrotherapist by inclination – hardly the most rigorous branch of medicine – who had, since 1828, been married to Mary Durham. She was thought to be anything between thirteen and twenty-six years older than he was: neither had counted their days very accurately. By 1858, the shadow of scandal hung vaguely around them, and it was even suggested that they had once poisoned a man and attempted to induce his wife to make a will in their favour, with a view to poisoning her later on. Perhaps this was only gossip, but, when they happened upon forty-two-year-old Isabella Bankes, a reasonably well-off spinster in the echo chamber of Notting Hill's lodging houses, it was as if the art had returned to their fingertips. Smethurst romanced Isabella without attempting to hide his behaviour from his wife, and eventually he ran away with her and married her (bigamously) in Battersea on 9 December.

The newly-not-quite-weds made their not-quite-marital home in Richmond; in March 1859, Isabella began to suffer with diarrhoea and sickness. Smethurst called in the doctors, who gradually came to suspect foul play, and the patient eventually expired on 3 May. The previous day, as a result of the suspicion against him, Smethurst had been arrested on a charge of attempted poisoning; Isabella's death merely converted the accusation into one of murder.

Now the scientists reached for their instruments. Some performed a post-mortem examination, finding that Isabella had been in the early stages of pregnancy at the time of her death. Others picked through her organs and her excreta for traces of poison. Dr Alfred Swaine Taylor, then the foremost medical analyst in the country, thought that he had detected arsenic in one of Isabella's stools; this he matched to the contents of one of Smethurst's medical phials, marked as containing chlorate of potassium. In addition, a small trace of antimony – somewhat below a lethal dose – was found in some of Isabella's organs.

The trial began in July, and then again in August, since the first running had to be abandoned when one of the jurors became ill. By this time, things appeared to be turning in favour of the defendant. Dr Taylor had ascertained – to his horror – that the arsenic reading was a false positive caused by an impurity in his test apparatus; and great scorn was poured on the idea that anyone who had died of antimony poisoning could have left behind them a liver which was, on testing, found to be entirely free of toxic agents. For every medical man who was prepared to testify for the prosecution, one was found for the defence. Serjeant Ballantine, leading the case against Smethurst, was forced to conclude, rather weakly, that Isabella had been poisoned by 'some poison or other', as if the absence of the expected clarity in this area could be forgiven or overlooked. Nevertheless, rather to everybody's surprise, the jury returned a verdict of guilty, and Smethurst was sentenced to death.

A reprieve followed – in fact, a pardon followed – when considerable anxiety was expressed about the security of this verdict. Isabella was known to have had a 'bilious' constitution, and her pregnancy had coincided with her fatal illness, so perhaps she was hyperemetic. If one threw out Taylor's evidence, as one apparently had to do, then there was no arsenic in the case, and there was no indication that Smethurst had obtained a supply of antimony. Much more likely was that the dyspeptic treatments of the local practitioners, administered to Isabella in good faith when Smethurst had commissioned assistance, had contained an underdose of antimony (at the time, this was far from unusual). Why had Isabella's vomiting pattern, as it were, remained the same irrespective of whether Smethurst was with her, down in Richmond, or up in London? This did not suggest that doses of anything nasty were being introduced into her food, and the case, it was soon realised, was irretrievably broken.

The Home Secretary contented himself with prosecuting the newly innocent Smethurst for bigamously marrying Isabella Bankes – this was a much easier campaign, but one which Smethurst nevertheless attempted to derail, claiming that his marriage to Mary Durham had been the bigamous one because *she* had been married to someone else at the time, and that his union with Isabella was therefore virtuous. This tactic failed, and Smethurst spent a tokenistic year in prison with hard labour. He had the last laugh, however, suing for Isabella's estate upon his release, and winning, to the chagrin of the authorities. He died, having remarried in 1873, and left his widow, Ann, less than £100, which indicated that whatever advantages he had gained from whatever happened to Isabella were largely expended by the time he met his own demise.

MWO

FURTHER READING

Parry, L. A., *Trial of Dr Smethurst* (Edinburgh: William Hodge and Company, 1931)

Bowen-Rowlands, E., *In the Light of the Law* (London: Grant Richards, 1931)

Smith, Madeleine (1835–1928)

It is little wonder that the case of Madeleine Smith has become a cause célèbre in the annals of Victorian crime, or that it continues to fascinate to this day. Madeleine possessed many of the attributes of a young woman of the present day – wilful, wayward and unashamedly sexually adventurous – yet she was born into a typical nineteenth-century family deeply immured in the Scottish Calvinist mores of the time. Her father, James, was a prosperous architect and, in addition to occupying a large house in Glasgow's Blythswood Square, the family also enjoyed a country villa, Rowaleyn, overlooking the Clyde. Madeleine's scandalous affair with Pierre Emile L'Angelier – a dapper, moustachioed clerk who rather fancied himself as a ladies' man – echoed the theme of many a melodramatic novel, with indulged lustfulness leading inexorably to female downfall. L'Angelier must have realised that, subject to the restrictive class system of the time, Madeleine was out of his league. He was also jealous, and not without good reason: when Madeleine's passion for him began to subside (a few months before L'Angelier's death), she became engaged to another, more suitable suitor, Mr William Minnoch. Nevertheless,

her affair with L'Angelier, during which they revelled in audacious clandestine meetings, endured until his death, which was due, it was forensically revealed, to a huge dose of arsenic.

Having arranged to meet Madeleine on the evening of Sunday, 22 March 1857, L'Angelier returned to his lodgings in the early hours of the next day feeling extremely unwell and vomiting profusely. He endured intense suffering, and by 11.15 a.m. he was dead. A search of his

Madeleine Smith. (Authors' collection)

belongings unearthed Madeleine's love letters – and his diary – and she was subsequently arrested and charged with his murder. Throughout their liaison, numerous letters were exchanged; those penned by Madeleine were coquettishly signed from 'Mimi' and were passionate and sexually explicit. When she was brought to trial on three criminal counts – since the fatal dose was considered to have been administered at the climax of an extended homicidal campaign – their content was publicly revealed and became the subject of prurient interest.

The trial was opened on Tuesday, 30 June at the High Court of Justiciary, in Edinburgh. Three judges presided over the proceedings, which lasted for nine days; every word and nuance of the evidence given by both prosecution and defence witnesses was reported. Not content with reading about the judicial theatricals, huge crowds gathered daily around the court in the hope of catching a glimpse of the notorious libertine as she entered and left the building. At twenty-one, Madeleine was an attractive, grey-eyed brunette with, it was said, a magnetic presence. She wore a brown silk dress, a white straw bonnet with ribbons and a black veil which she lifted, making no attempt to conceal her face. In her lavender-coloured kid gloves she clutched a small bottle of *sal volatile* and a handkerchief. Contrary to the impression given by the sentimental phrasing of her letters to her lover, she sat calmly in the dock; there were no bouts of weeping or hysterical outbursts. Such was her self-control that she sat dry-eyed whilst listening to details of the agonising death of L'Angelier – the man she had so passionately addressed as 'my own darling husband, my love, my all, my best beloved'. Madeleine was not permitted to speak, but she was ably defended by John Inglis, the Dean of Faculty, who in his closing speech conceded that his client *had* purchased arsenic, although she had done so quite openly – either for use as a skin lotion or to kill rats.

When the jurors returned a verdict of not guilty on one count and not proven on the other two, the court reacted with thunderous applause, echoed by the crowds outside. Arguments for and against the verdict were mooted ad infinitum not only in the press, but in the nation's ale-houses and clubs and at its firesides. But the question remained – was it a case of suicide or murder? It had been established that L'Angelier was a neurotic hypochondriac, prone to bouts of melancholia when disappointed in affairs of the heart, and often talking of suicide. Although there was no evidence that he had ever purchased arsenic, it was also suggested that, in addition to the arsenal of drugs he took for real or imagined indispositions, he was also, in the belief that it would enhance his virility, a secret arsenic-eater (not as uncommon as might be supposed – see Florence Maybrick). Although Mrs Mary Perry, his landlady and go-between, had testified that his diary contained references to other occasions on which he had suffered stomach pains after visiting Madeleine (caused, perhaps, not by cups of poisoned cocoa, but by his ingesting small doses of arsenic prior to love-making), this evidence had been deemed inadmissible. If he had suspected that Madeleine had poisoned him with a massive dose of arsenic that Sunday night – the measure taken in was estimated at eighty-two grains – then why had he not said so? Was it gallantry? Or was it a reluctance to admit that he had administered the dose himself, either intentionally or by accident?

Clearly, Madeleine had tired of L'Angelier and had set her sights on a more acceptable marriage to Minnoch. But would she have dared to kill him? She knew that he had a stash of incriminating letters which would reveal the scandalous nature of their affair. Not only would such exposure make her and her family into social pariahs – and give Minnoch every reason to call off the engagement – but it would also ruin any chance she had of ever entering into a respectable marriage in the society she inhabited, steeped as it was in religious dogma and tightly-bound by notions of respectability.

After her release, Madeleine lived a life that, though unconventional, was without further scandal. In London, in 1861, she married an artist, George Wardle, by whom she had two children. For a time she was involved with the avant-garde and the Pre-Raphaelite movement. She later lived in New York with her second husband, under the name of Lena Wardle Sheehy. Detailed accounts of her life can be found in numerous books; she died on 12 April 1928, aged ninety-three, and was buried in the Mount Hope Cemetery.

KC, MWO

FURTHER READING

Tennyson Jesse, F. (ed.), *Trial of Madeleine Smith* (Edinburgh: William Hodge and Company, 1927)

Blyth, H., *Madeleine Smith: A Famous Victorian Murder Trial* (London: Gerald Duckworth, 1975)

Sommer, Celestina (1827–1859)

The case of twenty-nine-year-old Celestina Sommer caused considerable controversy in Victorian England. Although the crime she committed was particularly brutal and, by its nature, guaranteed to horrify and enrage the general public, it was the question of her sanity that fired widespread and strongly held views, aired in the press through articles and letters and even mentioned during debates in the Houses of Parliament.

Many aspects of the drama were strikingly similar to those in the case of Louise Masset; both women were educated, musical, and had given birth to an illegitimate child that had imposed real or imagined restrictions on their pursuit of what they perceived as a respectable mode of life. They both lived in London and fostered their children with minders. Celestina's father, William Christmas, was a silversmith, and the family lived at King Square, Islington. On 20 December 1845, when she was in her eighteenth year, Celestina gave birth to her illegitimate daughter, Celestine, at the home of Mrs Julia Harrington, in Hackney, and the child remained there until she was ten years old, at a charge of ten shillings a month.

On 12 August 1854, at St Mary's Church, Islington, Celestina married Charles Sommer, a Prussian émigre who was an engraver by profession. Eighteen months later, at ten o'clock on the evening of 16 February 1856, Celestina took her daughter to her house at 18 Linton Street, in Islington, led the child down to the basement kitchen and from there to a coal cellar, where she cut her throat. Charles Sommer was not at home at the time but the young maidservant, Rachel Munt, lying awake in her bed in the kitchen, heard the crime being committed and later testified to hearing the muffled groans of the dying girl.

Alerted by Rachel's sister, the police discovered the body in the cellar and arrested Charles and Celestina Sommer; as Charles had not been in the house at the time of the murder he was subsequently released without charge. Initial press reports estimated the murdered girl's age as fourteen and stated that Celestina had, at first, said that the girl's father was her unnamed, deceased brother. She confessed to the killing shortly after her arrest.

Celestina Sommer's trial at the Old Bailey was held on Thursday, 10 April 1856, before Mr Justice Cresswell and Mr Justice Crampton; she was defended by William Ballantine. She was described in the *Daily Telegraph* as having 'the appearance of a girl of fifteen. She is of the most diminutive stature and her countenance does not exhibit the slightest appearance of ferocity.'

The young maid, Rachel Munt, was able to describe the murder of the girl in great detail, even recalling her terrified cries for mercy as her mother prepared to cut her throat. She also testified that the relationship between Celestina and her husband, Charles, was one of disharmony. 'He used to beat her,' she explained. 'She seemed very unhappy. I often used to see her crying.'

Evidence was given that, whilst in police custody, Celestina's behaviour had been bizarre. She talked to herself incessantly, comparing the theatrical performances of two contemporary Shakespearean actors – Charles, son of Edward Kean, and Samuel Phelps.

Although the jurors had been presented with a wealth of damning evidence against Celestina, William Ballantine urged them to consider the possibility that, at the time of the murder, she was not responsible for her actions. The jurors rejected this plea and found her guilty as charged: she was sentenced to death.

A petition for a reprieve was forwarded to the Home Secretary, Sir George Grey, by Mr A. H. Dymond, Secretary to the Society for the Abolition of Capital Punishment, with the result that the sentence of death was commuted first to transportation and then to penal detention for life. The case of Celestina Sommer remained controversial, and her reprieve was fiercely contested in the press and studied by 'alienists', a term given to proto-psychiatrists who specialised in the field of insanity and culpability in acts of violence. Some commentators suggested that she was spared the gallows because she was an attractive young woman, and the Home Secretary was vigorously challenged on that score.

Celestina spent six months in Newgate before being transferred to Millbank Prison in October. On 26 December the following year, she was sent to the notoriously harsh women's prison at Brixton. During her time at Brixton, her mental and physical ill-health was further exacerbated by the rigours and privations of prison life, cruelly contrasting with the middle-class comfort to which she had been accustomed in the well-appointed family home in North London. Her behaviour became more and more eccentric; she often sang very loudly and made inappropriate responses during chapel services and, predictably, became an object of amusement to the other inmates. She was often unwell and confined to the prison infirmary and, with her sanity eroded, she was sent on 9 November 1859 to the privately owned Fisherton House Lunatic Asylum, near Salisbury, where between 1850 and 1870, prior to the building of Broadmoor, many of the 'patients' had been convicted of murder and were classified as 'criminal lunatics'.

By this time Celestina had become incontinent: she was soiling her clothing and bed sheets. She was also clearly distressed and cried constantly. She died at Fisherton on 11 April 1859, aged thirty-one, barely three years after she had killed her daughter. There were no winners in this tragic case: a child, inconveniently born and unwanted throughout her short life, brutally murdered by her mother in the dark recesses of a coal cellar. Celestina's life was also ruined and cut short – her suffering in body and mind after the murder was surely as punitive and painful as any she might have endured at the hands of the hangman.

KC

FURTHER READING

Clarke, K., *Deadly Dilemmas* (London: Mango Books, forthcoming)

Staunton, Harriet (1841–1877)

The death of Harriet Staunton in 1877 was, without a doubt, extremely disturbing, but the actual cause of her demise remains debatable. Despite being of low intelligence and uncertain temperament, Harriet was raised by her mother to function reasonably well in society, and a substantial legacy from a great aunt ensured that she was able to indulge a love of fashionable clothes (although her abundant plaits of false hair were out-of-date, reminiscent of the eccentric Christiana Edmunds).

It was in 1873, when she was thirty-three, that she met twenty-three-year-old Louis Staunton, a dark-haired, moustachioed clerk to an auctioneer in Streatham, and his twenty-year-old girlfriend, Alice Rhodes, who was described in the press as a 'flabby-faced young woman'. Her sister, Elizabeth, was married to Louis's brother, Patrick Staunton. Louis saw Harriet and her money as an easy target, and for her part she was gullible and easily swayed by his advances, little knowing that her involvement with him would lead to her gruesome death. When Louis and Harriet announced their engagement, Harriet's mother tried to have her daughter detained in an asylum, but in this she failed and the marriage went ahead on 16 June 1875. Three weeks later, Harriet's mother called at the house in Brixton where her daughter was living but, shortly after, received letters from both Harriet and Louis informing her that she was not welcome. Separated from her mother and at the mercy of her husband, his girlfriend Alice, and Patrick and Elizabeth, Harriet became isolated and, deprived of sufficient food, her health deteriorated and she became unkempt. Her mental and physical condition became even worse after she gave birth to a son, Thomas, in March 1876.

By August of that year, Louis had set up home with Alice in a house called Little Grays, in Kent, and deposited Harriet and the child a mile away in Frith Cottage, ostensibly in the care of Patrick and Elizabeth. There she was confined to a squalid upstairs room, deprived not only of companionship but of even the most basic washing facilities. Predictably, the child also suffered and, on 8 April the following year, when he became ill, Patrick and Elizabeth took him to Guy's Hospital, in London, where he died the following day. Four days later, Harriet, in a wretched state, was taken to a lodging house at 34 Forbes Road, Penge, in south London. Her appearance was described as 'more like a corpse than a living woman', and by the next day she, too, was dead – the cause given on the death certificate was 'cerebral disease' or 'apoplexy'. However, at a subsequent inquest Harriet's body was found to be filthy, riddled with lice, and so malnourished that she weighed little more than five stones. The cause of death was changed to one of 'starvation and neglect'.

The murder trial of the Stauntons (Louis, Patrick and Elizabeth – along with Alice Rhodes) was opened at the Old Bailey on Wednesday, 19 September 1877, before Mr Justice Henry Hawkins. There was tremendous interest in the case, for it had all the ingredients of a Gothic horror novel – many of those who were permitted to witness the trial were fashionably dressed ladies who behaved as though they were at the theatre, some even observing the proceedings through opera glasses. Those denied entry gathered outside in vast numbers, well-versed in the full horror of the case through lurid newspaper reports. The prosecution was led by the Attorney General, Sir John Holker, but the accused were fortunate to have on the defence team the redoubtable advocate Edward Clarke, who went on to triumph in his defence of Adelaide Bartlett in 1886. Clarke was adamant that Harriet's death was not caused by malevolent neglect but by medical conditions such as tuberculosis, diabetes or meningitis and, in part, her own refusal to eat due to her alcoholism – although the post-mortem revealed 'no sign of intemperance'. The prosecution, however, produced the Stauntons' sixteen-year-old maidservant, Clara Brown, who (though she was later accused of perjury) gave a harrowing account of the cruelty inflicted upon Harriet by the four in the dock. Alice and Elizabeth wept hysterically while this testimony was being given. Despite Clarke's efforts, and finding themselves influenced by the perceived bias of the judge against the accused, the jurors followed the lead of the maid's testimony and, on 26 September, returned a verdict of guilty against all four defendants. Clarke's arguments for the defence, however, clearly registered with his medical peers, for a letter was published in *The Lancet* on 6 October, commending a petition signed by 700 physicians (including Sir William Jenner) and protesting at the jurors' disregard of the medical evidence of disease. This was presented to the Home Secretary, and, on 14 October, the death sentence on the three Stauntons was commuted to penal servitude for life; Alice Rhodes was released without charge.

Whilst in prison, Patrick Staunton died of consumption (in 1881); his wife, Elizabeth, was released in November 1883. Louis Staunton served the last period of his sentence in Dartmoor Prison and seemed to show some remorse for his heartless treatment of Harriet, but still insisted that her death was caused by her refusal to take food. He was released from Pentonville Prison on 16 September 1897, aged forty-six, after twenty years' imprisonment. He wrote a letter – widely published – in which he protested his innocence. Reports of his life post-prison vary: it seems that he married Alice Rhodes in Brighton in 1898; it is generally agreed that he died in 1934, aged eighty-three; there appears to be no consensus on the question of whether his last days were spent in Australia.

Clearly, Louis Staunton and his cohorts treated Harriet appallingly, and the imprisonment and deprivation they forced upon her must have contributed to her death. Whether this was intentional we cannot know; but the fact that they witnessed her distressing mental and physical deterioration without seeking medical care shows a barely believable degree of callousness towards an extremely vulnerable woman who had done them no harm.

KC

FURTHER READING

Atlay, J. B. (ed.), *Trial of the Stauntons* (Edinburgh: William Hodge and Company, 1911)

Cox, D., *Brotherly Love or the Cudham Quartet* (Buckingham: Barracuda Books, 1989)

Stead, W. T. (1849–1912)

A gadfly pricking at the skin of the establishment, William Thomas Stead, as editor of the *Pall Mall Gazette*, forged a style of investigative journalism which threatened to expose the corruption running in the bloodstream of the average Victorian institution, sometimes irrespective of whether it was there or not.

In the aftermath of the Maiden Tribute affair, Stead was prosecuted on charges of kidnapping and indecently assaulting the teenage Eliza Armstrong. He elected to defend himself at the Old Bailey. Across the well of the dock, appearing for the prosecution, were Sir Richard Webster (the Attorney General), Harry Poland and Robert Wright. These were distinguished foes, concerned in many of the late Victorian period's most celebrated trials, and, perhaps inevitably, Stead was convicted and sentenced to three months' imprisonment; he did not shirk his punishment, although he wore his convict status (predictably) as a badge of honour and remained largely unmoved to personal remorse for the sufferings of poor Eliza. In other prisoners, such an unapologetic and unreformed disposition would have been all but intolerable to the authorities, but Stead, a willing martyr to his campaign, held all the cards. He had established a popular niche, forcing the readers of his newspaper to confront genuine unfairness, mistreatment and abuse. A little collateral damage along the way was held to be unavoidable – it was eggs for omelettes in the offices of the *Pall Mall Gazette*, and sentimental attitudes to Eliza Armstrong's psychological wellbeing were not to be permitted to distort the grander message.

Restored to his editorship after his release from prison, Stead had little time to wait before another criminal cause loomed into his purview. In 1887, Stead decided that Israel Lipski had *not* murdered Miriam Angel, and the pages of his newspaper were again decorated with passionate invective, much of it of the most hot-headed and unreliable sort. Too many column inches were given over to what was nothing more than a red herring: Stead thought that, if he could find *another* sale of nitric acid, to someone *other* than Lipski, somewhere in the vicinity of Batty Street, at some point before – but not too long before – the murder, then this would cast doubt on the security of Lipski's conviction. Naturally, he found one, to an unidentified patron of Maximilian Buchner's shop on Houndsditch, a few minutes' walk from the scene of the crime. But Buchner sold pure nitric acid, buying it, pure, from his wholesaler. Lipski's acid – that is, the acid found on Miriam's body, in Lipski's mouth, on Lipski's coat, and in the bottle discovered in Miriam's bedroom – was an adulterated mixture of nitric and sulphuric acid. Charles Moore, from whom Lipski had bought his acid, sold an adulterated mixture of nitric and sulphuric acid from his shop on Backchurch Lane. Buchner's man was never in the frame, and this absence of reasonable attention to detail characterised Stead's frantic attempts to clear Lipski of a crime which the evidence clearly suggested that he had indeed committed. A succession of rumours found their way into print: Rosenbloom, for example – one of the two men whom Lipski had accused of the murder – was said to be shedding weight fast, and this was implied to be an indication of his guilt; Schmuss – Rosenbloom's co-conspirator in Lipski's baseless vision – was this, or that, or behaving this way, or that way. The details hardly matter to us; they hardly mattered to Stead.

On 21 August 1887, Lipski confessed to the murder: he was hanged the next morning. The *Pall Mall Gazette*, which had spent weeks tirelessly agitating for the case for Lipski's innocence, now, under the shameless headline 'All's Well that Ends Well', sought to justify its previous stance: 'Those who have imputed to us either in praise or in censure the usurpation of the functions of a Supreme Court of Criminal Appeal are entirely mistaken,' it declared. 'We neither merit the praise nor deserve the blame.' One cannot help but feel that those caught up in the tempest of Stead's journalistic tactics – an assortment of individuals not limited to Rosenbloom and Schmuss – might have found the question of whether the newspaper had '[usurped] the functions of a Supreme Court of Criminal Appeal' to be perfectly immaterial. As Eliza Armstrong could have told them, neither their reputations nor their feelings were ever likely to be taken into time-consuming and impulse-stifling consideration by the *Pall Mall Gazette*; trifles such as these were not visible from Stead's vantage point.

Stead died in 1912, going down with the *Titanic*, but, obligingly, he returned to the sphere of the living almost immediately in the form of a spirit and made regular appearances at séances in various parts of the globe for several years to come. As early as 1913, he had been introduced to a French medium named Madame Hyver by a mutual acquaintance (actually the Duchess de Pomar, who was also technically dead), and in 1919 he consented to pose for a photograph, surrounded by something that looked quite a lot like a blanket, but was probably ectoplasm. By 1921, after many years of unutterably banal conversation from beyond the grave, Stead had provided enough material to fill a book, and so one was published, 'by' him, 'through' Madame Hyver, and 'edited by' his daughter Estelle. Its typically uncompromising title was *Communication with the Next World: The Right and Wrong Methods: A Text Book*. Regrettably, so keen was Stead to dispense his advice to aspiring mediums – for example, 'After a difficult materialization a medium should bathe in salt water, hot or cold' – that he entirely neglected to say whether he had taken advantage of his status as a dead man to neaten some of the loose ends he left behind in life. Had he apologised to Rosenbloom and Schmuss, for example? Had he wept with Miriam Angel, averting his eyes discreetly from her tattered wings? Was Eliza Armstrong truly happy?

Perhaps we shall never know.

MWO

FURTHER READING

Plowden, A., *The Case of Eliza Armstrong* (BBC: London, 1974)

Stevenson, Thomas (1838–1908)

The foremost scientific analyst of the late Victorian period, plying his trade for the Home Office, Stevenson was a Yorkshireman who had developed his practice at Guy's Hospital, where he followed in the footsteps of Alfred Swaine Taylor, author of a potentially catastrophic chemical error in the case of Thomas Smethurst.

Stevenson did much to shore up the credibility of medical analysis in the years after his 1872 appointment to the Home Office, putting in regular appearances at major poisoning trials, several of which are discoverable elsewhere in this book. Adelaide Bartlett, Florence Maybrick, George Lamson and Thomas Neill Cream all suffered to greater or lesser extents from his diligence and curiosity, and the *British Medical Journal* described him as 'a wholesome terror to the would-be poisoner'.

Perhaps Stevenson's strangest case came at Huntingdon in 1898. Annie Holmes, a local widow of restricted means, had succumbed to a dose of strychnine early in January; from the circumstances, it appeared that she had imagined herself (incorrectly) to be pregnant, and had asked her cousin, Walter Horford, to provide something to procure a miscarriage. The packet of powder that she received in return proved fatal, and Horford (who, it was believed, Annie thought to be the father of the child) was arrested. Although the unsigned letter accompanying the powder gave certain reassurances – 'Take in a little water. Is quite harmless. Will come over in a day or two' – poor Annie had ingested ten grains of strychnine. Less than a grain and a half, Stevenson confidently testified, 'would certainly kill an adult', and he warned that fatalities often occurred at much lower doses, 'a quarter to half a grain'.

There was little doubt about the verdict. On 28 December 1897, Horford had acquired a poisoner's treasure trove at a pharmacist's shop: ninety grains of strychnine in powder form, a pound of arsenic, a fluid ounce of prussic acid, and a shilling's worth of carbolic acid. Since he was a farmer by occupation, the transaction raised no suspicion. In the wake of Annie's death, however, not all of Horford's poison stock could be accounted for. There was also the tantalising suggestion, never quite confirmed publicly, that Horsford had done away with three other people over the years, all by similar means. He was executed in Cambridge Prison in June 1898.

For Stevenson, the case enabled him to break the shackles of witness-box typecasting, but only to some extent. The story is a difficult one to confirm, but it is said that, at one point during the trial, 'one of the barristers upset the packet of strychnine ... Realising the danger of a single grain of the strychnine not being recovered, Justice Hawkins ordered Dr Stevenson to go down on his hands and knees and pick up every atom of the powder before he would allow the trial to be resumed.' Stevenson, though ever an obedient servant of the law, was sixty at the time. He survived the experience, and would go on to give evidence in the trials of Edwardian murderers such as George Chapman and Arthur Devereux before his death in 1908. His passing finally confirmed the handing over of the analytical flame from Guy's to Queen Mary's Hospital, and the path was cleared for the rise of the celebrated analysts of the early twentieth century (most notably, Bernard Spilsbury).

MWO

Swanson, Donald Sutherland (1848–1924)

On 13 December 1867, a Fenian bomb placed outside London's Clerkenwell House of Detention exploded, causing widespread damage to person and property alike and killing several people in the process (see The Clerkenwell Explosion). This bombing, an attempt to free a Fenian activist who was being held there, was one of many throughout the Victorian period, and drew attention to a new form of extreme political dissent: terrorism. The public were fearful of the ruthlessness and indiscriminate nature of what was essentially attempted mass murder, as was the head of the Metropolitan Police at the time, Commissioner Richard Mayne. The answer, Mayne thought, was to bolster the police presence in the metropolis, and so a mass recruitment drive was decided upon and executed.

In March 1868, a young Scotsman who was working as a clerk in London's Seething Lane area spied an advertisement in the *Daily Telegraph*. Within days, this son of a distiller from Thurso had written an 'expression of interest' letter to Scotland Yard, concluding, 'I am nineteen years of age and do not so much desire a large salary as a good opening at a moderate one.' It was obvious that this young man had the ability to see the bigger picture, something which the future Commissioner Sir Charles Warren similarly acknowledged when he later appointed him chief investigator in charge of the most infamous manhunt of the Victorian era, the chase for Jack the Ripper. After all, Donald Swanson was, as his contemporary John Sweeney once stated, 'one of the best class of officers'.

However, Swanson's future as a successful detective was not initially clear. Upon joining the Metropolitan Police he found himself working and living at A Division's King Street Station in Whitehall and, just six months into his new job, he courted trouble when he was late for evening roll-call at the section house.

This would not be the only occasion on which Swanson broke the rules in his early police years. In April 1869, he was cautioned by his superiors for accepting money from a prisoner, although he returned the shilling to the man the following day; the following February, a yet-again-late Swanson was caught clambering over the railings at King Street in an attempt to sneak back into the section house without being seen. Clearly, this was not a good way to start life in the police, but the young Swanson did show traits of promise. Like many good detectives, he exhibited ingenuity and a willingness to tread the fine line between formality and daring; he was a man who would not be trifled with.

A series of promotions in the early 1870s brought about transfers to Y Division (Highgate) and K Division (Bow), and by now Swanson's career was marked by discipline and respect. In 1876, Swanson found himself back in A Division as a detective, and the following year he received the first of many commendations for his work in a case of theft. While working on the case, Swanson liaised closely with Detective Chief Inspector George Clarke, who would later find himself embroiled in the Trial of the Detectives.

Another commendation, 'for energy and zeal displayed in making numerous enquiries in the case of Percy Lefroy Mapleton', saw Swanson awarded £5 in 1881; this was one of many notable cases he worked upon during his career. His reputation for discretion and thoroughness meant he was often called upon by his superiors to deal with delicate cases, such as the recoveries of the Countess of Bective's jewels and a stolen Gainsborough painting. However, it was his position as Commissioner Warren's 'eyes and ears' during the Jack the Ripper investigation which consolidated Swanson's place in the lasting consciousness of the public.

By November 1887, Swanson had risen to the rank of Chief Inspector within CID, Scotland Yard. Barely a year on, the most notorious serial killer in history began his despicable campaign. The public were panicked, Scotland Yard flummoxed. To aid the police on the ground, Warren called upon Swanson's ability to examine the minutiae of the case in the hope that he could bring structure to the complex investigation. His remit was to review every report made on the case and if necessary act upon it. This impacted heavily upon Swanson's working day. 'I had to be at the office at half-past eight in the morning,' he was to later state about that period. 'Then I had to read through all the papers that had come in, which took me till eleven p.m., and sometimes one and two in the morning; then I had to go to Whitechapel and see the officers — generally getting home between two and three am.' Swanson's deep involvement with the case has necessitated that the handwritten notes which he made in his own copy of Sir Robert Anderson's autobiography, *The Lighter Side of my Official Life* – famously naming a suspect for the murders as 'Kosminski' – are typically thought to go some way towards substantiating Anderson's bold statement that Jack the Ripper was positively identified by a witness.

Donald Swanson retired from the police in July 1903, taking time to indulge himself in his passion for fishing during summer jaunts back to his native Scotland. On 25 November 1924, Swanson died at the family home in New Malden, and was interred at Kingston Cemetery a few days later. His grandson, James, giving an indication of Swanson's capacities in later life, said of him, 'There was nothing old about him – he had a mind like a rapier.'

NRAB

Further Reading

Wood, A., *Swanson: The Life and Times of a Victorian Detective* (London: Mango Books, forthcoming)

T, U, V

Tanner, Richard (1831–1873)

Until 1842, the detective aspect of London's policing arrangements fell under the remit of the Bow Street Police Office, whose staff was better known as the Bow Street Runners. However, it was then decided that a detective team, consisting of one inspector and six sergeants, should be created and based in Scotland Yard. The Detective Department, as it was eventually named, would remain at the forefront of detecting crime in London for just over thirty years, until the scandal that was the Trial of the Detectives brought about a complete restructuring and the birth of the world-famous Criminal Investigation Department (CID). Rather than recruit new detectives, the Metropolitan Police retained the services of the Bow Street Runners – men such as Nicholas Pearce, Stephen Thornton and Jonathan Whicher – and over the years the Detective Department expanded to include, among others, a sharp-minded young man named Richard Tanner.

By all accounts, Tanner was an eager detective. One of the first cases to benefit from his enthusiasm was the Stepney Murder. The facts were these: the wealthy Mrs Mary Emsley was found brutally murdered at her home just off the Mile End Road on 17 August 1860. She owned numerous properties, which she rented out. Her income amounted to around £5,000 per annum, a substantial amount for the period. She hired Walter Emm as her rent collector, and he, alarmed after calling at Mrs Emsley's home for four days straight with no answer, contacted her solicitor. The pair went to her home and found Mrs Emsley dead from severe head injuries. The police were called for. When they inspected the house, they found that there were no signs of forced entry – a tell-tale sign that the victim knew her killer.

A former Metropolitan policeman, James Mullins, had worked for Mrs Emsley as a plasterer at many of her properties. He had been dismissed from the force for larceny, and soon suspicion turned upon him. However, no evidence could be found against Mullins, and so the investigation continued until the offer of a £300 reward for information drew the fateful attention of the murderer.

Upon hearing news of a reward, Mullins turned up at the home of Richard Tanner. Tanner invited him in, and Mullins told him that he had seen Mrs Emsley's rent collector, Walter Emm, acting suspiciously by moving some parcels around in a shed next to her house; Mullins guessed that they contained items stolen from Mrs Emsley's home. The next morning they went to the shed, along with Emm. Mullins was asked to point out the parcel which he had seen Emm move; he did so without hesitation. The parcel was opened and indeed found to contain items such as spoons, all belonging to Mrs Emsley. Emm denied all knowledge of this. He ought not to have worried, as Tanner, privately, had already begun to suspect that the parcel had been planted by Mullins beforehand.

Tanner then asked Mullins to point out where he was standing when he saw Emm's 'suspicious' act. Mullins stated that he was on the other side of the road. Tanner, looking at the line of sight from the spot towards the shed and noticing that it was not a direct one, asked a question to which he already felt sure that he knew the answer: how had Mullins managed to see what Emm was doing inside the shed from that vantage point? Mullins faltered. Soon, other items belonging to Mrs Emsley began to turn up: a small pencil case belonging to her had, for example, been bought by a barman from a woman he knew as Mrs Mullins shortly after the murder. A spoon similar to the ones found in the parcel in the shed was located at Mullins's home, along with tape which matched the tape wrapped around the parcel and a plasterer's hammer capable of causing the fatal injuries. Mullins was tried and convicted of Mrs Emsley's murder, and executed on 19 November 1860.

Tanner's nose for suspicion saw him assigned to his most famous case, the murder of Thomas Briggs, in 1864; here, he successfully tracked Franz Müller from Hackney to New York. A popular man, Tanner also had a nose for a good bet. Because of his interest in horse racing, Tanner was frequently assigned to make police arrangements at classic horse meets, including the Oaks, the Derby and the St Leger. By the late 1860s, Tanner's health had waned, so much so that he retired from the force in 1869. He retreated to Winchester, where he ran the White Swan Hotel. On 19 October 1873, aged forty-three, he died, leaving a wife and three children.

NRAB

Taylor, Louisa Jane (1846–1883)

After the death of her seventy-two-year-old husband in March 1882, it didn't take thirty-six-year-old Louisa Taylor very long to find a replacement meal ticket. By August she had ingratiated herself into the home of eighty-five-year-old William Tregillis and his eighty-one-year-old wife, Mary Ann, in their two-roomed flat in Plumstead, south-east London. As old friends of her late husband, the couple had offered Louisa – described as an attractive brunette – board and lodging in return for the care of Mary Ann, who was quite frail. William, who had recently spent time in an asylum, was generally a credulous and trusting individual; but he did notice that – soon after Louisa joined the household – his wife's health unexpectedly deteriorated, and a number of items went missing. Louisa was systematically fleecing the old couple and even suggested that, once Mary Ann was dead, she and William – and his pension book – might elope together. When the old man protested that his wife was still alive, Louisa predicted that Mary Ann would soon be dead. Her regular paramour, a watercress seller called Edward Martin, did not seem to enter the equation.

Within three weeks, Mary Ann had become so ill that a local physician, Dr Smith, was calling daily. Louisa persuaded him to prescribe for her a regular supply of sugar of lead (lead acetate), which she said she needed for her complexion. Meanwhile, Mary Ann began to vomit so badly that the doctor asked Louisa to provide samples for analysis, but she kept making excuses, saying that to do such a thing would be 'nauseating and disgusting'. The discovery of Louisa's treachery came after she accosted William as he left the post office, having drawn about £10 in back payments of his pension; she persuaded him to hand it over, saying that she would give it to his wife, but she was seen later in the street with the money in her hand. This seemed to switch on a light in William Tregillis's brain and, on Friday, 9 October, he summoned the police, accusing Louisa of theft. A police doctor was also summoned, and he, examining the stricken Mary Ann, found a blue line around her gums – a sign of poisoning. The discovery caused Dr Smith acute embarrassment: he had apparently been distracted from his patient's suffering by Louisa's prepossessing complexion.

On 10 October, Mary Ann made a formal statement accusing Louisa of poisoning her; a magistrate was ushered to the elderly lady's sickbed especially for the purpose. Louisa was subsequently brought before Woolwich Magistrates' Court charged 'with systematically administering sugar of lead or some other poison'. So ended the poisoning campaign; but, even though she was free of Louisa, Mary Ann could not regain her health, and she died on 23 October. At the subsequent inquest it was confirmed that the post-mortem carried out by the Home Office analyst, Dr Thomas Stevenson, revealed the presence of lead acetate. Four days later, Louisa appeared in court once more, this time on a charge of the wilful murder of Mary Ann Tregillis.

The trial of Louisa Taylor was opened at the Old Bailey on 14 December 1882, before Mr Justice Stephen (who, seven years later and in a state of precarious sanity, presided over the trial of Florence Maybrick). The defence objected to Mary Ann's bedside statement being read in court, but Mr Justice Stephen ruled it admissible. On Friday, 15 December, the jury returned a verdict of guilty; sentencing Louisa, the judge described her crime as 'a cruel, treacherous and hypocritical murder'. She was hanged by William Marwood at Maidstone on 2 January 1883 – the last woman to be executed at the prison.

Many women, fearing destitution, have been driven to resort to all manner of crime – prostitution, baby farming, theft and fraud – but Louisa seems to have chosen a different path. Her means of survival was to gain the confidence of elderly people before stealing from them; it was suspected that she may have hastened her husband's exit from the world before homing in on the Tregillises. Yet the rewards were far from lucrative. Had she succeeded in getting her hands on William Tregillis's pension, it would have realised a paltry sum, amounting to less than a pound a week in today's currency. One suspects that she was a heartless woman who used people purely for monetary gain and failed to form any lasting relationships – in this, she was reminiscent of another devious poisoner of the elderly, Catherine Wilson, who befriended her victims and, while supposedly caring for them, watched them die in agony. The public clearly felt that Louisa Taylor deserved to die: there were no heated debates in the press or fervent pleas for leniency. Nor was there any sign of Edward Martin, the watercress seller, who admitted regretfully that, on one occasion, he had unquestioningly purchased sugar of lead for

Louisa. Whilst awaiting execution, her only visitors were the prison chaplain and matron. Not a single friend could be found, and the execution failed to draw the vast crowds that normally gathered on these occasions. Only a few passers-by even bothered to look up at the black flag raised over the prison after her death.

KC

FURTHER READING

Smith-Hughes, J., *Eight Studies in Justice* (London: Cassell, 1953)

Terrorism

Terrorism begins in the memory. Even as late as the 1840s, echoes of the troubled years at the end of the eighteenth century persisted: in revolutionary France, 'terror' had been a state-sponsored programme of violence and oppression, and 'terrorism' was, therefore, synonymous with the brutality of a radicalised executive branch, or the careless despotism of mass participation, or a state apparatus which had grown out of proportion to the freedom of citizens. Manifestations of this sort of terrorism were to be avoided by sensible Britons, and early attempts to introduce local systems of policing often attracted resistance. One pseudonymous letter, sent in March 1840 to the *Reading Mercury*, reacted to the idea of a 'Rural Police' in these uncompromising terms: 'It is our duty most resolutely to oppose any system of terrorism from whatever quarter it may proceed, and in whatever shape it may appear.' The following year, the taking of the national census inspired considerable popular suspicion and opposition, particularly among those who remembered that 'God condemned David for the numbering of the people'. ('A paternal government should always know how many children it has to provide for,' countered the *Western Times*. 'Moreover there is some difference between our beloved Queen Victoria and King David.')

As time went on, terrorism became increasingly identified with the political dissension of the Irish separatist movement. Spectacles such as the Clerkenwell Explosion and the Phoenix

Park Murders tended to draw the battle lines; by 1883, all was in place for a sustained mainland dynamite campaign, concentrating on the capital and partly funded by sympathetic agitators in America. One series of blasts, on 15 March, aimed squarely at the heart of the establishment – Whitehall, even Scotland Yard itself. Two senior detectives narrowly escaped death (the desk at which Inspector Sweeney had been recently sitting was 'blown to pieces'), and 'curiously enough, a mass of documents dealing with the dynamite conspiracy' were lost. The response of the Yard was to formalise their arrangements for coping with the new threat: Special Branch was founded, its sole purpose to learn about and deter terrorist acts, or to find the perpetrators of any acts that *did* occur. At the Home Office, Robert Anderson, whose professional history included extensive anti-Fenian work in Ireland itself, was the figurehead of this new expression of determination, but the terrorists were equally resolute, hitting the railways and the underground system, the Carlton Club, and London Bridge. In January 1885, explosions occurred at Westminster Hall and the Tower of London, which was then a functioning military garrison. Nevertheless, the Yard claimed considerable success: cooperation with the port authorities (particularly Liverpool) was improved, and some plots – notably one to disrupt Queen Victoria's jubilee celebrations in 1887 – were safely snuffed out.

When the Fenians rested, Special Branch found themselves to be interested in other groups with similar methodologies. Anarchists and socialists began to find their voice, and, in 1898, Vladimir Bourtzeff and Klement Wierzbicki were sentenced to imprisonment after publishing a pamphlet in which they advocated the assassination of Tsar Nicholas II. The frame of reference had changed: as Sir Basil Thomson observed in his book *The Story of Scotland Yard*, the objectives of the terrorists of the 1880s made one yearn for the simpler political ideals of the previous generation:

> The Fenian movement [of the 1860s] had been regarded by Irishmen as a rising for independence. The movement of the eighties was intended to bring the British people to their knees and to force them to crave for mercy at the hands of Ireland.

Smashing the state had become a desirable aspiration, and acts of public violence went along with it, hand in glove. Occasionally, there were lone wolves, such as Martial Bourdin, a Frenchman who blew himself up outside Greenwich Observatory in 1894: Bourdin had connections with West End socialist clubs (such as the Autonomie Club), but it was not established that he had been at the sharp end of a wider conspiracy. By 1929, when J. F. Moylan came to write his own history of Scotland Yard, 'Indian agitators' and 'suffragettes' could be added to the list of dissident terrorist groups with which Special Branch officers had had to deal.

The gradual semantic shift in the meaning of terrorism did little to assuage official fears about terrorism's near-neighbour, civil disobedience. *Barnaby Rudge*, one of the early novels of Charles Dickens, evoked the Gordon Riots of the century before, and occasional flourishes of localised violence aligned themselves unobtrusively with the volatile national and international zeitgeist. The Jack the Ripper murders of 1888 occurred in a city whose socioeconomic characteristics were those of Paris in 1871, just before the Commune – as Philippe Marlière describes it, 'its western side a playground for the rich, the east an overpopulated slum'. The strange idealisation of the Ripper has sometimes led him to be cast as a social reformer with terrorist sensibilities, but nobody ought to give this idea any more consideration than it really deserves.

MWO

FURTHER READING

Thompson, Sir B., *The Story of Scotland Yard* (New York: The Literary Guild, 1936)

Thames Mystery, The (1873)

With a total length of over 200 miles, it is no surprise that the River Thames has proved an all-too-convenient receptacle for the evidence of murder (amongst other crimes and misdemeanours).

In 1857, for example, the press eagerly reported the discovery of a bag containing various bones and a small quantity of flesh, deposited by the river on one of the stone supports of Waterloo Bridge. News of supposed clues to the 'Waterloo Bridge Mystery' continued to be published for well over a decade, and in 1872 it was claimed that a soldier serving in India had confessed to the crime. Nevertheless, the case was destined to remain officially unsolved – although, in his 1910 memoirs, *The Lighter Side of my Official Life*, former Metropolitan Police Assistant Commissioner Sir Robert Anderson would claim that the victim had been identified as an Italian police agent whose embedded mission had become known to the republican revolutionaries with whom he had ingratiated himself.

By 1873, however, the 'Thames Carpet Bag Mystery', as it was also known, was about to become old news. On 5 September 1873, an officer of the Thames River Police located what was subsequently identified as the left side of a woman's limbless torso in the mud of the Thames foreshore in Battersea. At least a portion of an opposing half (some reports simply state 'a right breast') was soon retrieved close to the nearby Nine Elms railway station, and when this too was taken to be viewed by the assistant divisional police surgeon at the local workhouse, the pair were declared a match. The public's sense of horror would only have increased as further parts of the unfortunate victim were located: a pelvis in Woolwich, a segment of the left arm, again at Battersea, and a portion of the scalp and face in Limehouse, in the heart of east London's dockyards.

Examination of the various body parts (under the guidance of Dr Thomas Bond) elicited little more than the conclusions that they 'corresponded' to one another and that they appeared to have been 'neatly disarticulated'. Aside from the brief suggestion that an 'association of escaped lunatics' might have been responsible for the 'Thames Mystery', the identity of the victim, that of her murderer, and the cause of – and reason for – her death were to remain unknown. The newspapers would eventually move on, but this was not to be the last such grisly conundrum.

Seven months later, in June of 1874, another female torso was dragged from the river not far to the west of Battersea, in Putney. The torso, this time with one remaining leg in situ, had supposedly been partially dissolved in chlorinated lime (which, it turns out, is actually remarkably inefficient for such a task); but the subsequent inquest did not reach a verdict of 'wilful murder', and thus no criminal investigation was ever launched.

There followed a lull of nearly five years before the next comparable murder, when portions of the body of Julia Martha Thomas were thrown from Richmond Bridge by Kate Webster on 4 March 1879.

The Thames would continue to offer opportunities for the criminally inclined, but the next series of sequential discoveries to grasp public attention in a manner akin to 'The Thames Mystery' was a decade away – see the Thames Torso Murderer.

TNB

FURTHER READING

Fitzgerald, P., *Chronicles of Bow Street Police Office* (London: Chapman and Hall, 1888)

Whittington-Egan, R., *Mr Atherstone Leaves the Stage* (Stroud: Amberley, 2015)

Thames Torso Murderer, The (1887–1889)

By 1887, retrieving body parts from the River Thames was nothing new (see Kate Webster and The Thames Mystery). An escalation in such incidents, however, was to see four cases within a little over two years, and gave rise to speculation that Jack the Ripper was not the only serial killer stalking London's streets during the late 1880s.

The story begins in the Essex town of Rainham. There, on 11 May 1887, the legless lower portion of a woman's torso, wrapped in canvas, was spotted floating in the river close to the industrial area known as Rainham Ferry. Almost a month later, on 5 June, a thigh, similarly packaged, was discovered upstream at London's Temple Stairs. The upper portion of the torso resurfaced on the same day on the edges of Battersea Park.

On 30 June, a boy discovered an arm in the Regent's Canal in St Pancras; finally, on the next day, two legs were given over to the police, reportedly also dragged from the canal. Presumably, one of these legs was missing the aforementioned portion of thigh, as the investigating doctors confidently decided that all the pieces recovered belonged to the same body – a collection which was now complete, save for the head.

Nevertheless, the woman was never identified and little could be ascertained as to the circumstances of her demise beyond that the dismemberment had been undertaken by an experienced hand. Unable to identify a specific cause of death, the inquest recorded an open verdict.

The next discovery occurred at the headquarters of the Metropolitan Police, which ought to have been amongst the most secure places in the capital. Indeed, during the construction of their new offices at New Scotland Yard, the site was protected by hoardings and gates (but not, it transpired, always by a nightwatchman). And yet, on 2 October 1888, a further torso was found in the recently dug foundations, apparently matching an arm found three weeks earlier in the river at Pimlico (but not, it seems, a further arm found shortly after that one in Lambeth, which leaves a macabre loose end).

If the workmen were to be believed, the torso had been placed in the foundations at some point over the course of a weekend; however, the extent of staining found on a wall against which it had rested seemed to point away from this conclusion. So too would the later discovery of an lower leg and foot on the same site; an element of black comedy was introduced into proceedings when these were found not by an officer of the law but by a small dog belonging to a member of the public who had offered his assistance.

Once again, an inquest failed to reach a verdict of murder. It is difficult to guess whether the police would have been frustrated or relieved by this, or perhaps simply embarrassed by the whole affair.

Eight months passed before, on 4 June 1889, the lower part of another female torso was taken from the river in Southwark. Over the next two days a leg, in Chelsea, and a liver, on the opposite bank in Nine Elms, would follow.

The upper portion of the body was found in nearby Battersea Park on 7 June, but the Thames had not yet finished revealing its secrets. By 10 June, the extant pieces had been joined by a neck and shoulders, parts of both legs and feet, parts of the arms, parts of the hands, the buttocks, the pelvis, and – finally – a right thigh. The latter of these was discovered not in the river, but in the garden of Sir Percy Shelley. It seemed to have been thrown there from the street. It has not escaped attention that Sir Percy was the son of the author of *Frankenstein*, Mary Shelley.

The most disturbing aspect of this case, however, was that the victim had been pregnant at the time of her death – her uterus and a portion of placenta were amongst the recovered body pieces. The foetus was missing and, although a foetus was later discovered, contained in a pickling jar and floating in the river, medical opinion prevailed that the two incidents were unrelated. It remains a distressing mystery within a mystery.

By her clothing, and also by a notable scar, the victim was identified as Elizabeth Jackson; her common-law husband, John Faircloth, was questioned but eventually eliminated from the police's enquiries. Rumours of a suspicious sighting of a 'navvy' came to nothing. Elizabeth Jackson had an identity, but her killer was to remain at large.

Finally, at around 5.25 a.m. on 10 September 1889, PC William Pennett was passing along Pinchin Street, Whitechapel, when he spotted 'something that appeared to be a bundle' lying in an archway. In the event, the bundle was revealed to be a headless and bloodless torso. We can only imagine the surprise of three men found sleeping in the adjacent arches, as they were woken and questioned about the decomposing remains close by. One would admit at the subsequent inquest that he was 'not exactly sober' at the time. That may have been a blessing.

At the inquest, it was determined that the victim had been a 'stoutish' woman of between thirty and forty years of age. Additional wounds were also noted – cuts to the arms, perhaps due to the positioning of the body during its dismemberment, and a fifteen-inch incision into the abdomen. Death was estimated to have occurred at least twenty-four hours prior to discovery.

Unlike in the previous three cases, no further parts of the last body were ever located – and therefore it has no demonstrable link to the Thames. Nevertheless, senior police officials, including Sir Melville Macnaghten, felt compelled to offer their opinions on how the matter may have tessellated with the larger series: Macnaghten noted that the crime appeared 'very similar' to the Rainham and Whitehall cases.

Some theorists have since posited that Jack the Ripper and the Thames Torso Murderer were one and the same. This question was, in fact, explored at the time. At the close of the inquest into the Pinchin Street remains, Dr George Bagster Phillips – the divisional police surgeon for Whitechapel – was asked whether he felt that the torso exhibited any giveaway mutilations associating it stylistically with the demolition of Mary Jane Kelly, ten months earlier. His answer was that he did not.

Whatever the truth, it would appear that the career of the Thames Torso Murderer, if such a figure existed, and whoever he may (or may not) have been, came to an end on that September night in Whitechapel.

TNB

Further Reading

Trow M. J., *The Thames Torso Murders* (Barnsley: Wharncliffe, 2011)

Thomas, Sarah Harriet (1831–1849)

In February 1849, an eighteen-year-old maid named Sarah Harriet Thomas (who was described in a newspaper report as possessing 'great personal attractions') took employment in Bristol as a live-in servant to an elderly lady called Miss Elizabeth Jeffries. The wealthy sixty-nine-year-old spinster was known to be extremely cantankerous and eccentric, and she shunned society. Her bad temper and frequent ill-treatment of her servants ensured that she was incapable of keeping them for any length of time.

Before long, the old lady was found battered to death on her bed. The stone used in the attack was found in the fireplace, and the house had been ransacked with many valuable items of jewellery and silver stolen. The body of the victim's dog was found embedded head first in the privy. The police found Sarah, who had absented herself from her place of work, hiding in the coal-hole of her mother's cottage; there had been no attempt to hide the missing valuables. She was accordingly arrested, charged with the murder of her mistress, and taken to Bristol Gaol.

Whilst incarcerated, Sarah tried to implicate another servant in the crime, but the jury at the subsequent inquest returned a verdict of guilty against her, and she was transferred to Gloucester Gaol to await trial. Sarah's mother was charged with receiving stolen goods and detained in custody until she could be called as a witness.

On 3 April, the trial was opened before Mr Justice Platt at the Shire Hall, Gloucester; huge crowds gathered for the event. After Sarah was found guilty and sentenced to death, she was removed to Bristol Gaol to await her execution. Her mother immediately demanded Sarah's clothing, a request that was abruptly refused. Guarded in the condemned cell by four female turnkeys, Sarah was given a pen and some paper and spent much of her time doodling and drawing large letters of the alphabet. Several petitions for a reprieve – containing thousands of signatures from religious groups and residents of Bristol – were forwarded to the Home Secretary, but all pleas were declined.

Descriptions of the execution of Sarah Harriet Thomas are harrowing in the extreme. She fought desperately all the way from her cell, and had to be dragged to the press-yard by six turnkeys. The prison chaplain eventually managed to calm her a little by whispering in her ear and leading her towards the gallows with her fettered hand in his. The dreaded hangman, William Calcraft, had erected the scaffold on the top of the entrance to the gaol, in full view of the baying crowds below. Once she had been hoisted up the ladder, still struggling and shrieking, he pulled the hood over her face and withdrew the bolt. The behaviour of the crowd was despicable, with much jeering, swearing, and tossing of clumps of mud. After hanging for an hour, Sarah's body was placed in a re-used coffin containing the skeletal remains of Mary Ann Burdock, who had been hanged by Calcraft in 1835.

The degrading scenes at the execution sparked lengthy protests in the press against the barbarity of capital punishment, but other aspects of the case were rather more morally equivocal. Clearly, Miss Jeffries had been a thoroughly unpleasant woman and had treated her servants harshly, yet Sarah had chosen to retaliate with violence rather than simply walking away and finding employment elsewhere. Without a character reference, this would probably have proved difficult.

If proof were needed that Sarah's mother was not only morally deficient but also lacking in any maternal feelings, this was finally demonstrated by the fact that she and one of her other daughters were in the crowd that had gathered to watch Sarah's agony as she was dragged screaming to her ignominious death on the gallows.

KC

Tichborne Claimant, The

'The Tichborne Claimant' was one of the most infamous legal scandals of the Victorian period, beginning in the civil courts and finally stumbling with its civility exhausted into imprisonment. In an age of ingenuity and progress (but without the benefit of today's genetic forensics), no contemporary problem took longer to resolve.

Roger Charles Doughty Tichborne, the heir to a baronetcy and a country estate, was a fragile and rather effeminate figure who had, as far as anybody knew, gone down with his ship off the coast of Brazil in 1854. Still, his mother, the dowager Lady Tichborne, clung to the idea that he may have survived, and, in the early 1860s, following an international advertising campaign, it seemed that her devotion had been rewarded. Roger had apparently been identified, operating as a butcher under an alternative name in Australia.

However, as the reader may already have intuited, things were not quite so simple. The new Roger was a different physical specimen, bulky where his previous incarnation had been slight, taller than he was before, and inexplicably unfamiliar with key aspects of his prior existence. One of the few things to his credit was his tobacco pipe, which was discovered to be monogrammed with the initials of the *disparu*; this was hardly definitive, but nonetheless the new Roger – the 'Claimant' to the family inheritance – was hurried to Europe for an audience with Lady Tichborne, who gleefully declared herself persuaded of the unlikely miracle.

It hardly seems necessary to say that this second version of Roger was, in fact, no such thing. In Australia he had been known as Thomas Castro, and even this was a substitute persona, for he had once been known in Wapping, in the East End of London, as Arthur Orton. The appearance of Lady Tichborne's newspaper appeal had, according to legend, inspired in him a spasm of amateur sophistry, and he came to a realisation which he recorded in his diary in the sort of language which seemed, somehow, not to be the product of Roger's elite education:

> Some men has plenty money and no brains, and some men has plenty brains and no money. Surely men with plenty money and no brains were made for men with plenty brains and no money.

Trial proceedings inevitably followed, and the Claimant's supporters – not limited in number to the grieving and self-deluded mother – lined up against his opponents, who hoped that common sense would prevail. All manner of tests were devised with a view to settling the matter once and for all, but still the results demanded interpretation: could bookish Roger have forgotten that Caesar was Roman (the Claimant guessed that he was Greek)? And could any graduate of Stoneyhurst (where the 'boys talk of little else', as Oliver Cyriax wryly observes) have omitted to form an understanding of the meaning of the word 'quadrangle'? Even the unusual characteristics of the Claimant's retracted penis were considered – 'We hear your client is made like a horse,' said one of the prosecution lawyers to the Claimant's counsel. It was true – but the Claimant simply contended that he had always been built in this way, even when he had been Roger the first time around; and, since it was difficult to find witnesses who had taken particular note of this part of Roger's anatomy before his shipwreck, it was all but impossible to disprove it.

After a punishing and often eccentric legal ordeal, however, the Claimant's identity with the missing Roger was rejected by the jury, and he was promptly arrested on a charge of perjury. A second trial followed, recapitulating much of the contested evidence given at the first one. At length, Orton, as he was now (quite properly) called, was sentenced to confinement in dingy Dartmoor Prison – an ironic caricature of the privileged, Arcadian retirement to which he had once aspired.

MWO

FURTHER READING

Annear, R., *The Man Who Lost Himself* (London: Robinson, 2003)

Transportation

To begin, a personal indulgence: the present author's great-great-great-great uncle, Thomas Clawson, was transported to Australia in 1831, having been convicted in Southwark on 4 January of that year for stealing 'a drawer and thirty shillings in money' from one Elizabeth Gordon. His co-accused, John Lacey, was treated more lightly, sentenced only to be 'publicly whipped 150 yards, near where the felony was committed'. The defendants were described in *The Morning Post* as 'of diminutive stature, and each only fifteen years of age'.

By the advent of the Victorian period, transportation – the practice of disposing of one's criminal underclasses by dispatching them, as the chance arose, to the other side of the world – had a long and chequered history, and was starting to creak. It was a form of punishment that had become increasingly reserved for thieves (like Clawson); opportunistic burglaries, subsistence crimes and youthful indiscretions all invited speculation as to the justice of the penalty. Among these relatively trivial and often strikingly similar offences, a few exceptional cases stand out here and there. In October 1837, Ann Frances Bennett, a twenty-four-year-old woman of, surely, doubtful emotional wellbeing, was convicted at the Old Bailey on the following tortuous indictment: 'that she ... feloniously and maliciously, by fraud and force, did take away a certain female child, of the age of four months, named Catherine Gilson, with intent to deprive William Gilson and Mary Ann, his wife, the parents of the said child, of the possession of the said child'. She had stolen the baby from its sister, Emily, whom she had persuaded to go into a toy shop while she – Ann – waited outside to look after Catherine. 'I was not in a minute,' lamented Emily, giving her witness testimony, 'and when I came out she was gone.' Thirteen days passed before Catherine was restored to her parents, and by then her appearance had been so transformed by an unskilful haircut, general neglect and illness that her mother initially failed to recognise her. At her trial, Ann greeted her sentence – transportation for seven years – with the derisive rejoinder, 'You had better make it ten.'

So much for the first phase of the process. There then followed the journey to the southern hemisphere, a gruelling three-month experience characterised by tedium, with excursions above deck being allowed only occasionally for the purposes of washing oneself, one's clothes, or the deck itself. In their recent book, David Hayes and Marian Kamlish researched the voyage of Leopold Redpath, a perpetrator of railway fraud, finding that their man had recourse to a collection of newspapers to relieve the boredom; but even this option would have been unavailable to illiterate prisoners. More commonly, the typical traveller must have been more or less alone with his thoughts, in his hammock and in absolute silence from nightfall to dawn, with only his uncertainties and regrets for company.

The arrival of the prisoner in the Antipodes did not necessarily herald a new beginning, free of the emotional damage of the past. The idyllic surroundings of Norfolk Island, isolated in the South Pacific, had long since been requisitioned for the purpose of creating what Oliver Cyriax calls 'the ultimate in convict degradation'. Corporal punishment was the cornerstone of the penal colony's disciplinary system: in the case of prisoner Laurence Frayne, one dispensation of 200 lashes was scheduled to be delivered in four distinct batches, 'so that his back could be opened up time and again with special heavy-duty whips'. Alexander Maconochie, who arrived as governor in 1840, introduced a comparatively enlightened regime: the number of lashes administered went down by 90 per cent in year-on-year analyses, but it has been noted that the average number of lashes to which misbehaving convicts were sentenced actually went up when taken case-by-case; there were also reports of extra-judicial punishments that unsettle the modern reader. Even so, Maconochie extended an unprecedented level of trust to the prisoners in his care, incentivising desirable conduct, improving access to cultural experiences, developing a sense of community and, in general, treating them with a humanity which previous regimes had stripped away. If the success of these penal reforms is to be judged by any measure, perhaps it is not unfair to start with the fact that the prisoners no longer considered it worthwhile to participate in small-scale lotteries determining their parts in desperate murder plots. The practice had been for the two 'finalists' of the main lottery, as Cyriax ably puts it, to enter a tie-break, with the winner murdering the loser, and the remainder of the field (normally numbering about ten) identifying themselves as witnesses to the crime; all – with the exception of the deceased victim, assigned to his terminal role by the vagaries of fortune – would be shipped to Sydney for the trial, hoping to find a way to escape from custody (and, in the murderer's case, to escape execution).

The last convict ship sailed from Britain in 1867, arriving in Western Australia with a cargo of 281 men early in 1868.

MWO

FURTHER READING

Hayes, D. A. and Kamlish, M., *The King's Cross Fraudster* (London: Camden History Society, 2013)

Moore, J., 'Alexander Maconochie's "Mark System"' in *Prison Service Journal*, 198 (2011), pp. 38–46

Cyriax, O., *The Penguin Encyclopedia of Crime* (London: Penguin, 1996)

Trial of the Detectives, The (1877)

The father of modern policing, Sir Robert Peel, created nine standards upon which the Metropolitan Police founded their procedures and their reputation as the servants of the public. Known as the Peelian Principles, they were created to clarify police responsibilities, and to reassure a public fearful of an organisation which they perceived to be biased in favour of the powers that be, rather than towards the common man, woman and child. Point two of the Peelian Principles states – in paraphrase – that the ability of the police to perform their duties is dependent upon public approval of police actions. In 1877, that public approval was drastically waning, thanks to the actions of those who were paid to uphold the law, and who eventually broke it.

The story began in the Angel Hotel, in Islington, in November 1872, when a convicted forger and bookmaker named William Kurr met Scotland Yard's Detective Sergeant John Meiklejohn. The pair struck up an instant relationship, and when Meiklejohn 'advised' Kurr on how to manipulate London's betting laws, the fated union was sealed. Kurr also had an associate, Harry Benson, with whom Kurr ran confidence tricks. One 1876 scam involved the creation of a betting periodical called *The Sport and Racing Chronicle*, which claimed that a Mr Montgomery had devised a betting system so successful that bookmakers were now refusing to give him odds. Mr Montgomery, stated the *Chronicle*, was looking for third parties to invest money in the scheme; he would, by means of cheque payments, reimburse them. The only problems were that *The Sport and Racing Chronicle* was a front, and Mr Montgomery was fictitious, as were the cheque reimbursements. Matters came to a head when the banker for victim Madame de Goncourt became suspicious of her excessive withdrawals and reported the matter to her solicitor in London, who in turn contacted Scotland Yard. The jig was up for Benson and Kurr; however, this was just the tip of the iceberg.

Upon realising they were wanted, the two conmen went on the run. Scotland Yard sent out some of their best men to track them down, including a young Detective Sergeant named John Littlechild, but, just when they were ready to pounce, the fugitive pair vanished. Eventually, Benson was discovered and arrested; Kurr was later picked up in his native Scotland. It was at that stage that the reality of the situation hit those working in the Detective Department. Kurr and Benson claimed that they had been given help whilst on the run, and the revelation was to damage the Metropolitan Police so drastically that it was thought, at the time, that it would never recover. The aid which Benson and Kurr had received came from Scotland Yard's own John Meiklejohn.

Meiklejohn, who was by now a Detective Inspector, had been on Kurr's payroll ever since that fateful meeting at the Angel Hotel, and had been feeding Benson and Kurr details of the police's pursuit of them. In addition, one of the detectives sent out to hunt them down, Chief Inspector Nathan Druscovich, was also on Kurr's roster. Chief Inspectors William Palmer and George Clarke were similarly implicated, and all were arrested for corruption in September 1877, along with police solicitor Edward Froggatt.

The trial began at the Old Bailey on 26 October 1877 and set the record as the longest ever heard there. Benson and Kurr – both of whom had already been convicted of their own offences – appeared as witnesses against the policemen, as did others such as Superintendent Adolphus Williamson, whose signature had been forged on telegrams and documents by Meiklejohn and Druscovich. A verdict was reached on 20 November. Meiklejohn, Druscovich, Palmer and Froggatt were all found guilty; Clarke was cleared. Each of those convicted received a two-year prison sentence.

Upon his release, William Palmer became the manager of the Cock public house in Lambeth, dying from a bout of pneumonia on 8 January 1888. Nathan Druscovich became a private detective, ironically conducting investigations into bribery allegations during the Oxford parliamentary elections of 1880. He died from tuberculosis in December 1881. John Meiklejohn died at his South Hackney home in April 1912, after a failed attempt, in 1903, to take out a libel action against the former inspector of prisons Major Arthur Griffiths, who had accused him of accepting a £500 bribe.

The Trial of the Detectives exposed some uncomfortable truths to Scotland Yard, since it was clear that corruption had infiltrated the organisation. In 1879, Home Secretary Richard Ashton-Cross called for a report into the structure and practices of the Parisian detective force, thinking that it was a possible template from which the Met's detective team could be rebuilt. Responsibility for compiling the report fell upon the shoulders of a young lawyer from Sussex, Charles Edward Howard Vincent; when Howard Vincent had completed his assessment, Ashton-Cross asked him to form and head the new detective force. However, the public's disdain for the word 'detective' dictated that it had to be omitted from the new department's title: and so the creation of the world-famous Criminal Investigation Department came to pass.

FURTHER READING

Payne, C., *The Chieftain* (Stroud: The History Press, 2011)
Dilnot, G. (ed.), *The Trial of the Detectives* (London: Geoffrey Bles, 1928)

W, X, Y, Z

Wainwright, Henry (1838–1875)

Until the epithet was usurped by Jack the Ripper, Henry Wainwright was known as the Whitechapel Murderer, noted for a homicide of such business-like properties that its commission was separated from its discovery by exactly a year. In between, he stowed his victim under the floorboards of his warehouse, and hoped for his luck to hold.

Wainwright was the heir to a brush-manufacturing concern in Whitechapel, but, though his father (Henry senior) had been diligent in industry and had come eventually to some prosperity, Henry junior had no similar head for business. Instead, his thoughts became occupied by the incomplete charms of Harriet Lane. Enraptured by her delicate hands, and not entirely put off by the decayed tooth which made itself visible when she smiled, he wrote her soppy letters, and elevated himself and her to parody-royal status with the adoption of silly pseudonyms: he became Mr Percy King, and she was Mrs King. All this was necessary because Wainwright had a wife, Elizabeth, and several children, living apparently decently in Bow's luxurious Tredegar Square.

Gradually this delicate arrangement began to unravel. By 1874, Mrs King – properly Miss Lane – had begun to tire of her clandestine lifestyle; after two illegitimate children, and with no sign of Percy – Henry – preparing to place their relationship on a firmer footing, her dissatisfaction began to find its bitter voice. There were arguments, and Wainwright must have realised that, if his affair were to be revealed, he faced social ruin. This was particularly worrying, since for some months his financial circumstances had also been embarrassingly parlous. Bankruptcy seemed to be beckoning, and bluff confidence – Wainwright's typical trading currency – would not deter his creditors. By grim contrast, though, it seemed to have had pleasing effects upon one Alice Day. She, a ballet dancer hoping for preferment in Whitechapel's theatre scene, had recently found her way into Wainwright's affections, a victim of his unaccountable sexual gravity. Whichever way one looked at the situation, something had to give.

In early September 1874, Wainwright ceased funding Harriet Lane's modest tenancy at Sidney Square and, on the eleventh day of the month, and at the end of her tether with her distracted lover, she went to confront him at his warehouse at 215 Whitechapel Road. There, he shot her, wrapped a rope around her, and dragged her into a makeshift grave which he had hollowed out underneath the floorboards at the back of the premises. Onto the body he poured half a hundredweight of chloride of lime (which he had ordered the previous day). He replaced the boards and began an unlikely rumour, saying that Harriet had gone to Europe with a man named, rather strikingly, Edward Frieake. The real Frieake, an auctioneer working at Aldgate and a longstanding acquaintance of Wainwright's, wondered at this, but telegrams from seaports, apparently composed by Harriet, seemed to indicate that the story was true.

By September 1875, however, and with Harriet still conspicuous by her absence, Wainwright was under pressure again. His former lover had not disappeared as completely as he would have liked: her unpleasant scent, percolating upwards, hung in the air at the back of his warehouse. Worse, the warehouse itself was soon to be sold under a bankruptcy settlement; nothing was more likely than that the new owners would lift the floorboards to uncover the source of the foul stench. His hand forced by these circumstances, Wainwright waited until darkness had fallen on 10 September 1875, and then disinterred Harriet, chopped her into multiple pieces, and packaged her into bundles, swaddled in American oilcloth. The next day, he planned to transport the bundles to a disused address in Southwark, and, to this end, he enlisted the innocent assistance of one Alfred Stokes. When the time came, and with the packages continuing to stink, Stokes took advantage of Wainwright's only momentary absence and covertly examined the unpleasant cargo. A hand discontinuing at the wrist persuaded him that all was not well.

The story of Wainwright's capture is among the greatest in Victorian criminal history: a filmic, romantic mess of dismembered limbs; Wainwright's hansom cab rattling across London Bridge, smoke issuing freely from his great cigar; Miss Alice Day, seated with him in the carriage, reading a newspaper and obediently refraining from entering into conversation with her implacable paramour, who said that he wanted to think; Stokes, a previously loyal victim of Wainwright's financial implosion, dashing through the traffic somewhere behind the cab, and laughed at by the policemen at Leadenhall Street whom he begged to intervene. Only when the cab reached Borough was Stokes able to persuade a policeman to take him seriously. Pieces of Harriet Lane dropped from their oilcloth surroundings, and Wainwright was arrested. So was the unfortunate Alice Day, although she was later released.

Wainwright was tried at the Central Criminal Court and hanged at Newgate, four days

Henry Wainwright. (Authors' collection)

before Christmas 1875. Remorse was not his strong suit, and, just before making his final descent, he snarled at the assembled dignitaries and journalists, 'Come to see a man die, have you, you curs?' (See Gallows Declamations.) The true author of the seaport telegrams – Henry's brother Thomas, masquerading as Harriet at Henry's request – received seven years' penal servitude as an accessory after the fact to murder, and was perhaps lucky not to suffer something rather worse.

MWO

FURTHER READING

Irving, H. B. (ed.), *Trial of the Wainwrights* (Edinburgh: William Hodge and Company, 1920)

Oldridge, M. W., *Murder and Crime: Whitechapel and District* (Stroud: The History Press, 2011)

Waters, Margaret (1835–1870)

It was in June 1870, during police investigations into a number of infant deaths in Brixton, that thirty-five-year-old Margaret Waters was exposed as one of many women involved in the nefarious and widespread practice of baby farming. Widowed in 1864, she tried to earn an honest living as a dressmaker, but when this failed and she fell foul of money-lenders, she opened her house as a lying-in establishment. Before long, she turned to baby farming, a more lucrative version of a similar business. She advertised in *Lloyd's Weekly Newspaper,* and found no difficulty in extracting money from women desperate to off-load their unwanted babies.

At first, she acquired death certificates for the babies who died in her care – infant death was endemic from disease and malnourishment – but, as doctors and undertakers were expensive, she shortly decided to dispose of the bodies herself by dumping them in alleyways or under railway bridges. Alerted to her activities, a police officer searched her house at 4 Frederick Terrace and later described the hideous scene: there was, he said, an overwhelming smell and 'some half-dozen little infants lay together on a sofa, filthy, starving, and stupefied by laudanum.' Both Margaret Waters and her twenty-eight-year-old sister, Sarah Ellis, were arrested and initially charged with the murder of five children, though the case rested on the death of John Walter Cowen, who, on 17 May, at three days old, had been placed with Waters by his grandfather (the baby's mother had given birth at sixteen, bringing disgrace to the family).

John had been born a beautiful, healthy child but, after just three weeks with Waters, he was described as resembling a skeleton, too weak to cry or make a sound; he looked barely human, more like a shrivelled monkey. In an attempt to revive him he was taken to a wet nurse, but he died on 24 June. Of the eleven children found in the house, the five who had been 'adopted' were near death, whilst the older ones, for whom Waters was receiving a weekly fee, seemed reasonably fit and were deposited in the Lambeth Workhouse. Unlike Amelia Dyer, who, in 1896, was suspected of strangling as many as 400 children, Margaret Waters chose to ply her charges with opiates so that they died slowly of starvation, too weak even to whimper. She admitted to having taken charge of forty children altogether, and it was estimated that she had starved at least nineteen babies to death in this way.

The trial was opened at the Old Bailey on Wednesday, 21 September before Fitzroy Kelly, the Lord Chief Baron of the Exchequer, with Serjeant Ballantine prosecuting on behalf of the Attorney General. The details of the case were harrowing and the press coverage extensive. According to one report, the woman in the dock was not a coarse, hard-bitten harridan but a woman with regular features and a pleasing expression. Another asserted that 'she received a good education; she not only knows English well but is perfectly conversant with French, writes a good hand and, it is said, is a good musician and plays well on the pianoforte'. Ellen O'Connor, a thirteen-year-old maid living in the house, testified that Waters and Ellis would often go out at night with a child in their arms (saying they were taking it home) and return either empty-handed or having acquired a quite different child. While the jurors retired to consider Margaret Waters's fate, her sister, Sarah Ellis, was acquitted on the murder charge; she was, instead, found guilty of obtaining money under false pretences and sentenced to eighteen months' hard labour. By contrast, the gruesome and incriminating evidence given during the trial left little doubt as to the guilt of Margaret Waters, and she was sentenced to death. Whilst awaiting execution, she wrote a long statement in which she admitted fraud but denied any intent to murder, blaming the parents for wanting to get rid of their babies. The initial crime was theirs, she argued, and without them the business of baby farming would cease to exist. She was hanged by William Calcraft on Tuesday, 11 October 1870 at Horsemonger Lane Gaol. She went to the scaffold calmly, neatly dressed in a plaid dress and a silk mantle. She eloquently enunciated an extemporary prayer and shook hands with the prison chaplain, Calcraft and one of the warders before the bolt was drawn. She died without a struggle and was buried within the precincts of the prison. She was the first baby farmer to be executed in England, but her fate failed to serve as a deterrent and more were soon to follow.

KC

Watson, John Selby (1804–1884)

In 1922, Herbert Rowse Armstrong brought something new to the legal sector when he became the first – and only – British solicitor to be hanged for murder. Every profession had its pioneers, although some had more disciples than others: doctors, for instance, were always tempted into transgressions, failing to learn from the examples of those who had passed before them. The Reverend John Selby Watson was a trailblazer in the small dataset of homicidal classicists, and in the even smaller dataset of homicidal classicists in holy orders. An enthusiastic writer, Watson's translations of both Greek and Roman authors are still fairly easy to obtain (some have even made their way into digital form). He also pursued interests in religious history, biography and so on; his most interesting title was 1867's *Reasoning Power in Animals*.

A German publication issued in the wake of Watson's crime encapsulated his story in an understated manner, describing him as *ein unglücklicher Ehemann* – an unfortunate husband. This, however, was only part of the picture. Watson's marriage to Anne Armstrong had, it was true, drifted through familiarity and into contempt by 1870, and rumour held that his wife was 'endowed with a power of nagging which age had not withered, nor custom staled'. But the theme of her bitter complaints was usually financial. Watson had been headmaster of the Stockwell Grammar School in suburban south London since 1844, but the pay was unimpressive and the school had been in 'serious decline' for some time. At Christmas in 1870, the governors of the school decided that enough was enough, and released him to an unwanted retirement. There was little to fall back on: his only profitable book was a biography of Bishop Warburton, published in 1863, and from this he had derived 'something under £5'. In a precarious position, and with only one servant, Eleanor Pyne, left to protect the leisure of his unhappy wife, Watson threw himself into his work, readying a 'complete history of the popes to the Reformation, which would have filled two octavo volumes'.

At 4.00 p.m. on 9 October 1871, which had been an ordinary Sunday in the Watson household, Eleanor went out, leaving her employers in their library and on 'very friendly terms'; in fact, she considered this to be the Reverend and Mrs Watson's usual state of relations. By the time Eleanor arrived home again at nine that evening, however, Mrs Watson was absent, and supposedly 'out of town' overnight. Watson directed Eleanor's attention to some stains on the carpet near the library door. 'Your mistress spilled some port wine,' he said, nonchalantly, 'and in case you wondered what it was I have shown it to you.'

Mrs Watson did not reappear on the Monday, and, on the Tuesday, Watson revised the arrangements, now announcing that his wife was not expected back for another two or three days. In the meantime, Eleanor had become disconcerted by Watson's oracular hints about doctors – 'If I am taken ill, or if you find anything wrong, send for Dr Rugg ... I may require medicine in the morning' – and, finally, at midday on the Wednesday, she heard her master groaning in his room. Reaching him, she realised that he had lapsed into unconsciousness, having swallowed a small amount of prussic acid.

When Dr Rugg arrived, a letter (in Watson's handwriting) directed him to Mrs Watson's bedroom, next to the library. 'I have killed my wife in a fit of rage,' the note said, 'to which she provoked me; often, often has she provoked me before, but I never lost restraint over myself with her till the present occasion, when I allowed fury to carry me away ... I trust she will be buried with the attention due to a lady of good birth.' The body itself was covered by a blanket, and exhibited eight wounds to the head, apparently inflicted when Mrs Watson was beaten with the butt end of a pistol. The attack seems to have been performed from behind; the few abrasions discovered on Mrs Watson's arms were not the relics of a struggle, but were probably caused when Watson dragged her corpse to its hiding place.

Watson recovered from his dose of poison and stood trial early in the new year. His case ran parallel with that of Christiana Edmunds, and a good deal of discussion was stimulated in the press about the limits of criminal responsibility. It was difficult to know how to interpret Watson's uncharacteristic actions unless one believed him to be mad (see Insanity), but the jury could not be persuaded of this. He was found guilty of murder, with a recommendation to mercy on account of his age and previous good conduct; the Home Secretary waived the hanging, and Watson eventually shuffled off this mortal coil in 1884 after falling from his bunk at Parkhurst Prison on the Isle of Wight.

MWO

Webster, Kate (1847–1897)

On the afternoon of Tuesday, 4 March 1879, a tall, gaunt woman turned the corner into Rose Gardens, Hammersmith – a street in west London that was, at the time, little more than a rough track flanked by rows of workingmen's cottages. Kate Webster was no stranger to the street, for she had once lived there. Now, six years later, she had come to revisit old friends – Harry Porter and his wife, Ann. She was accompanied by a young boy, and carrying a black canvas bag of the sort a woman might use to carry vegetables from the market.

Born in Killane, Ireland, in 1847, Kate was raised a Catholic and married whilst still in her teens. She had four children, all of whom died in infancy. Turning to crime in order to survive the early onset of widowhood, she became a seasoned jailbird with a string of convictions for fraud and theft. She was also a compulsive liar, changing the details of her life many times to suit her circumstances.

Since leaving Hammersmith, Kate had lost contact with Annie Porter – until, that is, there came that knock on the door. Remembering Kate as rather shabby, her friend barely recognised her. She was now well-dressed and self-assured, and keen to tell of the remarkable change in her fortunes. She had also come prepared: from a pocket deep in the folds of her skirt, Kate pulled a bottle of whiskey, and the two women settled down to bridge the gap of the intervening years over a glass or two. Since the Porters had last seen her, Kate said, she had married again. Her name was now Mrs Thomas, and she had a young son called Johnny. She was a widow once more but, she confided, she had struck lucky, for an aunt had bequeathed her a house, one of a pair known as Vine Cottages, in Park Road, Richmond. Little did her hosts know that inside the innocuous-looking shopping bag which their guest had placed so carefully under the table was the recently-severed head of Mrs Julia Thomas, Kate's erstwhile employer, neatly wrapped in brown paper.

Later that evening, Harry Porter and his son, Robert, accompanied Kate to the railway station at Hammersmith. On the way they stopped off at various public houses, with Robert carrying the canvas bag, which was surprisingly heavy, from hostelry to hostelry. During one break for refreshments, Kate said that she had arranged to take the bag to a friend in Barnes, and she disappeared, alone, into the murky blackness hanging over Hammersmith Bridge. Twenty minutes later, she was back in the pub, minus the bag. That night, when she and Robert reached 2 Vine Cottages, Kate produced a heavy wooden box to take to a friend waiting for her on Richmond Bridge. Once there, Kate took the box from Robert and, moments later, he heard a splash as something hit the water below.

The following morning, a coalman found a wooden box stuck in the mud near Barnes Bridge. He gave it a good kick, but was horrified when the box burst open to reveal a mass of congealed flesh. A local surgeon confirmed that the contents were, indeed, portions of a woman's body, although the head and one foot were missing. The colour and texture of the flesh seemed to indicate that it had been boiled. On Monday, 10 March, a human foot was found in a dungheap on some allotments in Twickenham.

Meanwhile, Kate and her cronies were at 2 Vine Cottages supervising the removal of the furniture. The next door neighbour, Elizabeth Ives, owned both cottages, but had not seen her tenant, Julia Thomas, for two weeks. She knew that Kate, Mrs Thomas's surly maid, was still there – but where was Julia? When confronted, Kate became flustered and fled. After grabbing her son from the Porters' house, she travelled to Ireland, taking refuge at her uncle's farm in Killane. Subsequent police searches at 2 Vine Cottages revealed some charred bones, bloodstains and a 'fatty substance'; a warrant for Kate Webster's arrest was promptly issued. It did not take long to trace her, and she was arrested and charged with the murder of Julia Thomas. In July 1879, she was tried and convicted at the Old Bailey, although she swore that the guilty party was really a man named Strong, the father of her son. Then, attempting to forestall the death penalty, she announced that she was pregnant, knowing that the law would not allow the killing of an unborn child. Upon examination, however, her claim was proved to be false, and she was sentenced to hang. At Wandsworth Gaol on 29 July 1879, William Marwood obliged.

The closeting together of the crotchety Julia Thomas and the volatile Kate Webster was bound to end in disaster. Unaccustomed to legitimate employment, Kate was unable to cope with Julia's pernickety ways, and, when the old lady returned from church on the evening of Sunday, 2 March, something happened to cause Kate's smouldering resentment to flare into terrible violence. After killing Mrs Thomas, she proceeded to dismember her body and boil the pieces in the kitchen copper. That Kate Webster's crime was one of the most callous ever recorded cannot be denied – but what to make of the behaviour of her supposedly lawful friends, who had swarmed over the contents of 2 Vine Cottages like the proverbial maggots over a rotting corpse, never questioning Kate's entitlement to the bounty? Even Kate herself was not without her

Kate Webster. (Authors' collection)

enigmas. She was, without doubt, a born hustler, and yet she doggedly supported her son and, despite her miscreant ways, always ensured he was well cared for during her frequent terms of imprisonment. Needing to keep one step ahead of the police, he had eventually become a millstone around her neck – she could so easily have sold him to a baby farmer – but, even when she knew her arrest was imminent, she did not abandon him, choosing instead to take him to safety in Ireland.

The dénouement of this case is extraordinary. In October 2010, whilst workmen were excavating part of the garden belonging to Sir David Attenborough, in Park Road, Richmond, they unearthed a skull. It was suggested that this may be the missing head of Julia Thomas: the location was close to her former home and extended to the derelict site of the Hole in the Wall public house, which had been frequented by Kate Webster and her acquaintances. The skull was subjected to forensic tests and the results were presented at an inquest on Tuesday, 5 July 2011. The West London Coroner, Alison Thompson, formally identified the skull as that of Julia Thomas, and recorded a verdict of unlawful killing. This belated development tantalises the student of the Webster case. In her confession, Kate said that she gave the bag containing the head to someone on Hammersmith Bridge. Was that person the child's father – the man called Strong? Was he involved in the killing, or, at least, in disposing of parts of the body? Did Kate hand him the head before rejoining her friends in the pub in Hammersmith, and did he take it back to Park Road to bury it behind the Hole in the Wall, where it remained undisturbed for some 130 years?

KC

FURTHER READING

O'Donnell, E., *Trial of Kate Webster* (Edinburgh: William Hodge and Company, 1925)

Clarke, K., *Deadly Service* (London: Mango Books, 2015)

Whicher, Jonathan (1814–1881)

There is nothing new under the sun, as the saying goes, and less than is often assumed separates our concerns from those of the Victorians. Continuities are visible everywhere: in the case of Charles Dobell and William Gower, Victorian society's anxieties about the corrupting influence of criminal literature prefigured ours (although we normally assume that films and video games are more dangerous than silly books). Other, familiar tableaux are woven inextricably into the Victorians' vast tapestry: here, a needless and harmful panic about immunisations, and alarm about the ingredients of foodstuffs, and worry about the inscrutable intentions of foreigners; and there, almost ritually, a half-cheerful gripe about the traffic and the weather.

So it is with the fetishisation of detectives. Among these, Jonathan Whicher is currently the most prominent, though attempts have been made to bring others up to standard. Whicher owes his contemporary profile to Kate Summerscale's portrayal of him in her well-known book, *The Suspicions of Mr Whicher*. Here, Whicher unveils the mysteries of Road Hill (see Constance Kent), and his deductions feel like a secular kind of seeing, running parallel to the supernatural versions then beginning to penetrate Victorian drawing rooms. It is easy to be cynical about hyperbolic representations of the salaried officials of the past, but true crime, as a genre which can sometimes be criticised for its conservative moral orientation, ought to be particularly conscious of them.

Years afterwards, Whicher's failure in Constance Kent's case was said to have troubled him. An unidentified but 'celebrated sleuth', providing unremarkable copy for a Scottish newspaper, reported that he 'knew Inspector Whicher' and remembered 'listening to his bitter complaints over the way he was treated' in the wake of the affair. One sympathises, but perhaps the truth is more complicated: the 'celebrated sleuth' goes on to say that Whicher 'did not live to see the day when every one of his [Road Hill] "theories" – as they were contemptuously described – was proved to be accurate'. Of course, Whicher *did*, in fact, survive to learn the outcome of the case; the memory of the 'celebrated sleuth' had failed him, despite his supposed intimacy with the subject of his article.

Elsewhere, Whicher's reception has been not so much faulty as fallacious. He did not, as far as anybody knows, descend into alcoholic escapism in his later days; the iteration of him which appears on television does exactly that, but purely for the purposes of the plot, and because, structurally speaking, his (superimposed) dysfunctions confer upon him a rarefied sort of heroism, one unavailable to the tidily virtuous. We have certain expectations of narrative, but it is possible to take the view that this careless stylisation turns the historical Whicher into little but a fictional cliché. Still, the drunk can always be retconned out of his stupor if the need arises.

Similar transmogrifications tend to occur to Frederick Abberline, whose (imagined) substance misuse issues are now a routine feature of his posthumous representation – sometimes these are co-morbid with other psychological and behavioural irregularities.

MWO

Wilde, Oscar Fingal O'Flahertie Wills (1854–1900)

There is a famous photograph, apparently taken in 1893, of Oscar Wilde, the Irish-born 'man of letters', seated next to Alfred Douglas (later Lord Alfred Douglas), who was his friend, fellow writer, and lover. Wilde's hair is long but neat, his collar starched. A handkerchief pokes fashionably from the pocket of his striped jacket. His boots are immaculately polished. He holds a cigarette in his right hand, the wrist cocked while the corresponding elbow rests on a knee. The presentation is of a man who is poised, confident, and relaxed. It is a pose that is immediately familiar, a touchstone for numerous portrayals of Wilde since – every inch the aesthete.

To his left, Douglas sits clothed in pale trousers and a dark jacket, which – unlike Wilde's – is unbuttoned, revealing the waistcoat and shirt underneath. Sixteen years Wilde's junior, Douglas is slimmer and smaller in stature. His dress is less assured than that of his companion. He holds a straw hat in his lap, his left hand lying across the top, his right hand obscured behind it. Unlike Wilde, Douglas does not look at the camera.

Wilde is the star of the piece and he is well aware of it. Only his left arm hints at the greater significance which the composition may hold – outstretched behind Douglas's shoulders. Still, this may well be seen as simply a friendly gesture, were it not that history now tells us otherwise; for the treatment of the relationship between the pair would soon lead to the public humiliation of both, and, for Wilde, an imprisonment which would contribute to his early death, aged forty-six.

Oscar Wilde's misfortune began with libel – and also a sizeable element of hubris. By 1895, Wilde was successful and celebrated. Married since 1884 and with two sons, he had enjoyed popular (if not critical) success, particularly with his plays *Lady Windermere's Fan* and *The Importance of Being Earnest*. Trouble, however, was never far away.

Alfred Douglas's father, the Marquess of Queensbury, had long disapproved of his son's relationship with Wilde, which had begun shortly after the couple met in 1891. In April of that year, Douglas's father had sent a scathing letter to his son, stating that he would feel justified in 'shooting (Wilde) at sight'. The letter was signed 'your disgusted so-called father'. Four years later, on 18 February 1895, the Marquess tried to confront Wilde at a private members' club in Mayfair. Wilde was not present, but his irate visitor left him a (misspelled and grammatically troubled) calling card: 'To Oscar Wilde, posing somdomite' (see Homosexuality).

Recklessly, and to the consternation of many of his friends, Wilde decided to sue the Marquess for libel. He was effectively daring the Marquess to prove his accusation – an accusation Wilde himself knew to be true, irrespective of the spelling – and, since homosexuality was illegal, to implicate him as a criminal. Given his propensity for visiting 'Molly houses', or male brothels, it was also easily provable – the owner of such an institution was eventually prosecuted alongside Wilde on the strength of the information which came to light.

The trial opened on 3 April 1895. Wilde lost, with letters sent between him and Douglas proving a particularly powerful tool for the defence. The verdict compelled the authorities to bring their own charges against Wilde, and a criminal trial – *Regina* v. *Wilde* – began later in the month. The jury was indecisive, but a retrial the following month saw the once-admired writer not only found guilty but sent to the cells with cries of 'shame' ringing in his ears.

Wilde was sentenced to two years' imprisonment with hard labour, the maximum sentence available. He was briefly sent to Newgate and thence to Pentonville Prison. A petition was raised amongst Wilde's friends to have him released, but in the event a statement was released to the media stating that they were satisfied with his transfer to a more lenient regime at Reading Prison, and that it was felt that it would not be in the interest of art or humanity to protest further.

Their concern was warranted – the harsh conditions at Pentonville, and subsequently Wandsworth Prison, had taken their toll on Wilde, and the newspapers of the day carried regular updates on the sorry state of his health. If this gives the impression that he continued to be a popular cause célèbre with an undertow of public support then this is a false reading – during his transfer to Reading, Wilde was heckled and spat upon by waiting crowds.

Wilde was released in May 1897, and soon travelled to France, although not before enduring some truly pathetic incidents involving his being evicted from London hotels due to his shattered reputation, and later arriving at the house of his mother, exhausted and in despair. Many of his possessions had been auctioned following his conviction, and he was to spend the last three years of his life in penury.

Oscar Wilde died on 30 November 1900 at what he termed the 'utterly hopeless' and 'depressing' hotel in Paris where he had been living (under a false name) for some time. Alfred Douglas, with whom Wilde had been briefly reunited in 1897, acted as chief mourner at his funeral and paid the expenses, although (perhaps fittingly) even this remembrance attracted its share of controversy.

Sex between two men was decriminalised in the United Kingdom in 1967, although consternation remained as to the limits of the equality offered – the stipulation 'in private' being a particular bone of contention, much as it had been in 1835 during the trial of Pratt and Smith. Today, at least ten countries continue to pass capital sentences for the 'crime', at least two of which – Iran and Saudi Arabia – are known to carry out such sentences. Elsewhere, a greater understanding of the nuances of sexuality has developed, and today some academics debate whether Wilde and Douglas were ever exclusively homosexual.

In 2014, a copy of *The Importance of Being Earnest* that Wilde had gifted to the governor of Reading Prison sold for £55,000 at auction – a happier story than the sorry tale of Wilde's squandered possessions from 116 years earlier. Alfred Douglas, on the other hand, was imprisoned in 1924 after being found guilty of libel against Winston Churchill, following a claim published in the anti-Semitic journal *Plain English*, of which Douglas was the editor.

TNB

FURTHER READING

Ellmann, R., *Oscar Wilde* (London: Penguin, 1988)
Murray, D., *Bosie: A Biography of Lord Alfred Douglas* (London: Hodder & Stoughton, 2000)

Wilson, Catherine (1817–1862)

Catherine Wilson was born in Lincolnshire in 1817. Her life of crime began early when, aged fourteen, she was found guilty of a minor theft. She left home soon after and, it was said, 'openly lived a loose life'. Her erratic lifestyle led her to Boston, Lincolnshire, and by 1853 she had become housekeeper to Peter Mawer, a retired sea captain, who died under suspicious circumstances, leaving her both money and property.

Two years later, thirty-eight-year-old Catherine Wilson made her way to London with a man called James Dixon. They took lodgings in the home of Mrs Maria Soames at 27 Alfred Street, Bedford Square, and, the following year, Dixon became violently ill and died in acute pain. In October 1856, Mrs Soames, with whom Catherine was now on very friendly terms, became ill with similar symptoms, and died soon after. Since even these three deaths had caused no suspicion to be raised, Catherine Wilson went on to poison a Mrs Jackson, posing as a friend and confidante, and stealing £120 from her for good measure. Mrs Jackson, of course, suffered from all the familiar symptoms.

A year later, in 1860, Catherine found yet another victim, Mrs Ann Atkinson, a wealthy friend from Kirby, in Westmoreland, who came to stay with her in Kennington and who soon succumbed to the same symptoms. Catherine next attempted to poison her paramour, a Mr Taylor, with whom she had lived for four years, but, perhaps having a stronger constitution than her previous victims, he survived. By the spring of 1862, Catherine had found employment with a Mr Carnell as nurse to his wife, Sarah. Already in poor health, Sarah soon became very ill indeed and was treated most solicitously by Catherine Wilson. However, finding the medication she was given too revolting to swallow, Mrs Carnell spat it out and refused to take any more. This instinctive reaction marked the beginning of Catherine's downfall, and before long the heartless and manipulative serial poisoner was exposed. The Carnells were horrified to see that the liquid which Mrs Carnell had ejected had burned a hole in the bedding.

Some sort of corrosive poison was suspected, and the police were alerted. Catherine fled, but she was arrested six weeks later and stood trial for the attempted murder of Sarah Carnell. Chemical analysis determined that the medication which Catherine had given Sarah had contained enough sulphuric acid to kill fifty people, but her defence barrister, Mr Montagu Williams QC, argued that the pharmacist must have written the wrong prescription, and that Catherine had administered it in good faith. Incredible though it seems, she was acquitted; perhaps reassuringly, she was immediately rearrested and charged with the murder of Maria Soames.

The new trial was opened at the Old Bailey on Monday, 22 September 1862, before Mr Justice Byles, and, as in most poisoning cases, the prosecution was led by the Attorney General. The court soon learned the extent of the treachery to which Catherine Wilson had descended once she was installed in Mrs Soames's house. Practised in the art of affecting friendship for her own ulterior motives, Catherine and her landlady were soon on familiar terms and spent a great deal of time together chatting in the front parlour. Although she was behind with the rent after James Dixon died, Catherine remained in the house, no doubt already plotting to resolve her money problems by employing the craft that she had perfected. Throughout Maria's illness, Catherine appeared anxious to do all she could to alleviate her suffering; but yet, whenever Maria was given her medication, she complained of extreme pain and vomiting. When her victim finally expired, Catherine resorted to the classic ploy of suggesting that Maria had committed suicide, troubled by a debt that she could not repay. As Maria Soames's death had followed so soon after that of James Dixon, and since both had suffered similar symptoms, a post-mortem of his body was ordered. But no trace of poison was found, and Mrs Soames's body had provided equally negative results.

According to the medical evidence of Professor Alfred Swaine Taylor, however, there were certain vegetable poisons which would surrender no perceptible trace any more than forty-eight hours after death. He suggested that the poison administered had been colchicum, and thought that a number of small doses had been ingested – a large dose was more likely to be expelled from the body by violent vomiting and purging. Indeed, the doctor attending James Dixon had found a bottle in Catherine's room which contained colchicum. When asked its purpose, she had said that she was in the habit of giving it to Dixon as a treatment for rheumatism and gout.

At the end of a lengthy trial, Catherine Wilson was found guilty. Upon hearing the sentence of death, she showed no emotion whatsoever. No sympathy was expressed by the newspaper reporters, and public opinion was against her. Whilst awaiting execution, she wrote a personal plea for mercy to Queen Victoria, but this was, predictably, dismissed, and, on Monday, 20 October

1862, before a crowd of thousands, Catherine entered history as the last woman to be hanged in public in London. Even in her last moments, she protested her innocence.

After the execution, a particularly damning article was published in *Harper's Weekly*:

> From the age of fourteen to that of forty-three [*sic*] her career was one of undeviating yet complex vice ... She was foul in life and bloody in hand, and she seems not to have spared the poison draught even to the partners of her adultery and sensuality. Hers was an undeviating career of the foulest personal vices and the most cold-blooded and systematic murder, as well as deliberate and treacherous robberies ... Seven murders known, if not judicially proved, do not after all, perhaps, complete Catherine Wilson's evil career. And if anything were wanted to add to the magnitude of these crimes it would be found, not only in the artful and devilish facility with which she slid herself into the confidence of the widow and the unprotected – not only in the slow, gradual way in which she first sucked out the substance of her victims before she administered, with fiendish coolness, the successive cups of death under the sacred character of friend and nurse ...

Catherine Wilson seems to have had none of the passionate vanity of Christiana Edmunds, the coquettish allure of Adelaide Bartlett or the alcohol-induced bonhomie of Kate Webster. Yet she was an accomplished actress able to play the part of the comforting nurse or special friend with ease and plausibility. The motives for poisoning are usually jealousy, revenge or sheer hatred – but Catherine Wilson seems to have killed purely for money. She had perfected her style over many years, and it was with extreme cunning that she managed to poison Mrs Soames under the very noses of her two grown-up daughters. She was a classic poisoner, heartless enough to stand by and watch her victims suffer whilst giving the impression that she was doing her utmost to effect a cure, solicitous and cruelly duplicitous in equal measure.

KC

FURTHER READING

Clarke, K., *Bad Companions* (Stroud: The History Press, 2013)

Winslow, Forbes Benignus (1810–1874) and Lyttleton Stewart Forbes (1844–1913)

A pioneering psychiatrist (or alienist, in the contemporary formulation), as well as a prolific author and an honorary Doctor of Civil Law, Forbes Benignus Winslow would eventually find his reputation sullied by the so-called 'lunacy panic' of 1858 and 1859; in the 1860s he himself was incapacitated by a lengthy and mysterious illness, which may well have been nervous in nature. It would have been understandable: two highly publicised 'lunacy inquisitions', in 1858 and 1862, had severely damaged both his standing and his businesses.

Previously, however, Winslow had been held in high regard. Since at least as far back as 1843, when he contributed to the defence of Daniel M'Naghten, he had been concerned with the plight of 'lunatics' facing criminal charges, and a conversion to evangelical Christianity a few years later only strengthened his conviction against execution in such cases. This did not make him popular. In 1855, he published *The Case of Luigi Buranelli, Medico-legally Considered*, which remains one of the best sources of information on one of the Victorian era's most controversial executions.

Winslow's son, Lyttleton Stewart Forbes Winslow, would also become a noted alienist, and his name looms large, if not always sympathetically, in many of the most famous cases of the late Victorian period – the Jack the Ripper murders, into the investigation of which he attempted, unsuccessfully, to insert himself, and the trials of Amelia Dyer, Percy Lefroy Mapleton, and Florence Maybrick amongst them. His behaviour in the case of Mary Pearcey, in particular, is a study in opportunism, and the average reader of the newspapers to which Winslow wrote expressing his fervent belief in the insanity of the condemned woman would perhaps be surprised to learn that he had never actually seen or examined her. One particular letter, published in the *Standard* on 12 December 1890, was clipped for the Home Office files and then dutifully annotated into oblivion by civil servants whose awareness of the facts of the case – as one might expect – clearly exceeded that of the blustering Winslow. He was recently resurrected as the subject of a lecture at the Royal College of Psychiatrists, and presented as a man of sincere compassion who was trying to do his best for people in perilous circumstances; but other interpretations, simultaneously more cynical and more evidential, are available.

TNB, MWO

FURTHER READING

Wise, S., *Inconvenient People* (London: Vintage Books, 2013)

Workhouses

Take a short walk west from London's Elephant and Castle roundabout, and turn into Renfrew Road. The red-and-brown brick building to your right would previously have signified that you had arrived at Lambeth Workhouse. Part of the remaining site now houses a museum of cinema – fittingly so, given that a local child named Charles Spencer Chaplin spent time in the workhouse during the 1890s.

In the Victorian era, if you were poor, sick, or vulnerable – in other words, if you were exactly the kind of person most likely to consider committing a crime or alternatively most likely to fall victim to one – then the chances are that you would have been acquainted with the interior of places like Lambeth Workhouse. Lengthy interviews with the impoverished and needy were conducted on admission. Any belongings would be taken into storage, bathing (in any number of concoctions) was compulsory, and clothes were removed for disinfection, with workhouse-branded garments loaned in their place. Presumably, it was assumed that no one would consider such items worth keeping hold of, but this was not always the case. Mary Ann Nichols, conventionally considered the first victim of Jack the Ripper, was first identified through the Lambeth Workhouse petticoats that she was still wearing on the night of her death. Nichols had passed Christmas 1887 in the older partner institution to Renfrew Road situated in Black Prince Road.

The iniquities of workhouse life were frequently crystallised in the experiences of children, who often seem to have been treated as if they belonged to the governing poor law union rather than to the mother herself. A system of adoption, or 'boarding out', developed, and the placement of advertisements looking for new homes for destitute infants led, inevitably, to opportunities for nefarious activity. In 1891, Joseph and Annie Roodhouse were found guilty of a baby-farming fraud involving adopted children (they had come up against Inspector Frederick Abberline); while the extent of the Roodhouse's activities remains difficult to gauge, practices such as these quite deliberately zeroed in on children born in, living in, or destined for workhouses. Amelia Dyer certainly exploited the safeguarding inadequacies of the workhouse system in her own schemes.

For parents, fear of the emotionally and physically traumatic effects of workhouse life could also be a powerful motivating factor. In 1876, Lucy Lowe was found guilty of the murder of her newborn child. Aged thirty-seven, she had by the time of the murder been widowed once and deserted since, and she had two other children living in Bedford Workhouse. The Home Secretary accepted her supporters' pleas for mercy, and she was sentenced to life imprisonment in lieu of execution. In 1865, Eliza Adkins had been animated by similar maternal sentiments, drowning her son in a well because she was unable to bear the torment of being separated from him (by an iron grid, through which she could hear him crying) in Loughborough Workhouse.

In April 1842, a very curious case came before the Old Bailey. It involved a Mary Ann Dunn, accused of kidnapping a three-week-old child whose mother handed it over – but not for keeps – in a public house near Covent Garden. Dunn took the child to Croydon Workhouse and stated (incorrectly) that she had given birth to it whilst in the workhouse at Lambeth. Dunn's mother stated that the defendant (whose courtroom resistance was nothing if not robust) suffered from 'fits', and that these had worsened since her brother died; whether it was on this account, or simply because of the confusion which hung over the whole affair, the jury saw fit to acquit Dunn. The child was returned to its rightful parents, who hopefully exercised more caution from then on.

TNB

FURTHER READING

Fowler, S., *The Workhouse: The People, the Places, the Life behind Doors* (Barnsley: Pen and Sword, 2014)

Higginbotham, P., *The Workhouse Encyclopedia* (Stroud: The History Press, 2014)